Home Crafts

Marshall Cavendish London & New York

Published by Marshall Cavendish Books Limited
58 Old Compton Street
London W1V 5PA

© Marshall Cavendish Limited 1975, 1976, 1977, 1978

This material was first published by
Marshall Cavendish Limited in the
partwork *Encyclopedia of Crafts*

This volume first published 1978

Printed in Italy by Poligrafici Calderara Bologna

ISBN 0 85685 487 5

Introduction

Part of the joy of having a home is introducing your own personal touch, and what better way to do it than by making many things – from the rugs on the floor to the pictures on the wall.

This is exactly what Home Crafts will help you to do. Chapter by chapter you will find the basic craft techniques fully explained with imaginative, bright projects, each one beautifully illustrated with full colour photographs, easy to follow step-by-step instructions and detailed patterns.

Home Crafts begins with the basic needlecraft skills of curtain making and leads on to making quilts, cushions and simple upholstery. How to restore rush, cane and seagrass chair seats is carefully explained as are four methods of making colourful rugs and three styles of lampshades.

Colourcraft brings a rainbow into your home and tells you, among other things, how to use stencils and design with paint. There are chapters on woodwork and ropework so that you can introduce gorgeous finishes and interesting textures into your decor.

Papercraft explains how to create murals, work with decoupage and make pretty paper cut outs. Other chapters tell you how to create fanciful flowers from feathers and fabrics, work with shells, stones and seeds and how to fashion useful items from glass and acrylics.

Home Crafts is a book for every member of the family to enjoy time and time again. You can use it over and over to help you make your house truly your own.

contents

Needlecraft 1
curtains

Unlined & sheer curtains

Unlined curtains can work magic in the home, bringing a touch of brilliant colour to rooms which are dark or diffusing harsh light in bright rooms. Problem windows can have their problems solved, or a room given a special character with imaginative use of fabrics and window fittings.

Choosing the fabric

Unlined curtains show to best advantage with light filtering through them, and good fabrics for this are the coarsely woven linen and Dralon semi-sheers. Some of the beautifully patterned light-weight fabrics, such as lawn, look even better with the light behind them than when lined but it may be necessary to have a thicker roller blind between the curtain and the window for privacy at night.

Furnishing fabrics usually measure between 120cm (48″) and 127cm (50″) wide, while sheers and nets come in widths from 90cm (36″) to 300cm (120″) wide.

Man-made fibres have revolutionized the field of net curtains—they do not shrink or pull out of shape and some, such as Terylene, are resistant to deterioration from light. Use nylon tape and Terylene sewing thread for best results when using these fabrics.

Tapes and hooks

Before buying the fabric you need to decide upon the type of heading and track.

Gathering and pleating curtains is made easier by using special gathering tapes which are widely available in the shops. There are several different types: some produce a soft gather and others deep formal pleats.

The tape which produces soft gathers (fig.1) is designed to gather up one and a half to double the fabric width, therefore reducing the width of curtain by up to half. The more formal pencil and pinch pleating tapes (figs. 2, 3) gather up to three times the fullness of material reducing the curtain to one third its original width.

Curtain hooks are available in metal or nylon. Make sure the hooks are the correct ones for the tape and track being used. Most curtain tracks have their own range of runners.

Curtain tracks

Curtain tracks should extend the width of the window plus 15cm (6″) at each end, so that the curtains can be drawn back and away from the window to give maximum daylight. If the curtains are to overlap in the centre, two sections of track instead of one

Sheer curtains used with imagination— the sheers are matched to the curtains as well as the loose covers.

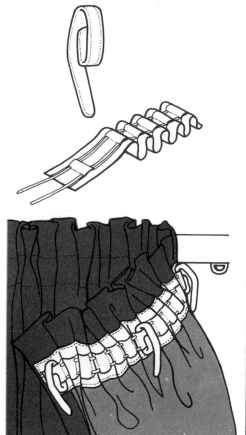

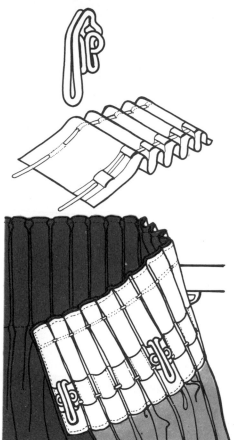

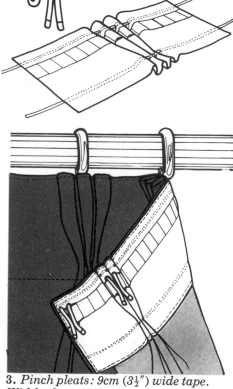

1. *Gathered heading: 2.5cm (1″) wide tape. Width of curtain required, one and a half to double length of track.*

2. *Pencil pleats: 7.5cm (3″) wide tape. Width of curtain required, two and a half to three times length of track.*

3. *Pinch pleats: 9cm (3½″) wide tape. Width of curtain required, two and a half to three times length of track.*

continuous piece will be required and 10cm (4″) extra should be allowed on the length of each track.

Each length of track will require two end stops to prevent the curtain hooks from running off.

Fabric requirements

To measure overall width of fabric needed. Measure the length of the curtain track and multiply by two for a simple gathered heading. To this add an allowance for side hems, usually 5cm (2″) on each side of each curtain. Add a further 15cm (6″) to each curtain width if they are to overlap in the centre. The total is the width of fabric needed for the pair of curtains.

For some windows it is necessary to join widths of material to achieve the overall width required. The chart shows the number of widths you will need for one of a pair of curtains for different sized windows.

Measuring the length of fabric needed. Use a steel tape or long rule to measure from the track to either the window sill or floor (fig.4). To this add 15cm (6″) for a double hem at the foot and up to 6.5cm (2½″) for the heading. The total, multiplied by the numbers of widths calculated above, will give the length of fabric required for one of a pair of curtains.

Widths of fabric required

Width of curtain area	Number of widths required per curtain (for simple gathered heading)
137cm (4′6″) and under	1
137cm–168cm (4′6″–5′6″)	1½
168cm–229cm (5′6″–7′6″)	1½
229cm–305cm (7′6″–10′0″)	2

Note: calculations are for 120cm (48″) wide fabrics.

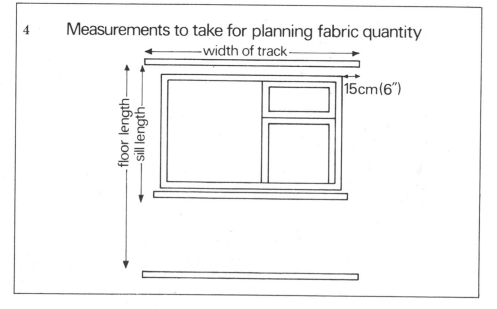

4   Measurements to take for planning fabric quantity

If the fabric has a repeated pattern, you will have to buy extra for matching the pattern at the seams on each curtain, and to ensure that the pattern falls at the same level on both curtains. To calculate the total fabric required start by checking the length of the pattern repeat, divide this measurement into the calculated length of the curtain to give you the number of pattern repeats for each curtain. If necessary round up the calculated length of the curtain to be a multiple of the pattern repeat.

If the fabric is not guaranteed pre-shrunk, allow about 5cm (2″) per metre (yard) and wash the fabric before cutting out.

Making the curtains
You will need:
The required length of fabric.
Matching thread.
Curtain tape and hooks.
Track and runners.
Tape measure and ruler.
Scissors.
Needles and pins.

☐ Lay the fabric on a large flat surface for cutting out—you must be able to see the complete curtain length at once. Use the floor if you haven't a table long or wide enough. Make the top edge absolutely straight by drawing a thread at right-angles to the selvedge, and then cut along the line. Alternatively use a T-square to obtain a straight line. Measure the curtain length from this point, draw another thread and cut along it. Cut the next length in the same way, matching the pattern if necessary (fig.5).

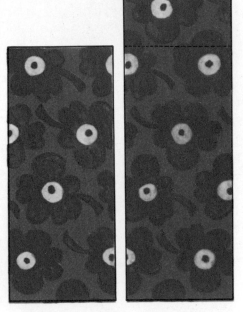

5. *Matching the pattern on two widths of fabric before cutting second length.*

☐ For a half width, fold one of the pieces in half lengthwise and cut down the fold.

Plain fabrics. Use a 1.5cm (½″) plain seam to join the pieces for each curtain, placing the right sides of the fabric together, selvedge to selvedge. If using half widths, place them to the outside of each curtain. Machine stitch the pieces together, using a loose tension and a fairly long stitch. Press the seams open and clip into the selvedges if they are tight, or cut off selvedges so that the curtain does not pucker.

Patterned fabric. Joining two pieces of fabric so that the pattern matches exactly needs a slightly different technique from that usually used on plain fabric. Begin by finding the same point in the pattern on both pieces of fabric.

☐ With right sides facing, pin the pieces together at this point, with the pin at right-angles to the edge (normally the pins are placed on the seam line parallel to the edge). Continue pinning the pieces together at about 5cm (2″) intervals, still placing the pins at right-angles to the edge. At

Floor length nets with a decorative border and pencil pleated heading.

about 30cm (12″) intervals turn the curtain to the right side to check that the pattern still matches. If it has started to slip, take out the pins and re-pin the pieces making sure you are not stretching either of the lengths.

☐ Tack the pieces together along the seam line in the normal way, but leaving the pins in position (if your tacking stitches are usually large, make them smaller for this). Still leaving the pins in, machine stitch, following the tacking line and removing the pins as you are stitching. Remove the tacking and press the seam open.

Side hems. Use 2.5cm (1″) double hems at the sides on unlined curtains as these are heavier than single hems and will prevent the sides from curling back. Trim off the selvedge or snip at intervals.

☐ To make a double hem, fold over the edge 2.5cm (1″) to the wrong side of the fabric, and then fold this over another 2.5cm (1″), so the raw edge is completely closed.

☐ Pin and tack the hem down and then slip stitch or machine stitch (if the fabric has a nap like velvet—hand stitch it using strong thread, as machine stitching might spoil the surface).

Attaching the tape. For soft gathered curtains turn over the raw edge at the top of the curtains 4cm (1½″) and tack down.

☐ Cut a length of curtain tape the width of each curtain, plus 5cm (2″) for turnings.

☐ Pull out about 4cm (1½″) of the cords from their slots at both ends of the tape. Knot the cords at one end, but keep the other free for gathering.

☐ Place the tape on the curtain so that it covers the raw edge centrally and the top edge of the tape is not more than 2.5cm (1″) from the top of the curtain (fig.6).

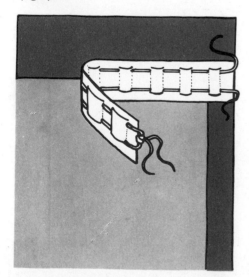

6. *Tape placed over raw edge at top of curtain with cords knotted at one end.*

☐ Tack along the top edge of the tape turning the ends of the tape under so that the knot is enclosed at one end, but the cords are free at the other (fig.7).

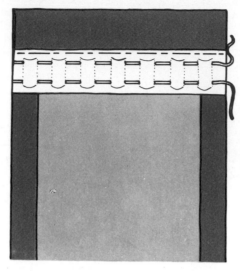

7. *Top of tape tacked to curtain with tape ends turned under.*

☐ Tack down the tape along the bottom edge. Machine stitch, outside the cords, along both edges of the tape. (Stitch in the same direction to prevent any drag which would show on the finished curtain). Stitch down the ends. Remove all the tacking and press.

For pinch pleats and pencil pleats: turn over the raw edge at the top of the curtain 1.6cm (⅝″), then make up as for soft gathered curtains but place the top edge of the tape 3mm (⅛″) from the top of the curtain.

Gathering the curtains. Pull the fabric along the cords until it is all at the knotted end. Pull out again to the right width, distributing the gathers evenly (fig.8) and knot the cords to secure the width.

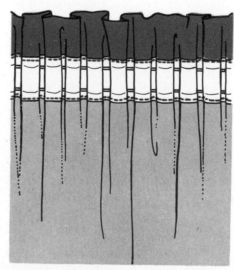

8. *Curtain gathered with the fullness distributed evenly.*

☐ Catch the knot to the tape with a few stitches to prevent it from hanging down, but do not cut off the surplus cords. When the curtains need washing or cleaning, the gathers can be released by unpicking the catch stitches and untying the knot.

☐ Insert curtain hooks (fig.9) into the pockets at each end of the curtains, and at 7.5cm (3″) intervals when assembling gathered headings.

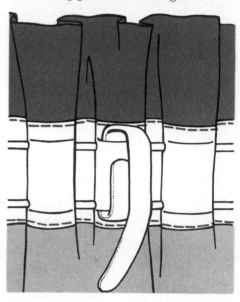

9. *Insert hooks into tape at about 7.5cm (3″) intervals.*

☐ For pencil pleats the hooks are also inserted at 7.5cm (3″) intervals but for pinch pleated headings the special hooks are inserted where indicated on the tape.

Making the hem. Hang the curtains for a few days before taking up the bottom hems, as some fabrics may stretch during this time.

☐ When you are ready to do the hems, mark the line for the length at each side of the curtain while it is still hanging. Full-length curtains should finish 2.5cm (1″) above the floor to allow them to hang properly and prevent them dragging and wearing through. Sill-length curtains should either just clear the sill, or be about 2.5cm (1″) below the sill so that the curtains hang outside it.

☐ Take down the curtains and mark the hemline with pins using a wooden rule to make sure an accurate measurement is achieved.

☐ Turn the hem up and tack loosely along the edge of the fold through one thickness of fabric.

☐ Turn in the raw edges half the depth of the hem allowance to make double hems. Tack them down and machine or hand stitch.

☐ Remove the tacking and press the hems and then the complete finished curtains.

Lined curtains

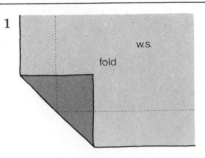

1a. *Mark the hemline and turn up the corner as shown, press.*

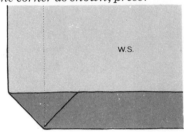

1b. *Turn up the hem on the fold line and press.*

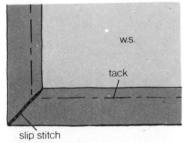

1c. *Turn in the side on the fold line. Tack, press and slip stitch corner.*

Well-lined curtains contribute a feeling of warmth and luxury to a room. The curtains will hang well and the lining also helps to insulate the room.

Velvet, brocade, silk, satin and many cottons or fabrics made from man-made fibres should be lined to prevent the fabric from fading and rotting.

Fully-lined curtains have the linings stitched to the curtain round the two sides and bottom. An attached lining prevents dirt and dust from getting between the curtain and lining fabric, giving more protection to the fabric and making it last longer.

If the fabric is washable the lining can be made detachable so that the curtains can be washed. There is a tape designed especially for this, so that the curtain and lining are attached to the same hooks.

The previous section on curtain making gives information on curtain tracks, tapes and hooks, also how to measure for the quantity of curtain fabric required, how to match the pattern in the curtains and join any seams. Make sure that the pattern is printed correctly on the grain of the fabric otherwise this can present problems when making the curtains.

Pale blue lace curtains lined with fabric in a darker tone to accentuate the design of the lace.

With all fabrics try to cut with the grain of the fabric.

Choosing fabric for lining

Traditional linings are made from fine cotton sateen in a neutral colour. This fabric blends well with most curtain fabrics and although light weight, is closely woven and firm enough to protect the curtains without being too bulky.

Curtain lining fabric is usually 120cm (48″) wide and must be pre-shrunk. Some curtain fabrics with an open weave or in a light colour will need matching lining, such as white linings for white fabrics.

If you prefer to have lining in a colour to match your curtains and cotton sateen is not available in the colour, choose a fabric that is pre-shrunk, closely woven and light in weight or dye cotton sateen to the colour required before making up.

You will need:

The calculated quantity of curtain fabric (see the previous section on unlined curtains).

The same quantity of lining fabric if it is the same width or the re-calculated quantity of lining if the width differs.

Matching thread for fabric and lining.

Heading tape. Measure the width of each ungathered curtain and add 5cm (2″).

Special lining tape, if required for detachable linings, to the measured width of each curtain, plus 7.5cm (3″).

Curtain track, stops, runners, hooks.

Steel tape and ruler.

Sharp scissors and pins.

Cord tidy, one for each curtain.

Sewn-in linings

Preparing the curtains

☐ Cut out and sew any seams to make the width required.

☐ If the curtains are to hang just below the sill turn in 4cm (1½″) at the sides and bottom of the curtain, tack and press.

☐ Mitre the two bottom corners and, using matching thread, slip stitch by hand (fig.1).

☐ Using matching thread, serge stitch by hand round sides and bottom (fig.2).

☐ For floor length curtains tack the sides and bottom, but only finish the

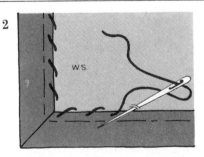

2a. *Work serge stitch from left to right in matching thread.*

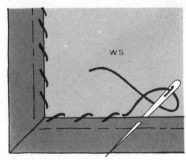

2b. *Pick up raw edges then pick up a few threads of the curtain.*

Beautifully made curtains with a pinch pleated heading and fully lined.

two side seams to about 20cm (8″) from the bottom as the curtain should be hung to drop before the hem is finally finished.

Preparing the lining
Before cutting do not try to draw a thread on lining sateen, square it up on a table or use a set-square. Cut off or snip all selvedges.

3. Lining folded back and a locking stitch worked to keep the two layers together. Pick up two or three threads at a time.

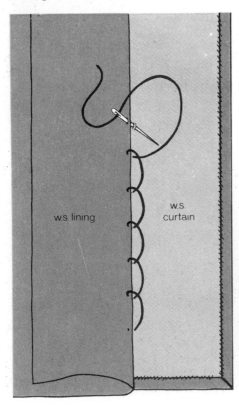

w.s. lining   w.s. curtain

Short curtains, lined and with a plain gathered heading.

☐ Cut the lining the same length as the curtain fabric.
☐ Join widths together to make lining the same width as the curtain. Make a plain seam with right sides together taking 1.5cm ($\frac{1}{2}$″) seam allowance; press open. Snip any selvedges.

Locking in the lining
A lining is locked to the fabric to prevent the lining falling away from the top fabric when the curtain is hanging.
☐ Place the curtain on a table with the wrong side facing up.
☐ Lay the lining on top of the curtain, with the wrong sides together—the raw edges of the lining should be flush with the curtain all round, so trim the sides and lower edge by the required amount.
☐ Fold back the lining at the centre of the curtain and lock the lining to the curtain by making long loose stitches. The stitches must be loose to avoid puckering (fig.3). The locking should start and end 15cm-20cm (6″-8″) from both top and bottom.
To help work the stitches in a straight line make a crease mark on the fold of the lining with your thumb.
☐ Locking is usually worked at 30cm (12″) intervals across a curtain. So if the curtain is 120cm (48″) wide there would be three rows of locking, one down the middle of the curtain and one to each side.
☐ When the locking is completed, fold in the lining at the sides and bottom of curtain for 2.5cm (1″), mitring corners. Tack.

☐ Make a line of tacking stitches across the curtain 15cm (6″) from the top. This is to keep the lining firmly in place until the heading tape is attached.
☐ Slip stitch lining to curtain round the two sides and bottom for short curtains, but for floor length curtains slip stitch the sides only, using matching thread. Allow floor length curtains to hang before finishing.

Attaching the tape
☐ Having decided upon the heading preferred, measure the length of curtain again from hem to planned position of heading tape. The hook position on the curtain in relation to the rail will determine the length required.
Floor length curtains should hang to 2.5cm (1″) above the floor.
☐ Attach the tape as described in the previous section on unlined curtains, turning in top and lining together.

These full length curtains on a narrow window, have been fully lined and a pencil pleated heading attached. They are held back with chains at about window sill level.

Detachable linings

Making the curtains

Measure, cut and make the curtains as in the previous section.

Making the detachable lining

Finished linings should be 2.5cm (1″) smaller on either side and 2.5cm (1″) shorter than the curtains when the lining is in position.

☐ Carefully measure and cut out the curtain linings.

☐ Join the widths or half widths where necessary, with 1.5cm (½″) plain seams and press open. Snip the selvedges every 10cm (4″).

☐ Make side hems by folding over

4a. *The cord is pulled free and knotted at one end.*

4b. *End folded under and machine stitched across cords.*

5a. *Top raw edges of lining enclosed between the two layers of tape.*

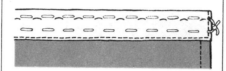

5b. *Cord ends are knotted to prevent them disappearing inside tape.*

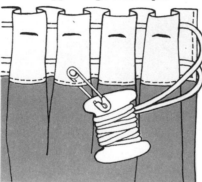

6. *Linings gathered up and cord held in place with a cord tidy.*

7. *Hooks threaded through both curtain and lining.*

2.5cm (1″) and then another 2.5cm (1″). Tack and machine stitch. Do not sew the bottom hems.

Attaching the lining tape

☐ To prepare the tape, pull free 4cm (1½″) of the draw cords at one end and knot the cords together. Trim off the surplus tape to within 5mm (¼″) of the cord (fig.4a).

☐ Fold under 1.5cm (½″) of the knotted raw end and machine stitch across the fold, stitching through the tape to secure the knotted cords (fig.4b).

☐ With the right side of the lining fabric and the corded side of the lining tape facing you, slip the top raw edge of the lining between the two sides of the tape, leaving 2.5cm (1″) of tape free at the prepared end (fig.5a).

☐ Pin and tack the lining into position on the tape. The underside of the tape is slightly wider than the top, so that when stitching from the right side both sides of the tape will be caught in the stitches.

☐ Fold under the surplus tape at the prepared end, level with the side hem edge of the lining, to give a neat edge.

☐ Machine stitch the tape to the lining, finishing the unprepared end in the same way as before but leaving the cords free for gathering. Knot the loose ends to prevent them disappearing back into the tape (fig.5b).

☐ Gather up the lining to match the gathered curtains and wind the surplus cord on to the cord tidy. Attach the cord tidy to the lining tape with a safety pin (fig.6).

Attaching the linings to the curtains

☐ With the wrong sides of curtain and lining together, insert the curtain hooks through the buttonholes at the top of the lining tape, then through the pockets in the standard heading tape on the curtain before turning the hooks into their final position. Both the curtains and their linings will hang from the same hooks (fig.7).

Finishing the lined curtains

Note: For a perfectly finished straight hem you must take great care.

On some long curtains it is possible to finish the hem without detaching the lining and taking the gathers out, but unless you are very careful you may find the hem does not hang well.

☐ Hang the lined curtains from the curtain rail and mark the correct length of the linings with a row of pins. The linings should be 2.5cm (1″) shorter than the curtains. Take down the curtains and detach the linings.

☐ On each lining, unwind the cord from the cord tidy and pull out the gathers. Lay the lining on a large flat surface and turn up the hem to the line of pins. Catch-stitch the hem by hand.

☐ Attach the finished linings to the curtains again and re-hang. Check that the linings are the correct length.

Hand-stitched pinch pleats

When you are making curtains from expensive fabric it is always worth taking the extra trouble of finishing them by hand. This chapter shows you how to make beautiful hand-stitched pinch pleats which are sometimes known as a French heading.

Although it is possible to form pinch pleats with a heading tape, hand-stitched pleats are crisper and stay crisp for longer. Also the hooks used are stronger than those used with heading tapes which is an advantage for heavy fabrics such as velvet.

Materials

Buckram is used to stiffen the pleats and heading. Buy the sort made specially for curtain headings, which is white, 10cm (4″) or 12.5cm (5″) wide, and will not lose its stiffness if washed or dry-cleaned. Do not buy the kind of buckram sold for pelmets. This is usually orange (from the stiffening agent used) and cannot be washed or cleaned because the colour runs.

Allow enough buckram to fit the unpleated width of each curtain.

Hooks from which to hang the curtains are always sewn on by hand. Sew-on hooks, as they are called, are brass and have a small hole at the base of the stem for the stitching (fig.1a).

For curtains intended to cover the curtain track when closed, hooks with long stems and a hole at each end may be used to help stiffen the heading (fig.1b). Buy one hook per pleat, plus one hook for each side edge of the curtains. For sewing on the hooks and for stitching the headings, buy button-hole twist in a colour to match the curtain fabric.

Fabric amounts

For the length of the curtains use a steel rule to measure from the base of the curtain runner, where the hook will be placed, to the sill or floor as required. Add 15cm (6″) for a double hem at the foot and 1.5cm (½″) for the heading or, if the curtain is to cover the track when closed, add 1.5cm (½″) to amount required to cover track. Add a further 11.5cm (4½″)—or the depth of your buckram plus 1.5cm (½″)—for turnings at the top of the curtains.

For the width of each of a pair of

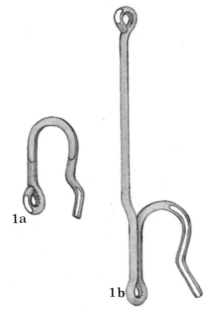

1a. *This type of sew-on hook can be used with all curtain tracks.*
1b. *Use long-stemmed hooks where you wish the curtains to cover the track.*

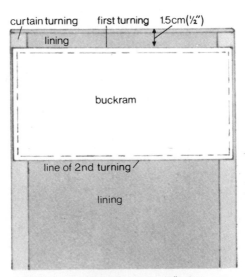

2. *Buckram placed 1.5cm (½″) from top.*

curtains, measure the length of the track and allow at least this measurement as the width in each curtain plus 5cm (2″) on both sides for the side hems. If you have to join widths of fabric to make up the required width it is easiest to base your calculations on full or half widths because any extra width can be incorporated into the curtains. Allow an extra 1.5cm (½″) or the width of the selvedge, if this is more, for each width being joined (turning allowance). Where you have three or more curtains to one window, calculate the width of each curtain as follows: measure the length of the track each curtain is to span and allow double this width in each curtain plus the allowances previously described.

The total. To calculate how many widths of fabric will be required for each curtain, divide the fabric width into the required width of the curtain and round up the amount to the nearest half or full width. Multiply this figure by the required length to give the minimum fabric required for each curtain.

☐ If the fabric has a pattern, calculate the amount of extra fabric required for matching it on each width, as described in the first section on unlined curtains. Add this to the minimum amount of fabric and multiply by the number of curtains to give the total amount of fabric required.

Calculating the pleats

The spaces. The total width of the spaces left at each side edge of the curtain and between each group of pleats must add up to the required finished width of each curtain, plus 2cm-4cm (¾″-1½″) more for ease. Each space may be 10cm-15cm (4″-6″) wide.

☐ Decide the width you wish the spaces to be and divide this into the required finished width of the curtain to give the number of spaces.

The pleats. Because there is a space at each side edge of the curtain, there is always one less group of pleats than the number of spaces.

☐ Start by subtracting the required finished width of the curtain from the unpleated width of fabric (less allowances for turnings and side hems). Into the remaining width divide the number of pleats to give the amount allowed for each pleat.

Making the curtains

Make the curtains with either sewn-in or detachable linings as described in the previous, section on curtains but do not, of course, attach heading tape. (Lining tape may be attached to detachable linings which are made up in the same way as for curtains with heading tapes.)

☐ Cut a length of buckram to fit the width of each curtain. Place the buckram on to the wrong side of the curtain to come exactly 1.5cm (½″) from the top edge. Pin and tack all round (fig.2).

Elegant pinch-pleated heading made to cover curtain track by Sanderson.

□ Fold over the top edge of the curtain (and lining if this is sewn in) on to the buckram for 1.5cm ($\frac{1}{2}$") and machine stitch through all thicknesses.

□ Machine stitch through all thicknesses along remaining three sides of the buckram.

□ Turn the folded edge of the curtain again for the depth of the buckram and tack. Slip stitch the side edges.

□ Mark the positions of the pleats accurately on the right side of the fabric with pins or tailor's chalk to the depth of the second turning.

Forming the pleats. Working with the right side of the curtain towards you, place the marked edges of each pleat together with wrong sides facing. Pin along the mark to the depth of the second turning. Machine stitch through all thicknesses along this line (fig.3).

□ Fold the fabric contained in each pleat into three equal pleats as shown in fig.4 and press the folds firmly with your fingers. Using the buttonhole twist backstitch by hand through all thicknesses just below the bottom edge of the buckram (you can feel this bottom edge easily).

□ Oversew the top of each section individually (fig.5).

Sewing on hooks. Place each hook in turn on the wrong side of the curtain in line with the seam line of the pleat and leaving the depth of the heading between the top of the hook and the top of the curtain.

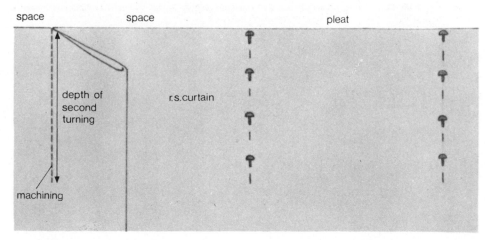

3. *Pleat formed by stitching marked edges together with wrong sides facing.*

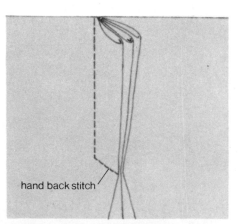

4. *Three equal pleats formed.*

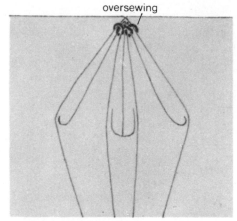

5. *Pleats oversewn at top.*

□ Using buttonhole twist double, oversew the hooks to the curtain through the holes at the bottom and then, on long-stemmed hooks, up the stems and round the holes at the top (fig.6). Fasten off securely.

□ Place the hooks for the side edges of the curtain about 5mm ($\frac{1}{4}$") in from sides and the same distance from the top of the curtain as the other hooks. Sew on as before. The curtains are now ready for hanging.

Hand stitching gives pinch-pleated headings a distinctive crispness.

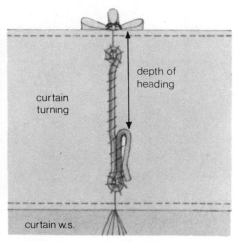

6. *Long-stemmed hook stitched in place.*

18

Needlecraft 2
quilts & cushions

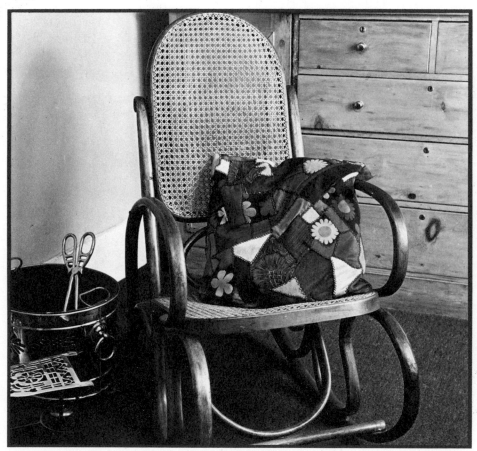

Four-piece duvet set

Duvets or continental quilts are an increasingly popular form of bedding, devised from the warm feather beds characteristic of Germany and Eastern European countries. These quilts not only replace the top sheet and blankets, but they are easy to handle, light to sleep under and retain heat exceptionally well. Duvets are available with a number of different stuffings: goose down, feathers and a mixture of feathers and down; also synthetics such as polyester mixtures. Of these, pure down is the most superior but all will give a warm comfortable covering. Because of their simple rectangular shape, it is very easy to make a duvet cover and less expensive than buying one. A complete matching set comprised of valance, bottom sheet, pillowcase and duvet cover can be made.

There are many interesting ways of making the set attractive and individual: plain or printed fabrics can be used or appliqué worked using a motif from the curtains. Alternating panels of contrasting fabrics could also be used.

Bed sizes

Quantities and instructions are for two standard sizes of bed.

Single bed size: 90cm x 190cm (3′x 6′3″).

Small double bed size: 135cm x 190cm (4′6″x 6′3″).

Individual quantities are given for each piece of the set, made from either 178cm (70″) wide sheeting for a single size, or 228cm (90″) wide sheeting for a double size.

Sheeting in a polyester and cotton mixture is preferable as it is quick drying and requires little or no ironing. Unless otherwise stated, instructions given are the same for a single bed or

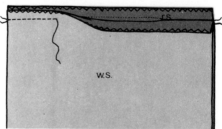

1. Leave opening for Velcro or zip.

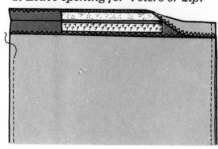

2. Stitch fastening into opening.

double bed, the base standing 30cm (12″) from the floor.

1.5cm (½″) turnings have been allowed unless otherwise stated.

Duvet cover

Size: the average size of a duvet is 137cm x 198cm (54″x 78″) for a single bed and 198cm x 198cm (78″x 78″) for a small double bed.

The duvet cover should be about 5cm (2″) larger all round than the duvet. This enables the duvet to move freely inside the cover.

There are various ways of fastening the cover, but the easiest and most popular are Velcro or a zip fastener.

You will need:

Single duvet cover: 4.30m (4⅝yd) of 178cm (70″) wide fabric.

1m (40″) of 2cm (¾″) wide Velcro or 75cm (30″) zip fastener.

Matching thread.

Double duvet cover: 4.30m (4⅝yd) of 228cm (90″) wide fabric.

1m (40″) of 2cm (¾″) wide Velcro or 75cm (30″) zip fastener.

Matching thread.

Cutting out

☐ For a single cover cut two rectangles 150cm x 211cm (59″x 83″).

☐ For a double cover cut two rectangles 211cm x 211cm (83″x 83″).

Making up

☐ First prepare the bottom end of the cover to take the Velcro or zip.

☐ Neaten with a zigzag stitch the two raw edges and turn 2.5cm (1″) to the wrong side and press.

☐ With right sides facing, stitch these two edges of the duvet cover together along this crease line leaving an opening in the centre of the seam the length of the Velcro or zip (fig.1).

☐ Insert the zip into the opening or stitch the Velcro to each side of the opening (fig.2).

☐ Press the turnings open for a zip or to one side if using Velcro.

☐ With right sides facing, stitch the remaining three sides together taking 1.5cm (½″) turnings. Trim the turnings at the corners and neaten them together with a zigzag stitch.

☐ Turn the cover through to the right side and press lightly.

Fitted bottom sheet

A fitted bottom sheet with elastic corners will fit neatly over the mattress and will not slip out of position; it will also crease less than a plain unfitted sheet.

You will need:

2.75m (3yd) of 178cm (70″) wide fabric for single and 228cm (90″) for double bed size.

1m (40″) of 1.5cm (½″) wide elastic.

Matching thread.

Cutting out

☐ Cut a rectangle of fabric to the size

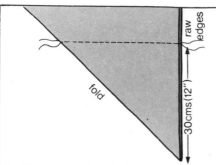

3. Stitching a fitted sheet corner.

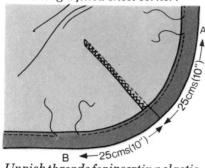

4. Unpick threads for inserting elastic.

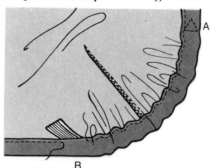

5. Stitch down elastic to gather corner.

of the mattress plus 38cm (15″) all round. The figures allow for an easy fit.

Making up

☐ With right sides facing, fold each corner of the rectangle so that the raw edges lie together on top of each other forming a point.

☐ Stitch across the corner 30cm (12″) from the point (fig.3).

☐ Cut off the point to within 5mm (¼″) of the stitching line and neaten the raw edges together with a zigzag stitch.

☐ Work a small hem all around the outside edge of the sheet; first turn under 5mm (¼″) and then 2cm (¾″). Machine stitch close to the fold.

☐ At each corner measure off 25cm (10″) to each side of the dart; this section will form a channel for the elastic. Unpick a few stitches at each point, A and B (fig. 4). Cut a 25cm (10″) length of elastic and thread through the channel from A to B. Secure the ends of the elastic by stitching small triangles over each end, through all thicknesses (fig.5). Stitch the opening. Press.

☐ Repeat with the other three corners then fit the sheet over the mattress.

Valance

The valance is a frill of fabric attached to a rectangle of matching fabric or calico, and placed under the mattress so that the frill hangs to the floor, covering the base of the bed and the legs.

The length of the frill should be about double the three sides of the bed, unless you wish the frill to go all around in which case it would be double the four sides of the bed.

You will need:

For a valance which goes round three sides 30.5cm (12″) finished depth:

4m (4½yd) of 178cm (70″) fabric for single bed.

4m (4½yd) of 228cm (90″) fabric for double bed.

3m (3yd) of 1.5cm (½″) wide tape for ties.

Cutting out

Remember that 1.5cm (½″) turnings are allowed throughout.

☐ First cut a rectangle of fabric to fit the top of the bed, plus 1.5cm (½″) all round.

☐ For the frill cut 6 strips of fabric each from the full width of the fabric 33.5cm (13½″) deep.

Making up

☐ With right sides facing, stitch the frill pieces together into one long strip. Neaten raw edges together with a zigzag stitch and press to one side.

☐ Trim frill to the required length.

☐ Work a small double hem taking 1.5cm (½″) along one long edge of the frill (this is the bottom of the frill) and across the two short ends, mitring corners.

☐ Divide the frill into eight equal parts along the remaining long edge (fig.6).

☐ Work two rows of gathering through each section.

Attaching the frill to the base.

Neaten the top end of the base cover with a small 1.5cm (½″) hem.

☐ Measure and divide the remaining three sides of the base cover into eight equal parts and mark with pins.

☐ With right sides facing, gather and pin the frill to the base cover, matching the pins on the frill to the pins on the base cover (fig.7). Pull up the gathering threads and distribute the fullness evenly. Tack and stitch. Neaten the turnings together with a zigzag stitch and press towards the frill (fig.8).

For a strong finish and to make sure the frill hangs correctly you can add another row of stitches. Work from

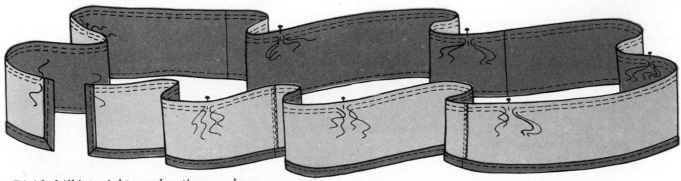

6. *Divide frill into eight equal sections as shown.*

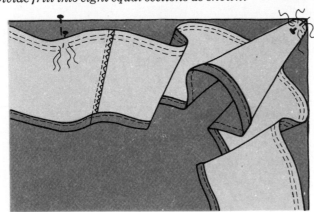

7. *Connect frill sections to corresponding top sections.*

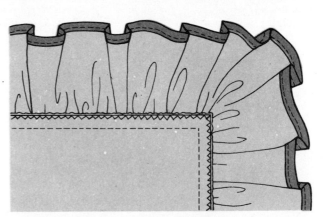

8. *Press gathered seam towards frill.*

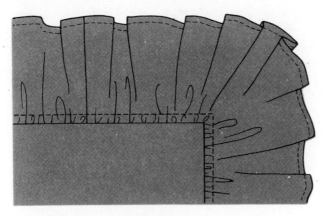

9. *Topstitching through all thicknesses is optional.*

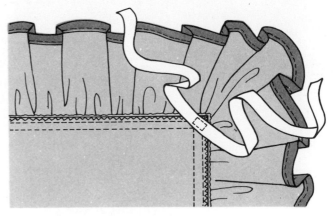

10. *Attach tape to valance corners. Tie these to posts.*

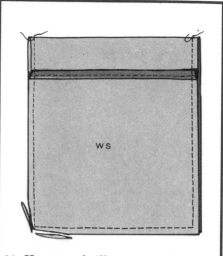

Lightweight duvet with colourful covers makes a welcoming bed!

11. *Hem top of pillowcase sections and then sew sections together.*

larger rectangle by stitching a small double hem, taking 1.5cm ($\frac{1}{2}$") turnings.
☐ Make a 1.5cm ($\frac{1}{2}$") double hem on one short edge of the smaller rectangle.
☐ With right sides facing, place the two rectangles together with raw edges level. Fold the extending flap on the larger piece down over the smaller piece as shown (fig.11).
☐ With right sides facing, stitch the two rectangles together on three sides, leaving the finished ends open.
☐ Trim the turnings at the corners and neaten the raw edges together with a zigzag stitch.
☐ Turn the pillowcase to the right side and fold flap to the inside.

right side and tack the frill through seam allowance through all thicknesses. Then with one edge of the machine foot to the stitching line, stitch through all thicknesses (fig.9).
☐ Cut the tape into four equal lengths and stitch the centre of each piece to a corner of the valance on the wrong side as indicated (fig.10).
☐ Place the completed valance on the base under the mattress and tie the tapes around the legs of the bed, under the frill.

Pillowcase

For a pillow about 70cm x 50cm (27" x 19")
You will need:
70cm ($\frac{3}{4}$yd) of 178cm (70") wide fabric.
Cutting out
☐ Cut out two rectangles, one measuring 89cm x 55cm (34$\frac{1}{2}$" x 21") and the other 75cm x 55cm (29" x 21").
Making up
☐ First neaten one short edge of the

Right: detail shows neatly fitted corners and completed valance.

American patchwork quilts

More importance is attached to the art of making patchwork quilts in America than in any other country. Traditionally, the neighbourly custom of 'quilting bees'—parties at which women gathered to help in the final work in making quilts—lent great social significance to this craft.

No bride's bottom drawer was considered complete without thirteen quilts. The first twelve were made throughout a girl's adolescence, and the last was the marriage quilt itself, adorned with a heart and completed at a quilting bee during which the betrothal was formally announced.

The block method of quilt construction which evolved in the 19th century—and was greatly aided by the invention of the sewing machine in about 1850—is not the only form of patchwork practised in America. It is, however, the most common method, probably by virtue of its being so economical in terms of both time and material.

Basically, the block method consists of piecing scraps of fabric together in a geometric pattern to form a square section or block. (The term 'piecing' simply means the sewing together, edge to edge, of small pieces of cloth.)

When enough blocks have been worked to make up a complete quilt, they are sewn or 'set' together, either directly adjacent to each other or separated by strips or blocks of plain fabric.

This method obviously reduces the sewing time, particularly as no paper patterns are required and the straight seams involved lend themselves especially well to machine sewing.

Although it is possible to piece and set the blocks by hand in back stitch and using papers, this is a much more laborious process than machine stitching which enables you to run up blocks at a speed unknown to many other forms of patchwork.

In addition to these practical advantages, the block method permits enormous scope for design and invention. There are two stages of design—that of the blocks themselves and that of the arrangement of the blocks.

There are hundreds of traditional patterns to follow. The importance given to their colourful names is another characteristic of American patchwork. The possible combinations of geometrical shapes are innumerable and constitute a refreshing change from the popular English hexagon.

It is advisable to start by following a traditional pattern. First master piecing—then create your own designs.

Left: this superb bedspread, made up entirely of Winged Square blocks, is a fine example of the importance of planning a colour scheme.

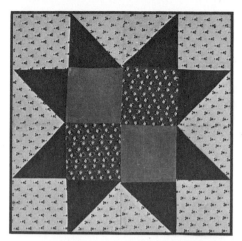

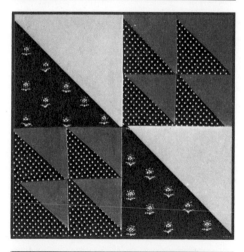

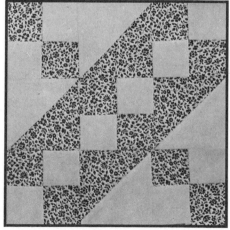

Planning

Before you embark on constructing a quilt, it is important to plan your design if the end result is not to be confused or messy. Indeed, simple patterns are often the most successful. Measure the bed you intend covering from top to bottom and from side to side. If you wish your quilt to reach the floor on three or all four sides of the bed, add this measurement—from the top of the bed to the floor—to your calculations where appropriate.

If you are to obtain a regular design all over the quilt, rather than a random effect, it is obviously important to check that you have enough of each fabric to be used. It is safer to overestimate your requirements, especially if you are using scraps of old material which you will not be able to match up if you run out.

It is advisable to experiment with a few sample blocks. This may help you choose a design, and will give you practice in sewing straight seams. In addition, you will then be able to calculate the area of cloth that a given block takes, and can estimate roughly how much of each fabric is needed for the total number of blocks required.

Building blocks

There is no correct size for blocks. They can vary from 15cm (6″) to 60cm (24″) square. The most common size, however, and probably the most manageable, is 25cm (10″) to 30cm (12″) square. Whatever design and size you choose, accuracy is of the utmost importance. The secret of success is to use window templates, which let you plan the pattern exactly, allowing 6mm (¼″) for seams.

On the wrong side of fabrics chosen for the block, pencil along both outer and inner lines of the template. Cut along the outer line—the inner line will act as a seam guide. In this way, you will obtain accuracy both in cutting the patches to be pieced together and in seaming. Quilt piecing is a craft of precision; tiny inaccuracies may throw your pattern out—blocks will not be exact squares, corners will not match up.

Start constructing your block according to the design you have chosen, being careful to follow seam guides. Open up and press each seam flat as you go. Spraying the assembled patches lightly with spray starch is a quick and efficient way of obtaining flat units.

Four examples of pieced blocks.
From top to bottom: Saw-tooth Star, Double Four-patch, Flock of Geese, (three of the four-patch family) and Road to California or Jacob's Ladder (one of the nine-patch family).

The actual piecing of the blocks will obviously vary slightly according to the pattern chosen. A general rule, however, is to join any triangles first to form squares, and then to build up the squares to form bigger and bigger units. A good example of this is the construction of the Windmill block (fig.1).

1. *Sew triangles together.*   *Join squares in pairs.*   *Make up first square patch.*   *Final four-patch block.*

It is a good idea to pin the points at which the seams meet, as you go, to ensure that the lines of the pattern match. If these basic principles are followed, there are no patterns based on squares and triangles that cannot be assembled.

Most pieced blocks belong either to the four-patch (fig.2) or to the nine-patch (fig.3) family. As their names imply, they involve either four or nine basic units, which can be subdivided in any number of ways.

Other blocks can be made by using a combination of piecing and appliqué, or by using appliqué alone. If you use appliqué, planning is once again very important before you begin.

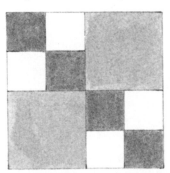 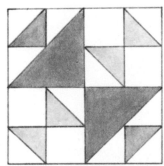  

2. *Simple four-patch block.*   *Old Maid's Puzzle.*   *Broken Dishes.*   *Indian Hatchet.*

3. *Basic nine-patch block.*   *Bear's Tracks or Bear's Paw.*   *Jack in the Box.*

Setting
The final design of the quilt depends on the arrangement of the blocks. Joining the blocks is known as 'setting'.

Blocks can be joined side by side to create an unbroken pattern over the whole quilt. Road to California blocks, for example, may not be very striking individually but they create an exciting pattern when set together. Windmill and Broken Dishes are also particularly attractive set in this way for a repetitive all-over result.

This way of setting can create a messy effect, however, particularly as the finished article is to be quilted. Quilting tends to be confused or concealed on all-patchwork quilts.

It is often advisable, therefore, to set each block beside a square of plain material—using a window template to cut it out exactly the same size—to obtain a checker-board effect (fig.4). Appliquéd blocks in particular are shown at their best set in this way so that the complete pattern of each individual block stands out boldly.

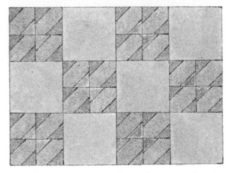

4. *Alternate pieced and plain blocks.*

Another way is to alternate pieced or appliquéd squares and plain squares diagonally, using half squares at the sides to obtain straight edges (fig.5). Alternatively, pieced blocks may be alternated with appliquéd blocks. Another method of setting which also throws each block into relief is the use of lattice bands, usually about 8cm (3″) wide excluding seams, which separate and frame each block (fig.6). This is sometimes known as sash work. Lattice strips, cut on the straight of the fabric, can also be set diagonally, again using half blocks at the sides (fig.7).

5. *Alternate blocks diagonally.*

6. *Blocks separated by lattice bands.*

7. *Diagonal lattice strips.*

Finishing

When sufficient blocks have been set to make the required quilt, they can be bordered with a simple frame of plain material, bound with bias tape or even decorated with a pieced border—made up in a similar way to the blocks.

The finished article can then be lined and quilted. Quilting by blocks should be done by hand to avoid puckering the patchwork. No frame is necessary. Quilting is displayed at its best where pieced or appliquéd blocks have been alternated with plain squares. The design of the pieced or appliquéd blocks should simply be followed by small running stitches while the plain blocks may either echo the patterned blocks or introduce a totally new idea.

Detail of Shoo Fly bedspread.

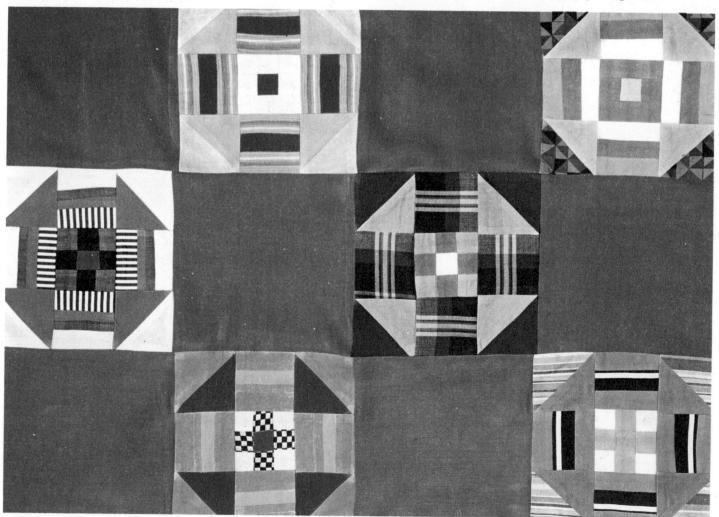

crazy patchwork quilts

Crazy patchwork is one of the simplest forms of patchwork, demanding little skill in stitching or planning. It consists of sewing unhemmed scraps of fabric on to a foundation fabric in a random fashion. The raw edges are then covered with embroidery which prevents them from fraying.

A superb quilt of random patches worked in blocks and embroidered.

The time devoted to the embroidery depends very much on the individual. The method of working can range from the most elaborate hand worked embroidery to a machined zigzag stitch.

Crazy patchwork is thought to have originated in America in the 17th century as an economical method of making quilts. Crazy quilts were often created out of warm woollen fabrics, frequently cut from old clothes. The great advantage of this method was that virtually any scrap of fabric—whatever its size or shape—could be used, and that it was quick and simple to execute.

Crazy patchwork did not become popular in England until the mid 19th century. Towards the end of the last century, the nature of crazy patchwork underwent a radical change. It developed from its lowly origins to a luxurious and elaborate affair, particularly in Victorian England. Sumptuous silk and velvet fabrics were used, which, in spite of their own rich texture and colour, were almost hidden by decorative embroidery worked in silk and metallic threads. Ribbon, braid, beads and sequins were also incorporated.

The crazy patchwork of today has returned to its former simplicity for practical reasons of rapidity and durability. It is often made up of cotton fabrics which, as for all patchwork, are the most suitable, especially if the article is to undergo constant use and frequent washing.

A mixture of fabrics is possible since the foundation fabric bears much of the strain, but the resulting work will not be so strong. An excess of embroidery and decoration can also weaken the patches and makes cleaning more difficult.

Method

The initial preparation and assembly of patches for crazy patchwork is extremely simple. It should appeal to anyone who lacks the patience necessary for other forms of patchwork, many of which demand careful and time-consuming planning.

The foundation

You will need a strong but light-weight foundation fabric that is not too stiff, such as a fine cotton fabric. The backing fabric must be the size of the finished article.

It can be made up of a single piece of fabric or several pieces of fabric joined together in back stitch or straight machine stitch to make up the required size. Economize by using the good parts of worn sheets or large sections of discarded dresses.

Alternatively, the patchwork may be made up in sections which are later joined together when they are com-

Detail of quilt opposite illustrates the rich variety of stitching used to decorate the velvet patches and to keep the edges from fraying.

pleted. This approach is based on the same principle as the American method of quilt construction by blocks, as has been described in the section on American patchwork quilts on page 25.

Whatever method is employed, the foundation fabric should be ironed before any patches are applied to ensure that it is quite flat.

The patches

You will need as many different scraps of fabric as possible. You can continue collecting additional scraps as work progresses if you have no definite overall pattern in mind.

Patches can be of virtually any size and shape. Ensure that they do not show signs of wear. Iron them flat and trim off any frayed edges and irregular ends.

Design

Unless a particular colour scheme is desired, no initial planning is needed. Although the pattern is a random one, a balance of light and dark shades and of relative sizes and shapes of the patches is required if the result is not

to be too disorganized and messy.

It is therefore advisable to plan the arrangement of about a dozen patches at a time as you work. Try overlapping them, and move them around until you are satisfied that they look right in relation to each other and to any work already completed. A predominant colour randomly interspersed helps to strengthen the design.

It is also possible to work to a pre-arranged pattern—a specific colour grouping of patches, for example, or sections of crazy patchwork, each framed by bands of a single colour. If you intend to approach crazy patchwork in this way, work out your design on paper, and then mark it out on the foundation fabric as a guide.

Applying patches

Lay the first few patches on to the foundation fabric, overlapping them by 1.5cm ($\frac{1}{2}''$). It is usual to start working in one corner of the foundation fabric with a right-angled patch, but this is not a strict rule.

When you have decided on the arrangement of the first few patches, pin them to the foundation. Working on the right side and starting with the first patch, sew it to the foundation with an even running stitch round its raw

Crazy quilt (right) achieves regularity by intermixing solid squares (see detail).

A modern example of crazy patchwork designed and made by Kathleen Smith.

edges. Sew round the raw edges of each of the adjoining patches in turn. Where patches overlap, make sure that you stitch through all the layers of fabric, including the foundation fabric, so that the raw edges cannot slip out. Remove the pins as you work, and continue adding patches until you have covered the foundation fabric.

An alternative method is to apply the patches with a straight machine stitch. Use a fairly long stitch and check your tension to ensure that there is no 'pull' on the patches. You must be particularly careful about this if you are using fabrics of different weights within the same piece of work.

Whichever method you choose, the next stage—intended to hide both the stitching and the raw edges—is the same.

There is a third method of application, however, which combines the covering of the raw edges. This is to use a machine with a swing needle. Simply pin the patches on to the foundation fabric and, using a fairly wide zigzag stitch, sew them to the foundation following the raw edges.

It is advisable to go over the edges a second time using a closer zigzag stitch for extra strength and to guard against fraying if the article is to be washed frequently.

Embroidery

Unless you have used the last method of applying patches, the raw edges of the patches need to be covered with embroidery to prevent them from fraying. The basic hand worked stitches for this process are feather stitch and herringbone stitch and they should cover both the raw edges and the initial stitching. This additional stitchery will also strengthen the patchwork fabric. The use of a single colour thread throughout acts as a unifying factor and gives a degree of consistency to a random design. There are many kinds of embroidery stitch and thread that can be used. Experiment, adding beads and ribbons as in Victorian quilts for a rich, elaborate effect.

Finishing

Crazy patchwork results in a thick, heavy article which is virtually impossible to quilt. It is sufficient simply to line it—preferably in a shade to echo a predominant colour in the patchwork.

Traditionally, the edges of a piece of crazy patchwork were simply turned under and the lining was attached by two rows of running stitch round the edges. You may prefer to bind the edges of the patchwork or to add a decorative fringe, frill or braiding for a final flourish. Any such edging should be in keeping with the overall effect of the work, and should not overpower it.

Basic stitches

Feather stitch (fig.1) is worked in a vertical line from top to bottom. The stitch should be centred on the raw edge of the patch to be covered.

☐ Bring the needle from the left of the raw edge to the right and take a small vertical stitch as shown in fig.1a, catching the thread under the point of the needle.

☐ Take the needle back to the left of the raw edge and make another small vertical stitch, again catching the thread under the needle.

☐ Continue making a series of stitches to the right and left of the raw edge in turn, catching the thread under the needle each time (fig.1b).

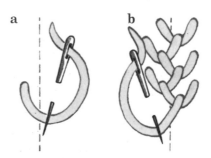

a   b

Herringbone stitch (fig.2) is worked from left to right. Again, the stitch should be centred on the raw edge being covered.

☐ Make a series of small horizontal stitches to the left, above and below the raw edge in turn as shown.

simple cushion making

Add an individual character to any room with cushions sewn by you in your own choice of fabric. Make them in a variety of shapes, sizes and textures, in colours to blend with your decor. Cushions also make a useful way to display other techniques, such as patchwork, appliqué and quilting.

The fabric

Most fabrics can be used for flat

cushion covers (those without welts), although very fine fabrics usually need backing and can be difficult to work on. If you intend to pipe the edges of a cushion do not use a loosely woven fabric as the cord will show through.

How much fabric? For a plain (un-piped) flat cushion decide on the size of your cushion cover and allow at least twice this amount, plus 1.5cm (½″) extra all round for turnings. For a

30cm (12″) flat square or round finished cover you will need a piece of fabric at least 33cm x 66cm (13″x26″).

Allow an extra 45cm (½yd) of fabric if you intend to pipe the edge of the cover. This amount of fabric, although some wastage is involved, avoids too many joins in the casing strip.

For a well-filled, professional looking cushion make the cover 1.5cm (½″) smaller all round than its pad.

Plain flat square cushion

You will need:
A cushion pad.
Fabric as above.
Matching thread.

☐ Keeping the straight of grain, cut two pieces of fabric to the calculated size.

☐ With right sides together, tack and machine stitch around three sides.

☐ On the fourth side fold down the seam allowances on to the wrong side of each section and press. Trim the stitched corners (fig.1). Neaten turnings and turn right side out. Press.

☐ Insert the pad and slip stitch the opening neatly by hand. These stitches can be easily removed when the cover is washed.

Rectangular cushions are made in the same way.

1. *Square cushion stitched on three sides with corners trimmed.*

Plain flat round cushion

It is necessary to make a paper pattern to make sure of an accurate curve. Use the pin and string method (Design know-how 1, page 28) to draw a semi-circle on a large sheet of paper. Make the distance between pin and pencil equal to the radius of the finished cover, plus 1.5cm (½″).

You will need:
A cushion pad.
Fabric as above.
Matching thread.

☐ Fold fabric in half lengthways on straight of grain. Place the pattern with the straight edge to the fold. Pin into place and cut along the curved line only. Mark grain line along fold with tacking.

☐ Cut another piece of fabric in the same way.

☐ With right sides together, grain lines matching, place the two sections together. Tack and machine stitch 1.5cm (½″) from the edge all round the cover, leaving an opening of about one quarter of the circumference to turn through.

☐ Clip small V-shapes to within 3mm (⅛″) from the stitching at 3cm (1″)

A whole heap of cushions in various shapes, sizes and fabrics.

intervals all round (fig.2).

☐ Finish off as for a square cover.

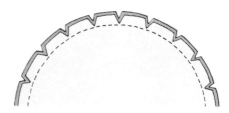

2. Round cushion stitched and clipped.

Piped cushions

Piping should be attached before the cushion cover is made up. It is not a good idea to pipe flat round cushion covers as these do not keep a good shape when the pad is inserted.

Zipper foot. To attach piping successfully by machine it is necessary to use a zipper or piping foot on your sewing machine. This is made in one piece, instead of split as with the standard foot, enabling the stitching to be worked close to the piping.

The cushion cover is usually inserted into the machine with its bulk on the left and the turnings of the seam under the foot. The needle should be to the left of the foot which is pressed up hard against the piping cord.

Keep the foot in this position throughout the sewing. At the corners, leave the needle down, lift the foot and turn the fabric round to the new position. Lower foot and continue sewing.

Piping consists of a cord covered with bias-cut strips of fabric and is stitched into a seam.

Piping cord is usually cotton and made up of three strands. It comes in a range of thicknesses and number 2 or 3 is most suitable for cushion covers. As the cord is liable to shrink, buy about 25cm (¼yd) extra. Boil the cord for about 5 minutes and dry it thoroughly before use to ensure that it is fully shrunk.

☐ Cut and join enough 4.5cm (1½″) wide bias strips to fit the perimeter of the cover, plus 10cm (4″).

☐ Lay piping cord, slightly longer than the strip, centrally along the wrong side of this strip. Fold the edges together, with the cord in the middle. Tack or machine stitch casing firmly round cord to within 3cm (1″) of each end, keeping the stitching as close as possible to the piping (fig.3).

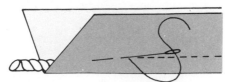

3. Casing tacked round cord.

☐ Starting in the middle of a side, pin the casing all round the edge on the right side of one cover piece. The raw edges of the folded casing must be level with the raw edges of the cover. At each corner, clip into the casing seam allowance to within 3mm (⅛″) of the tacking stitches of the casing. This will make the piping lie flat (fig.4).

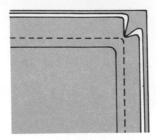

4. Casing pinned in place.

☐ To make a neat join in the piping, unfold the untacked portion of the casing at each end and overlap them by 1.5cm (½″). Adjust the overlap to fit the cushion cover exactly. Join the ends as for bias strips, trimming to 6mm (¼″).

☐ Overlap the cord for 3cm (1″) and trim off the excess. Unravel 3cm (1″) at each end and cut away two strands from one end and one strand from the other. Overlap and twist together the remaining three ends and oversew or bind them firmly (fig.5).

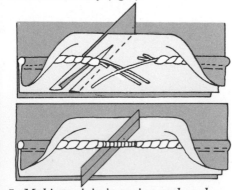

5. Making a join in casing and cord.

☐ Fold over casing and tack round joined cord. Tack piping to cushion.

☐ Place the second cover piece on top of the piped piece, with right sides together and enclosing the piping. Tack and machine stitch the cover together along three sides, stitching as close as possible to the cord.

☐ Finish as for a plain cover.

Left: piped patchwork cushion.

Two ways to insert a zip

When a cover needs to be removed frequently for washing you may prefer to insert a permanent type of fastening, such as a zip fastener.

Zip fasteners are best kept for use on cushions with straight sides as a zip fastener is inclined to distort the shape of a round cushion.

The methods given here are for piped cushions but plain cushions can be treated in the same way.

Zip fastener stitched by hand. This is a very neat way of putting in a zip.

☐ Make up the cushion in the usual way but stitch along the fourth side for 3cm (1″) at each end. Fasten off the stitching securely. Turn the cover right side out.

☐ Press under the turning along the piped edge if piping has been used.

☐ Place the piped edge over the right side of the closed zip so that the folded edge of the turning lies centrally along the teeth of the zip.

☐ On the right side of the cover tack along the gulley between the piping and cover (fig.6).

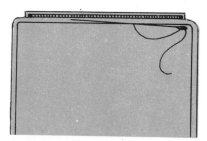

6. Tacking along the gulley.

☐ Fold under the unpiped edge of the opening and put it on to the zip so that it meets the piped edge. Tack in position close to the edge of the zip teeth, curving the stitching into the fold at the top and bottom.

☐ Using double sewing thread, prick-stitch the zip to the cover along the tacked line. Prick stitch is like a spaced back stitch, but on the right side of the fabric the stitches should be extremely small (fig.7).

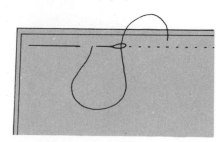

7. Working prick stitch.

Zip fastener stitched by machine. With the cover inside out, place the zip face downwards on the piped edge of the opening, with the teeth as close as possible to the piping cord.

☐ Tack and machine stitch the zip to the turning and piping only, close to the teeth, using a zipper foot (fig.8).

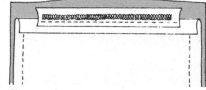

8. Zip stitched to piped edge.

☐ Turn the cover through to the right side and place the other folded edge over the zip to meet the piped edge.

☐ Tack and machine stitch the cover to the zip tape 1cm (⅜″) from the fold; take the stitching across to the fold at each end (fig.9).

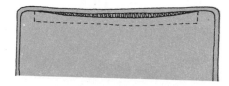

9. Zip machine stitched in place.

☐ Undo the zip, turn cover to the wrong side and snip into the stitched-down turning at each end.

If you prefer, the zip can be inserted before the other three sides are stitched.

Cushion pads

Many large stores sell square and oblong cushion pads in a wide range of sizes. It is, however, quite possible to make your own pads in the size and shape you want.

Filling. Down is the most luxurious and most expensive filling and feathers are a good alternative, but many people today prefer to use a synthetic filling which has the advantage of being washable.

Kapok, shredded foam and foam chips are cheaper fillings, but kapok can give a lumpy look and foam becomes hard after a time.

Pad covers. These can be made from sheeting, calico or any inexpensive, firmly-woven fabric, but if you choose feathers or down for the filling it is essential to buy a down-proof fabric for the pad cover.

Making up. Make the cover in the same way as a plain cushion cover, remembering that it should be 1.5cm (½″) larger all round than the outer cushion cover. Turn through to the right side and press.

☐ Stuff the cover with filling so that it is plump but not hard, paying particular attention to the corners.

☐ Pin the folded edges of the opening together. Then tack and machine stitch close to the edge.

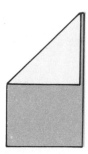

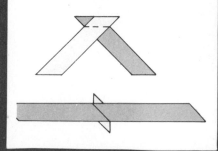

cushions & bolsters

The previous introductory section covered techniques for making plain and piped flat cushions and for inserting zip fasteners into cushion covers. This chapter explains how to make bolsters and cushions with welts.

Cushions with welts

This type of cushion has a strip of fabric separating the top section from the bottom; it can be piped or left with plain edges, and can have a soft filling or be made from a foam rubber pad for a firm seating cushion. It can be made to almost any shape that you choose.

The fabric. The range of suitable fabrics for a soft cushion is as wide as that for flat cushions.

If you are making a firm seating cushion which will have a lot of wear, use a medium weight furnishing fabric recommended for loose covers.

How much fabric? The easiest way of estimating this is to draw a cutting chart to scale on graph paper; eg take one small square on the graph paper to represent 3cm (1″). By measuring the length of the completed layout you will be able to see how much fabric you will need for a plain cushion.

If the cushion is to be piped, allow extra fabric for this. About 45cm (½yd) should be sufficient to pipe the top and bottom, but this depends on the size of the cushion.

To make a cutting layout. Draw a straight line to represent the width of the fabric. Draw a line at right angles to each end of the first line. Then draw on the shapes of the cover pieces: a top and bottom, and either separate welt strips for each side of the cushion or one long strip to go right round the cushion (plus a little extra if possible) if the cushion does not have corners, eg a round or oval cushion. Add on 1.5cm (½″) seam allowance all round each piece (fig.1).

Note. Pieces should be cut on the straight of grain. If the fabric has a pile or one-way design this should run from back to front on the top and bottom pieces and from top to bottom on the welt.

Piping. A cushion with a welt looks better if it is piped. Make up piping and attach it to the top and bottom sections (see page 34 for this technique), before joining them to the welt.

Zip fastener. If a zip fastener is to be inserted into a square or oblong cover, insert this between the welt and one side of the bottom piece of the cover before attaching the top piece.

Alternatively the zip can be inserted into the centre of one welt section or centrally on the bottom section. In

Making a welted cushion is an excellent way to display a piece of work, like this delightful needlepoint embroidery.

either case the relevant section should be cut in two equal pieces of half the finished size plus a 1.5cm (½″) seam allowance all round each piece.

Cushion pads

Soft cushions. Square, round and oblong cushion pads with welts can be bought ready made but if you prefer, or if you want a more unusual shape, it is quite easy to make your own pad.

Make the pad cover in the same way as the outer cover, making it 1.5cm (½″) larger all round than the outer cover. Do not pipe the edges. Suitable fabrics and soft fillings are discussed on page 35 in the previous section.

Firm cushions. Foam rubber pads are sold without covers and can be cut to a different shape, if required, with a large pair of sharp scissors or a sharp knife, depending upon the thickness of the foam. Stick a paper template of the

exact shape required to the top of the piece of foam with small pieces of sticky tape, draw round this with a ball-point pen and then cut out the shape.

It is advisable to make an inner covering for a foam rubber pad to protect the foam and prevent the outer cover from sticking to it.

The pad for a firm welted cushion should be the same size as the outer cover so that the edges of the outer cover sit neatly on those of the pad. A good tip is to cut the outer cover the same size as the pad cover but to make very slightly larger turnings—about 3mm (⅛″) larger on the outer cover—to ensure a snug fit.

1. *An example of a cutting layout with the top, bottom and four separate welt sections drawn in position.*

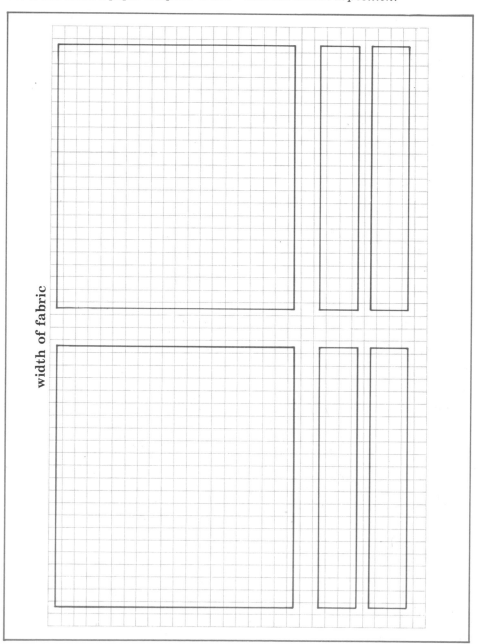

width of fabric

Round cushions

You will need:
A cushion pad.
Fabric for cover as above.
Piping cord (optional).

To make the cushion. Make a circular paper pattern for the top and bottom of the cushion to the finished size, using string the length of the radius to draw the first quarter circle arc.

☐ Pin the pattern to the fabric, following the cutting chart, and cut out a top and bottom piece in fabric, not forgetting to add 1.5cm (½″) seam allowance all round. Cut a strip for the welt to the required depth, by the length of the circumference of the circular pattern (multiply the radius by 6.3 for this measure), plus 1.5cm (½″) seam allowance all round. (If you have enough fabric it is advisable to allow a little extra on this length which can be trimmed away later if necessary.)

☐ Fold the top and bottom pieces in half and mark the centre back of each piece with thread.

☐ On the welt piece work a line of stitching along each long edge on the seam line. Snip into these edges at 2.5cm (1″) intervals, almost to the stitching. This ensures a neat fit when the welt is attached to the top and bottom pieces.

☐ With right sides together, pin one long edge of the welt to the top piece, 1.5cm (½″) from the edge. Start pinning at the centre back, matching the centre back mark with a point 1.5cm (½″) from one short end. Continue pinning until the welt is pinned right round the top and then pin in the welt seam (fig.2).

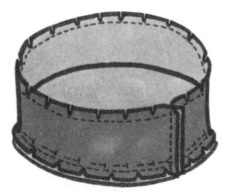

2. The welt pinned on to a round cushion top, with welt seam pinned in.

☐ Stitch the welt seam and trim the seam allowance on the second short end to 1.5cm (½″) if necessary.
☐ Tack and stitch the welt to the top, taking 1.5cm (½″) turnings.
☐ Snip 'V'-shaped notches almost to the stitching at 2.5cm (1″) intervals in the circular piece and press the turnings on to the welt.
☐ Pin the bottom piece to the welt, making sure that the grain runs the same way as on the top section. Tack

and stitch, taking 1.5cm (½″) seams, leaving about one third of the edge unstitched to turn through. Notch and press turnings as before.
☐ Turn cover to the right side, insert pad and slip stitch opening.

Square cushions

You will need:
A cushion pad.
Fabric for cover as above.
Piping cord (optional).
Zip fastener (optional).

To make the cushion. Cut out the pieces for top, bottom and welt of cushion on the straight of grain to the sizes given in the cutting chart (the finished size plus seam allowance).

☐ Take two side strips and join them along one short edge taking 1.5cm (½″) turnings. Taper stitching into the corners 1.5cm (½″) from the beginning and end of each seam (fig.3). Join the

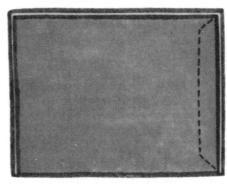

3. Two welt strips stitched together before attaching welt to a square top.

other strips to these two in the same way to make a continuous strip for the welt. Press turnings to one side.
☐ With right sides together, pin the top section of the cover on to the welt, matching corners of the top to welt seams. Tack and stitch (fig.4).

4. The top section of a square cushion cover stitched to the welt.

☐ Attach the bottom piece to the welt in the same way, but leave one side open to turn through. Make sure that the grain runs in the same direction on the top and bottom.
☐ Turn cover to the right side, insert pad and slip stitch opening.

Bolsters

The basic bolster shape is cylindrical, and can be piped or decorated with braid, or other trimming.

The fabric. Choose a closely woven, medium or heavyweight fabric, such as velvet, corduroy, firm tweed, linen or heavy cotton. A loosely woven fabric like soft tweed is unsuitable as it will pull at the seams.

How much fabric? Decide on the length and the diameter of the ends. You will need enough fabric to cut a piece to the length of the finished bolster, plus 3cm (1″) for turnings, by the length of the finished circumference of the ends (see Design know-how chapter 1, page 28), plus at least 3cm (1″) for seaming, and two circles with a diameter 3cm (1″) larger than that of

A poppy motif applied by machine adds interest to a simple striped bolster.

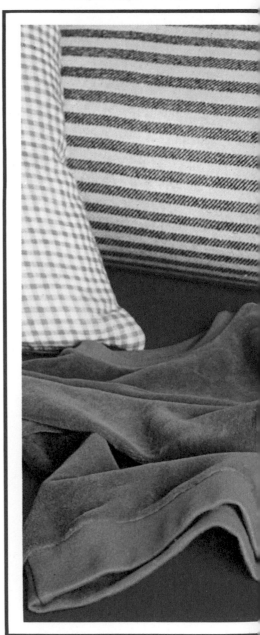

the finished ends. Draw the pieces to scale on a cutting layout to calculate the amount of fabric required.

Piping. This should be made up and attached to the ends before joining them to the body section.

Zip fastener. If you wish to use a zip fastener insert this into the seam of the body section before the ends are stitched into place.

Bolster pads

Soft bolster pads can be bought ready made in a limited size range. If you wish to make your own pad, make the cover in the same way as the outer cover but do not add piping. It should be 1.5cm (½") larger all round than the outer cover (fabrics and fillings can be the same as for ordinary cushions).
Firm bolster. Foam rubber pads are sold without covers. It is advisable to make an inner cover for a foam-rubber pad for the reasons described for a cushion with a welt, and the same making up points apply.

To make a bolster

You will need:
Fabric as above. Piping (optional). Zip fastener (optional). A bolster pad.

☐ Make a circular paper pattern the size of the finished ends (see Design know-how chapter 1, page 28).

☐ Pin the pattern to the fabric, following the cutting layout, and cut out the two ends, not forgetting to add 1.5cm (½") seam allowance all round. Cut a strip for the body section of the finished length, plus 3cm (1") for seams, by the length of the circumference of the circular pattern, plus 3cm (1") for the seams. (If you have enough fabric it is advisable to allow a little extra on this measurement which can be trimmed off after joining if necessary.)

☐ Fold and mark the ends as for the top and bottom of a circular cushion.

☐ On the body section work a line of stitching on the seam lines at the sides of the bolster.
Make 'V'-shaped notches at 2.5cm (1") intervals almost to this line of stitching. This makes it possible to ease the body section on to the ends.

☐ Stitch the body seam, leaving an opening of half to three quarters of its length in the centre to turn through.

☐ Pin the body section to the ends as if fitting the welt on to the top of a circular cushion (fig.2).

☐ Tack and stitch the ends into place taking 1.5cm (½") turnings.

☐ Make 'V'-shaped notches at 2.5cm (1") intervals on the circular pieces and press the turnings on to the body section.

☐ Turn cover to the right side and insert pad. Slip stitch opening.

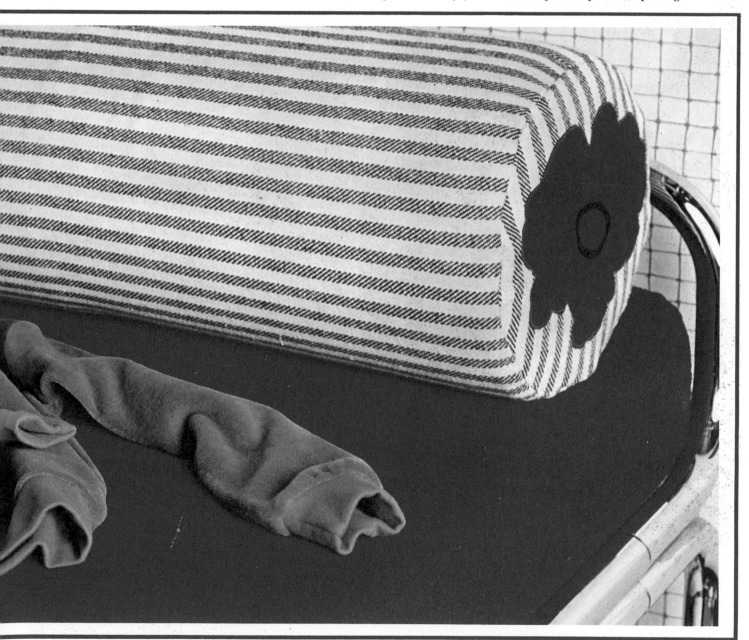

'soft sculpture' cushions

What is soft sculpture? First of all it is a form of three-dimensional art. The term is applied to a wide range of objects, usually sewn from cloth and padded in some way. Sometimes it is described as 'toys for adults'—a cup of coffee or a typewriter made from foam rubber and towelling, or a huge pea pod made of the shiniest of satin and filled with soft wadding. Some objects are definitely furniture—a padded

reclining figure to lean on or a headboard for a bed, using quilting techniques to turn an everyday item into a piece of sculpture.

Most of all, soft sculpture is fun—so enjoy yourself. Start with some delicious candy cushions. Patterns for two sorts of chocolate and a bonbon are given in this chapter, but you can easily adapt them to make a selection of your own favourites.

Cushion pads. In the instructions for the chocolate cushions the filling is placed directly inside the satin cover, which means it is not removable. If you prefer you can make a separate cushion pad to go inside the satin cover, making the pieces of the pad cover 1.5cm ($\frac{1}{2}$") larger all round than the outer cover.

To make the rose petal chocolate cushion

You will need:
1.4m ($1\frac{1}{2}$yd) of 90cm (36") wide brown satin for the 'chocolate'.
45cm ($\frac{1}{2}$yd) of 90cm (36") wide pink satin for the rose petals.
1kg-1.35kg (2lb-3lb) kapok or use a synthetic filling for stuffing cushion.
45cm ($\frac{1}{2}$yd) of 61cm (24") 55gm (2oz) synthetic wadding for rose petals.
Strong fabric adhesive.
Matching thread.
1.6m ($2\frac{3}{4}$yd) of 122cm (48") wide lining fabric (optional).

☐ Make paper patterns for the cushions and the rose petals by enlarging figs. 1-4 (see Design know-how chapter 4, page 112). Seam allowances of 1.5cm ($\frac{1}{2}$") included on pattern.

☐ Cut out four cushion top pieces and one cushion base piece in brown satin on the straight grain.

☐ Cut out two of each petal section in pink satin, and one of each in 55gm (2oz) wadding.

☐ Place two cushion top pieces with right sides facing and stitch together on one side only from A-B. Join the other two top pieces in the same way. Snip 'V'-shaped notches at 2.5cm (1") intervals along the curved edges, almost to the stitching.

☐ Place these two pieces together and stitch along the remaining two side seams. Press seams open.

☐ With right sides together pin the base piece into place, matching the corners of the base to the seams of the top. Stitch the base to the top leaving one side open to turn through. (Leave two sides open if you have made a cushion pad.)

☐ Trim corners and turn cushion to right side.

Delicious candy cushions made in satin add a touch of luxury to a simple room setting. Designed by Felicity Youett.

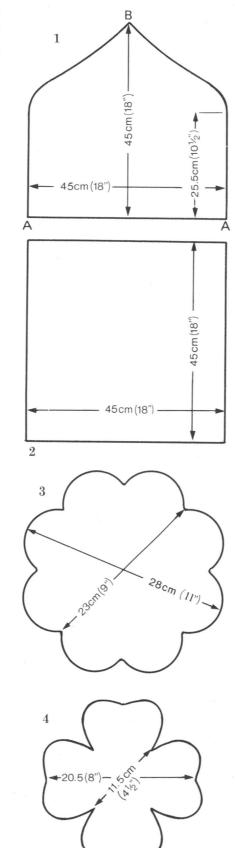

1. *Cushion top piece — cut 4.*
2. *Cushion base piece — cut 1.*
3. *Lower petal section.* 4. *Upper petal section. Cut two of each in satin and one of each in interfacing.*

☐ Insert filling until the cushion is firm (or insert the pad). Then slip stitch the opening.

☐ Place the satin pieces for the larger petal section with right sides together on top of the wadding section. Tack and stitch through all thicknesses, all around the edge. Trim the wadding away close to the stitching and trim the seam allowance on the satin to 6mm ($\frac{1}{4}$").

Make clips into the edge, at the angles, almost to the stitching.

☐ In the upper thickness of satin only, cut slits as shown (fig.5). Turn the petals right side out.

☐ Work lines of top stitching to make four petals (fig.6).

☐ Make up the smaller petal section in the same way and add three more lines of top stitching on each petal (fig.7).

5. *Slits cut in upper thickness.*

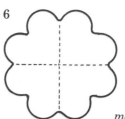

6. *Topstitching makes four petals.*

7. *Topstitching on smaller petals.*

☐ Glue the two petal sections together at the centre with the slit side of the smaller section to the unslit side of the larger one, making sure that the slits are completely covered. Oversew the two sections together at the centre.

☐ Glue the larger petal section to the centre of the top of the cushion, covering the slits. Turn back the petals and oversew to the cushion at several points close to the glued centre.

simple
upholstery

drop-in chair seats

This and the following chapters on upholstery show how all kinds of chairs and even sofas may be stripped and re-upholstered to make attractive furniture which looks good and lasts for years. It does not matter if the seating is grubby, the springs bare or the stuffing is sagging. Any piece of upholstery can be made as good as new: dining chairs, fireside chairs, buttoned chairs, chesterfields and even padded headboards.

With modern materials such as foam rubber the craft of upholstery is made easier for the amateur. With a little practice and patience, you will be able to renovate all kinds of upholstered furniture, both traditional—stuffed and sprung—or modern. Some of the tools you will need are similar to carpenters' tools and most are quite simple to use.

The best introduction for the complete beginner is to re-make the drop-in seat of a dining chair. These chairs can often be bought cheaply in junk shops and usually need only a bit of work on the seat to bring them back into use.

Equipment

Tape measures are used for measuring off pieces of fabric etc.

A shabby chair ready for a new seat.

Shears, which are really sharp, are essential for cutting out fabric and other materials such as webbing and hessian.

Mallet and ripping chisel for lifting the heads of tacks when removing old upholstery. The tip of the chisel is blunt to prevent damage to the frame and should always be driven in the direction of the grain and inwards from corners.

Tack lifter for pulling out the tacks once the heads have been lifted. Alternatively, you can use a pair of carpenter's pincers or pliers or the claw end of a hammer.

G-clamp, two for holding the chair base to the work surface.

Upholsterer's hammer with face of about 1.5cm ($\frac{5}{8}''$) and claw at other end. A reasonable substitute would be a carpenter's 'pin' hammer. A cabriole hammer is a specialized tool which is used for fine tacking along polished edges and carving.

Web strainer is used for stretching the webbing across the seat of the chair to prevent it from sagging. The simplest type of strainer is a piece of hardwood about 25cm x 7.5cm x 2.5cm (10"x3"x1"), slightly waisted for a good grip, with a groove at the end to give leverage (fig.1, left). Other more elaborate versions have a slot into which the webbing is inserted (fig.1, middle and right). Alternatively, a narrow piece of hardwood round which the web can be wrapped and pulled taut is efficient if you have a strong wrist.

Tacks are used to attach the various materials to the frame (nails should never be used). Use 1.2cm ($\frac{1}{2}''$) fine or 1.2cm ($\frac{1}{2}''$) 'improved' for a drop-in

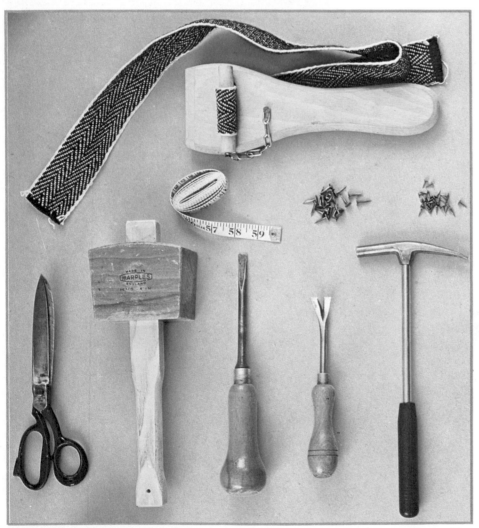

Upholsterer's tools and equipment. Bottom row, left to right: shears, mallet, ripping chisel, tack lifter, cabriole hammer. Top: web strainer, tacks, tape measure.

seat. 1.5cm ($\frac{5}{8}''$) tacks are used for the webbing on easy chairs.

Plastic wood for filling old tack holes if these are going to show.

Cloth-backed strong tape 4cm ($1\frac{1}{2}''$) wide and to the length of the perimeter of the chair seat plus 10cm ($4''$).

Adhesive with latex base for attaching the pad.

Webbing. This is placed across the seat frame in strands, running in both directions, and supports the padding. Most chairs have two strands each way (fig.2a), but the wide, early-Victorian type of chair may need three each way or two by three or four (fig.2b). To estimate the amount you need, slit open the fabric covering the underneath of the seat and buy enough to make the same arrangement.

The highest grade of webbing is made from pure flax and is black and white with a twill weave. Other grades of black and white webbing are made from mixtures of jute and cotton or hemp, and sometimes linen threads are woven into the selvedges to strengthen them. Plain or striped brown webbing is a cheaper grade made from jute and is not recommended for dining chairs. Rubberized webbing, such as Pirelli, can be used but is more expensive.

This re-upholstered chair has a new seat and is ready for many years of wear. Supplied by C.H. Frost Ltd.

1. *Different kinds of web strainer.* **2a.** *Two strands of webbing.* **2b.** *Some chairs need several webbing strands.*

Padding. Foam biscuit, 1.2cm ($\frac{1}{2}''$) larger all round than the size of the chair seat x 5cm ($2''$) deep. Old dining chairs were usually stuffed with wool on horsehair but this is expensive, hard to find and difficult to use, and foam padding is perfectly suitable for the purpose. Latex (rubber), which comes in cavity, plain and pin-core sheets, is the best to use, but polyester foam is adequate and less expensive.

Calculating the fabric

For the main cover choose fabric which is hard-wearing, simple to clean and easy to work with. It should have a firm, close weave and be colour-fast. Fabrics with a smooth finish will keep clean longer than those with a pile or nap (velvet or needlecord, for example) which hold dust, cling to clothes, and have to be allowed for when the cloth is cut. Avoid using those fabrics which have a large pattern or motif which would need to be placed centrally on the seats and so be wasteful in material.

To calculate the amount of fabric needed for each chair measure the length and width of the seat (at the widest part) and allow a piece at least 15cm ($6''$) longer and wider so that the fabric can be turned over the seat frame. You will also need a piece of hessian and two pieces of linen (or calico) 5cm ($2''$) wider and longer than the seat.

Stripping the seat

Cover the work surface with newspaper, remove seat from chair base and secure the seat, upside down, to the work surface with G-clamps.

Using the ripping chisel and mallet start to drive out the tacks holding the bottom hessian and cover fabric. To do this, place the tip of the chisel behind the head of the tack and drive it out, working with the grain of the wood. Use the claw side of the hammer, or a pair of pliers or pincers, to pull it out completely. It is essential to work *with* the grain to prevent it from splitting.

Next, turn the seat over and remove the cover and stuffing. Cut any twine ties with scissors. Strip off the hessian and webbing in the same way. If there is no webbing and plywood has been used as a base, remove all the nails holding this.

As you work, note the way the webbing was originally placed, the side of the frame to which it was tacked, and the part of the frame which was uppermost when finished. Examine the frame carefully and remove all old tacks. If necessary treat wood worm with Rentokil or Cuprinol.

If the new covering fabric is thicker than the original, the frame should be planed down a little to compensate for the extra thickness.

Replacing the webbing

Space the webbing evenly as shown (fig.2a). If there is an uneven number of webs, start with the centre web running back to front (fig.2b).

Without cutting off a length of webbing, place the end of the webbing on the top of the frame on the back side. Fold over approximately 1.2cm ($\frac{1}{2}''$), tack down with five tacks in a staggered formation (three in a straight line along the edge of the fold, then two slightly in towards the inner edge of the frame), giving a shallow 'W' shape (fig.3).

Stretch the webbing across to the front of the frame, pressing the edge of the strainer on the side of the frame to give leverage (fig.3). Tack the webbing, again using three tacks in a straight line (fig.4). Cut off the webbing with 2.5cm ($1''$) to spare, turn it back over the first tacks and tack again with two tacks so that the five tacks are on the same shallow 'W' formation as before (the first three tacks will be hidden by the fold).

Place the other pieces of webbing from the back to the front of the frame in the same way, then secure the side webbing (which runs across the seat), interlacing it with the other webbing (figs. 2a and 2b, overleaf).

To cover the webbing before attaching the padding, fold over 1.2cm ($\frac{1}{2}''$) on one side of the hessian and, with the fold uppermost, tack it to the back of the seat frame with 1.2cm ($\frac{1}{2}''$) tacks. Strain it tightly to the front and temporarily secure with three tacks. Repeat this at the sides, keeping the grain of the fabric straight. Then, working from the centre of each side towards the corners, place tacks about 4cm ($1\frac{1}{2}''$) apart. Turn up the raw edges and tack these down (fig.5).

Attaching the padding

Cut four pieces of tape equal in length to the sides of the foam, plus 2.5cm ($1''$). Fold the tape in half lengthwise and crease firmly. Glue one side of the folded tape to the perimeter of the foam, positioning the crease as shown (fig.6). When this is completely dry, place the foam on the hessian, tape side uppermost and, holding it firmly in position, tack free edge of tape to frame.

As the foam is slightly larger than the seat, it will make a dome in the centre, giving a rounded shape to the finished seat. An additional piece of foam can be placed under the centre area provided the edges are tapered; this will give an even higher dome.

For a better foundation on which to place the final cover, the foam should be covered with a piece of calico or

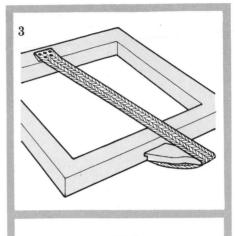

3

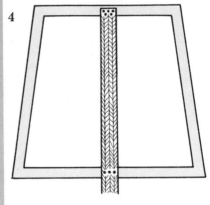

4

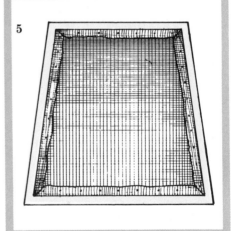

5

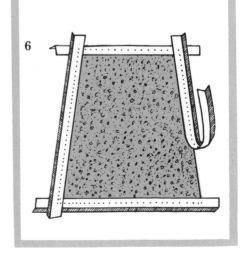

6

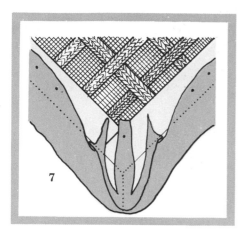

3. *Five tacks in a 'W' formation. The strainer is pressed on the seat frame for leverage.* **4.** *Webbing is secured with tacks in a row.* **5.** *The webbing is covered with hessian which is tacked to the seat frame.* **6.** *One side of the tape is glued to the perimeter of the foam.* **7.** *Fold up the excess fabric into a double pleat at the corners before covering bottom of seat.*

linen. Attach this with 1cm ($\frac{3}{8}$″) fine tacks to the outside edges of the seat frame and cut off the raw edges close to the tacks.

Attaching the final cover

Make centre marks on the base of the frame at front and back and centre marks on front and back edges of covering. Then place the cover fabric on the work surface with its wrong side facing uppermost. Put the seat, foam side down, centrally on the fabric and turn up the edges of the fabric on to the bottom of the seat frame. Line up the centre marks on covering and frame, then temporary tack the covering into place, only driving the tacks half-way down. When satisfied that the covering is well placed, hammer down 1cm ($\frac{3}{8}$″) tacks at 2.5cm-4cm (1″-1$\frac{1}{2}$″) intervals.

At the corners make a double pleat as shown in fig.7. Start by pulling down the point tightly and tacking it. Fold the excess fabric into inverted pleats and tack these down. Cut off any excess fabric and then cover the bottom of the seat with the remaining piece of linen or calico.

Fold under the raw edges and tack the calico to the frame, covering the tacks and raw edges of the seat fabric, spacing the tacks evenly. Replace the finished seat in the chair frame and tap it down lightly for a good fit.

Upholstery is a satisfying craft which rewards the time and care involved in it. After mastering the techniques given here and the next two sections, you may feel inspired to go on to more complicated projects.

Dining chairs spring & stuff

Victorian dining chairs can often be bought quite cheaply from a junk shop and you can turn them into something both useful and decorative simply by re-upholstering them and giving a little attention to the woodwork, especially to check for the presence of worm. Value can also be increased by re-upholstering in the traditional way with springs and horsehair. Don't start by tackling antiques—anything over one hundred years old—that's a job for the experts. In this chapter a chair is stripped, the webbing replaced, the springs attached and the chair stuffed. In the next Upholstery chapter the edges are stitched, the second stuffing inserted and the chair finally covered with a top cover and finished off.

Tools

The tools required are listed on page 44. In addition, you will need:

Coil springs: four 10cm (4″) in 12mm (gauge 10) wire.

Regulator. This is a type of needle 20cm -25cm (8″-10″) long which helps to form the stuffing into a good shape. It has one pointed and one flat end. A kitchen skewer could be used for this purpose, although if you are planning to do a lot of upholstery it is worth investing in the proper tool which is not expensive.

Needles. For making the bridles you

These chairs (above and left) have been re-upholstered using traditional springing and stuffing techniques. This kind of chair is an ideal candidate for renovation and new upholstery and will give you many years of wear.

will need a spring needle which is a heavy-duty needle 13cm (5″) long, curved along its length, so that it can be pulled in and out easily. For stitching the edge you will need a 25cm (10″) straight upholsterer's needle which is pointed at both ends.

Materials

Stuffing. Horsehair is the traditional stuffing but, because it is difficult and expensive to obtain today, it is often mixed with hog hair. Old hair mattresses can sometimes be bought cheaply at jumble sales or from junk shops. If you tease out the hair before washing it will return to its original life and springiness.

Alternatively, use Algerian fibre. This comes from the Algerian palm grass and, provided that it is teased out thoroughly, it makes a good, inexpensive stuffing.

For a small chair with about 7.5cm (3″) depth of padding you will need about 1kg (2lb) of either type of material.

Webbing. Buy sufficient to replace the original webbing; plain brown twill weave or upholsterer's webbing.

Most ordinary chairs will need three or four strands of 5cm (2″) webbing placed back to front plus two strands across the seat.

Twine, a very strong, smooth string made from flax and hemp, is used for

Stripping the upholstery: remove the tacks on the underside of the seat.

Underneath the top and inner covers there is a hair stuffing; lift this off.

Cut the stitching (above) and remove the twine holding the springs (below).

making bridle ties round the edge of the seat which help to hold the stuffing in place. Twine is also used for stitching on the springs and for stitching up the edge, another process which holds the stuffing in place and ensures a straight and firm edge.

Laid cord, a thicker twine, used for lashing the springs.

Scrim, a loosely woven material which is used for covering the first layer of stuffing. Allow enough to cut one piece the same size as the seat plus 15cm (6″) larger all round to allow for the depth of the padding.

Calico is used for covering the second layer of stuffing; you will need a piece approximately the same size as the scrim.

Wadding is used over the calico to prevent the stuffing from working through; allow the same amount as for the scrim.

Canvas, a heavy furnishing variety, is used over the springs. You will need a piece the size of the seat plus about 2.5cm (1″) all round for turnings.

Main cover. It's wise to choose a dark colour in a proper upholstery grade fabric which will wear well and not show the dirt quickly. Patterned fabrics or those with a raised surface stay crisper-looking for longer than plain fabrics. Allow the same amount as for the scrim.

Stripping the upholstery

Follow the method described on page 46 under Drop-in Seats. As you work, make notes or sketches of the way the original top cover was attached, the number of springs and webbing strands and the height of the original padding. If you wish, the padding can be made a little higher or lower.

Check that all the old tacks have been removed from the frame. You should fill the old holes with plastic wood to give a firm basis for the tacks. Repair the frame and treat it for woodworm, if needed, and let the fluid dry completely before you start work.

The chair stripped of stuffing, springs and webbing. Take out remaining tacks.

Replacing the webbing

The webbing is the basis for the rest of the upholstery and must be secured tautly and really firmly. As the chair has springs the webbing is attached to the underside of the frame. You will find it easier to turn the chair upside down on the work surface.

Use the webbing straight from the roll. Without cutting it, fold over the end for 2.5cm (1″) and place it centrally on the back rail so the cut edge is uppermost and the fold is 1cm ($\frac{1}{2}$″) from the outer edge of the rail as shown in fig.1. Tack down, using five 15mm ($\frac{5}{8}$″) improved tacks placed in a row about 1cm ($\frac{1}{2}$″) from the fold, with the line of tacks staggered in the form of a shallow 'W'.

1.

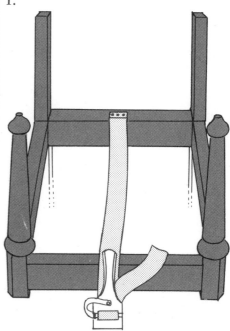

1. On a chair with a sprung seat webbing is attached to the underside of the frame. Tack down on the back rail and stretch the webbing across to the front using the web strainer.

If the wood tends to split use 1cm ($\frac{1}{2}$″) fine tacks instead (fig.1).

Stand on the opposite side of the chair by the front rail and, using the web strainer, put the webbing down in position on the front rail. Press the edge of the strainer on the side of the frame to give leverage. If the frame is polished use a pad of wadding to prevent damage from the strainer.

Tack down on the rail through the single thickness of webbing, using three tacks placed in a row.

Cut off the webbing 2.5cm (1″) from the tacks.

Turn back the excess over the tacks, placing them in a staggered 'W' formation as before.

Attach the remaining strands from the back to the front in the same way, then secure the side webbing (which runs

49

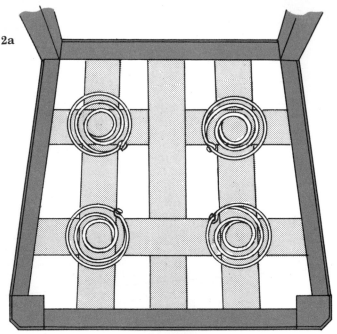

2a

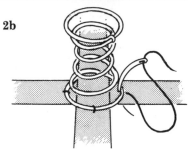

2b

2. *The springs are arranged in a square on top of the webbing before sewing down with a spring needle and twine.*

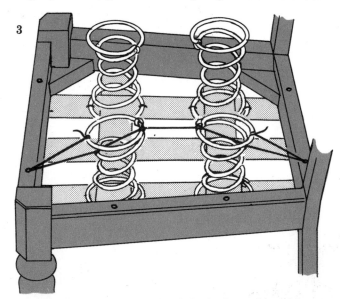

3

3. *Above: the springs are firmly lashed together with twine and attached to the frame to prevent them moving in the seat. Below: one way of winding twine round springs.*

4

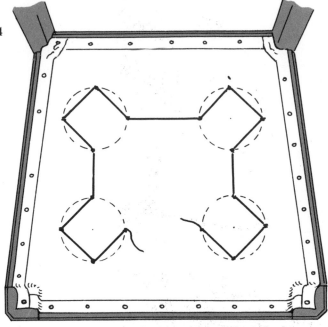

4. *The springs are covered with canvas and stitched in a similar way as they were attached to the webbing. Use the spring needle and make a single knot at each stitch.*

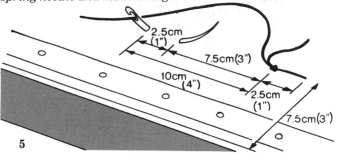

5

2.5cm (1")
7.5cm(3")
10cm (4")
2.5cm (1")
7.5cm(3")

5. *Bridle ties are stitched on the canvas to hold the stuffing.*

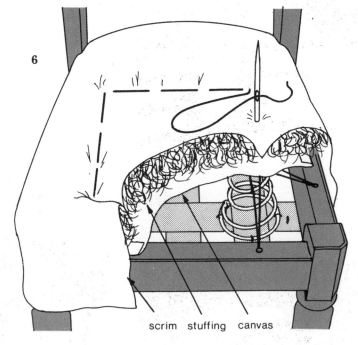

6

scrim   stuffing   canvas

6. *Stitch the scrim to the canvas with needle and twine. This process anchors the stuffing in middle of chair.*

50

across the seat), interlacing it with the first strands.

Attaching the springs

The springs must be sewn to the webbing, and then lashed together securely at the top to prevent them from moving about in the seat. This lashing also gives the chair a rounded shape.

Turn the chair the right way up and evenly space the springs in a square on top of the webbing intersections (fig. 2a).

The beginning and ends of the springs should be towards the middle.

Thread the spring needle with a long length of twine.

Using the fingers of your left hand to feel the positions of the spring from the underside of the chair, insert the needle into the webbing from underneath so that it comes out level with the outside of one spring. Pull the needle through, leaving a short tail of twine, and insert it into the webbing again from the top, catching the bottom ring of the spring with a single stitch (fig.2b).

Knot the tail of the twine to the length pulled through, but do not cut it.

Still with the needle on the underside of the chair, move to the other side of the ring and stitch it to the webbing there.

Move back to the outside again and make another stitch. This makes three stitches in all, in a 'V'-shape.

Without cutting the twine move to the next spring and repeat the operation. Continue round in this way for the remaining springs then make a knot to finish off and cut the twine.

Lashing the springs. Attach two 15mm ($\frac{5}{8}$") improved tacks on all four sides of the frame, each one in line with the centre of a spring, hammering them half-way in.

Cut off enough cord to stretch twice around the frame. Leaving a tail which will stretch easily to the top of the nearest spring, plus a couple of inches for knotting, tie the cord round a tack on the back rail, and hammer the tack in.

Working towards the front of the chair, take the main length of cord to the nearest spring and knot it round the coil which is second from the top of the nearest side. Take it through the spring to the other side and knot it round the top coil. Use a clovehitch knot (fig.7).

Move to the other spring in the row and knot the cord round the top coil on the nearest side, keeping the distance between the springs the same as at the bottom. Take the cord through the spring and knot it round the coil which is second from the top on the front edge. Tie it off tightly round the tack on the front rail and hammer it in (fig.3).

Take the tail of cord at each tack back to the nearest spring and tie it round the top coil on the outside, pulling tightly so that the spring slightly leans down towards the frame.

Repeat this process on the other pair of springs with the cord running parallel to the first length, and then again with two lengths running across the chair. The springs will now have a rounded shape.

The main stuffing

The canvas. Centre this over the springs. Fold over 2.5cm (1") on one side of the canvas and place this centrally on the back rail with the raw edge uppermost. Tack down 15mm ($\frac{5}{8}$") tacks, placing them 2.5cm (1") apart and 1cm ($\frac{1}{2}$") from the fold. Fit it neatly round the back uprights, cutting if necessary, as described in Upholstery chapter 2, page 434.

Smooth the canvas over the springs by pulling it quite taut and temporarily tack it to the front rail through a single thickness, keeping the grain of canvas

7.

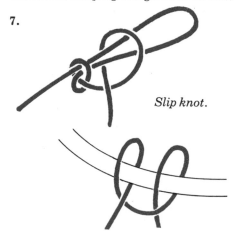

Slip knot.

Clovehitch knot.

absolutely straight. Smooth out the canvas to the side rails, and temporarily tack through the single thickness.

When satisfied that the canvas is completely smooth and the grain straight, hammer the tacks in completely. Trim off the excess canvas to within 2.5cm (1") of the tacks, then fold this over and tack it down at about 5cm (2") intervals.

Stitch the springs to the canvas in a similar way as they were attached to the webbing, but make a single knot at each stitch to lock it in position (fig.4).

To make bridle ties for the stuffing, thread the spring needle with enough twine to go 1½ times round the chair. The stitch used is rather similar to back stitch. Start by making a stitch in the canvas about 2.5cm (1") long and 2.5cm (1") from the edge. Pull it through, leaving a 7.5cm (3") tail. Tie the tail in a slip knot (fig.7) to the main length at

the point where it emerges from the canvas.

Go forward and insert the needle about 10cm (4") away, but pointing it backwards. Pull it out about 7.5cm (3") from the starting point (fig.5). Leave the stitch on top of the canvas loose enough for a hand to be inserted.

Continue round the whole edge in this way, making sure that a 2.5cm (1") stitch falls at each corner. You may have to adjust the length of the bridles to do this.

Finish off by tying a knot.

Stuffing. Take a handful of stuffing and tease it out thoroughly, removing any lumpy pieces. Put it under one of the bridle threads, working it together well to prevent lumps. Do this for all the bridles, then fill the middle with more stuffing, teasing it well to make an even shape and to overhang the edge slightly by the same amount all round.

Scrim. Place it centrally over the stuffing and fix one temporary tack in the middle of each side to hold it. Put two other temporary tacks either side of the central tack. At this stage the scrim should be rather loose on the surface of the stuffing.

Thread an upholsterer's needle with a long piece of twine and stitch through from the scrim to the canvas in a rectangle about 7.5cm (3") from the edges of the seat. To do this, pass the needle through the scrim and stuffing and pull it out between the webbing on the underside of the chair, leaving a tail of twine on top for tying off. As soon as the needle is completely through the canvas, keep the unthreaded end pointing down, and push needle back through the canvas with the threaded end 1cm ($\frac{1}{2}$") further on. Withdraw it on top and tie to the main length in a slip knot.

Push the needle back into the scrim making a stitch about 7.5cm (3") long on top. Continue round in this way, leaving a 1cm ($\frac{1}{2}$") gap between stitches (fig.6).

Pull the twine tightly so that the scrim is pulled down and be careful not to catch the springs as the needle passes through. Even out any lumps in the stuffing with the regulator. This process anchors the hair in the middle.

Remove the temporary tacks securing the scrim to the frame—on the front of the seat first, then the sides, and lastly the back. Even out the hair which is along the edges of the seat. Add more if necessary to make a fat roll which just protrudes beyond the edge of the frame. Tuck the raw edge of the scrim under the hair, smoothing it over the roll. Use 10mm ($\frac{3}{8}$") tacks to fix the folded edge of the scrim to the chamfered edge of the frame. Do not pull it too tightly over the roll.

Dining chairs stuff & stitch

In the last chapter on upholstery a dining chair was fitted with webbing, the springs attached and lashed and the main stuffing inserted and covered. In this chapter the process is completed by stitching the edge, putting in the second stuffing and then finally covering. Your chair is now ready for use.

Stitching the edge

This is done in two stages. The first, which is called blind stitching, pulls enough stuffing to the edges to enable a firm edge to be built up. The second stage, top stitching, forms a roll from this section of stuffing. The roll has to be really firm because the covering fabric is pulled over it, and any unevenness would spoil the shape.

Start the stitching at the back on the left side of chair and work round seat anti-clockwise to include back.

To do the blind stitching thread the upholsterer's needle with a good length of twine. Insert the unthreaded end of the needle into the scrim just above the tacks and about 4cm (1½″) from the corner. Insert the needle into the stuffing at an angle of about 45°. It will emerge on the top of the chair about 5cm (2″) in from the edge and 1cm (½″) nearer the corner.

Pull the needle through, stopping as soon as you see the eye, so that it is not completely withdrawn. Push it back into the stuffing again, altering the angle so that it emerges through the side on the same level as where it first entered, but 2.5cm (1″) nearer the corner. You have, in effect, made a V-shaped stitch or loop in the stuffing (fig.1).

Pull the twine through so that there is a tail of about 7.5cm (3″). Tie to main length with a slip knot and pull tight. Insert the needle about 5cm (2″) further along the edge, slanting in the same way as before and bringing it out on the same level on top as the first stitch. Bring it down again at an angle to emerge on the side about 2.5cm (1″) back. Before withdrawing the needle completely, wind the twine hanging in a loop below it, around the needle twice. Pull needle right through.

Put the unthreaded end of the needle into the centre of the chair top to anchor it temporarily. Hold the edge of the stuffing with your left hand so that the fingers are on the top and the thumb is on the side. Wrap the twine around your other hand and pull the stitch really tight, pressing down with your left hand at the same time; you should be able to feel the filling being pulled towards the edge.

Continue working around the edge in this way, being careful not to place the twisted section of a stitch so that it has to go around a corner. To finish, knot the twine carefully and tightly.

Correct any unevenness in the stuffing with the regulator, then re-thread the upholsterer's needle with a long length of twine.

Top stitching is similar to blind stitching, the main difference being that the needle is completely pulled through on top of the stuffing so that a stitch can be made on top. This means that the needle should be inserted vertically into the scrim and not inclined to the left as with blind stitching. Starting at a corner, insert the needle about 4cm (1½″) away and about 1cm (½″) above the blind stitching. Push it through so that it emerges on top about 2.5cm (1″) in from the edge.

Re-insert the threaded end of the needle about 2.5cm (1″) to the left of this point, keeping it parallel to the first entry so that it emerges 2.5cm (1″) away (fig.2).

Tie the end of the twine in a slip knot as before. Insert the needle again and complete the stitch, reinserting it about 2.5cm (1″) to the left as before so that it is just short of the first stitch. Before withdrawing the needle completely from the second half of the stitch, wind the twine around it and then pull tight in the same way as for blind stitching. Continue all around

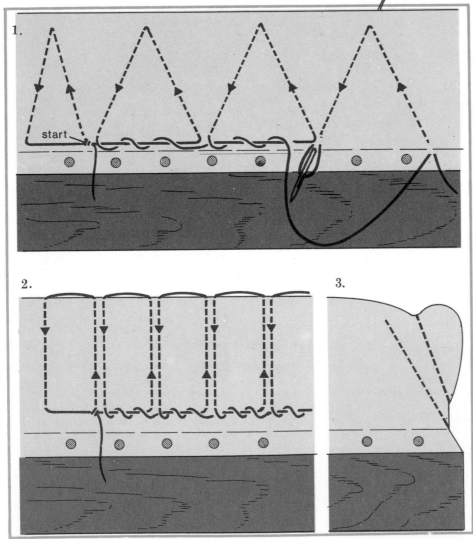

1. *The loop made by blind stitches pulls the stuffing to the edge of the seat.* **2.** *Top stitching forms the stuffing into a roll.* **3.** *A profile of the stitches.*

the edge in this way. The stitches on top of the chair should form a continuous line, following line of chair.

The second stuffing

Make bridle ties in the scrim as with the first stuffing. Fill the cavity which has been formed by the roll edge with more stuffing tucked under the bridle ties, and cover the chair with a piece of calico, temporarily tacking this with 10mm ($\frac{3}{8}$") fine tacks to the front of the frame, then the back and lastly the sides.

If the original upholstery finished on this face, rather than on the underside of the chair, be careful to place the tacks clear of the line where the wood begins to show. Cut into the calico at the back corners to fit around the uprights of the chair back, tucking in the surplus fabric between the stuffing and the leg of the chair.

After the calico has been positioned, tack it in place.

If the front corners of the chair are rounded, make a double pleat or an inverted pleat (as in the photographs), or a single pleat if the corner is square. To keep a smooth line the calico has to be pulled hard over the roll edges, but be careful to keep the grain of the calico absolutely straight, putting most of the pressure from back to front, as illustrated, rather than from side to side.

The top cover

Cover the calico with wadding to prevent the stuffing from working through. Cut a piece of cover fabric on the straight grain large enough to cover the seat in the same style as the original upholstery. Temporarily tack it down with 10mm ($\frac{3}{8}$") fine tacks through a single thickness. Finish the corners as for the calico cover, using the flat end of the regulator to make a smooth finish at the back.

Tack down.

Trim off the excess fabric.

Finishing off. If the cover was attached to the front face of the frame the raw edge and tacks can be hidden with braid, stuck on with a latex adhesive such as Copydex. Mitre the braid at the corners and cover the 'works' under the seat with black hessian, cut to the exact size plus 6mm ($\frac{1}{4}$") turnings, tacked into place.

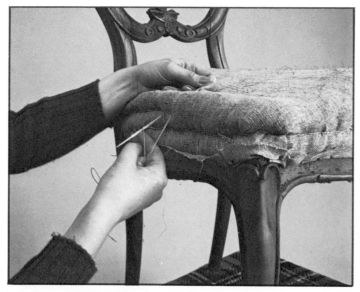

Working top stitching anti-clockwise round the seat.

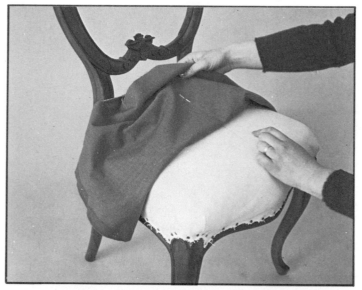

Checking that the grain of the cover fabric is straight.

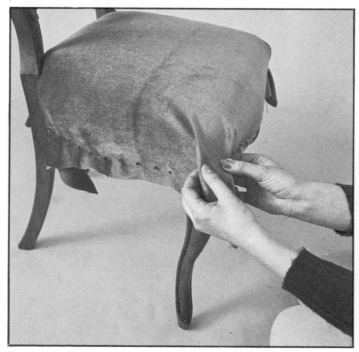

Finishing off the corners in a double pleat.

The re-upholstered chair: elegant and ready for use.

Rolled edges

The basic techniques of upholstery can be applied to easy chairs and sofas. In most cases the construction of traditional upholstery is the same: webbing which spans the frame and supports the upholstery; springs (on larger pieces of furniture); hessian which acts as a foundation for the stuffing. The method of application of all these materials is quite easy to adapt to suit your own piece of furniture.

The next stage of upholstery, however, may cause difficulties. It is the formation and stitching of the stuffing into the roll edge. This is an essential process of nearly all traditional upholstery and it is also a process which requires practice.

Roll edges

These are made wherever the upholstery is 'over-stuffed'. This does not mean where there is too much stuffing but where the stuffing is built up on the frame so that the sides of the stuffing are at right angles to the frame rather than sloping away from it. Roll edges are made around seats of dining chairs, chaise-longues and easy chairs, around the fronts of arms and around some backs of larger easy chairs (fig.1). All these are positions of heavy wear on the upholstery. If the roll was not there the top edge of the stuffing would not hold its shape, the surface would become lumpy and uncomfortable as the edge stuffing was pressed back, and the cover fabric would wrinkle and crease.

When making a roll edge by traditional upholstery methods, the stuffing is applied in two layers. The first layer is the main layer, using two or three times as much stuffing as the second layer. It is the first layer which is covered with scrim and moulded and stitched into the roll edge. The second layer is a 'topping up' over the scrim and helps form the final dome shape of the padding. (Types of stuffing are described in Upholstery chapter 3, page 468.)

In modern upholstery the roll edge has been substituted by foam rubber or by a manufactured roll of stuffing which is tacked to the edge of the frame—but neither of these gives as much wear as the traditional stitched roll.

Forming the roll

If you have already tried to make a roll edge, you probably discovered that it was not difficult to make it firm, but that it took much more skill to form the stuffing into an even depth and into a shape which followed the line of the frame.

An essential factor in achieving these qualities is the sight line.

Sight line. This is an imaginary line which lies along the edge of the stuffing where the horizontal surface becomes vertical. If these two surfaces met at right-angles, for example, the sight line would be the angle. On a curved surface the sight line lies in the centre of the curve.

The sight line must be the same distance from the frame all along and it should also be immediately above the line of the frame. If you were to stand above a chair looking down at a seat, the outside edge of the seat would fall on the sight line and this edge should also follow the line of the frame (fig.2). It may help you to find the sight line if you draw a guideline on the scrim before you start to add the stuffing.

☐ To do this, lay the scrim over the hessian on the appropriate surface, matching the centre points of each side to those on the hessian and temporary-tacking to hold it in place on the frame.

☐ Using a felt-tipped pen, draw round the edge of the frame on the scrim (fig.3).

☐ Remove the scrim from the frame and draw a second line outside the first, leaving a margin equal to the desired depth of stuffing plus about 1.5cm ($\frac{1}{2}$") for ease.

☐ Leave another margin of at least 2.5cm (1") outside the second line for turnings and trim off the excess scrim.

1. *Some of the places where roll edges are made to give firmness and shape.*

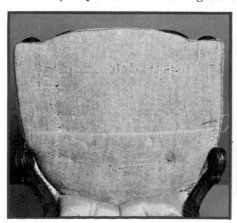

2. *Sight line drawn on edge of seat.*

3. *Drawing round edge of frame.*

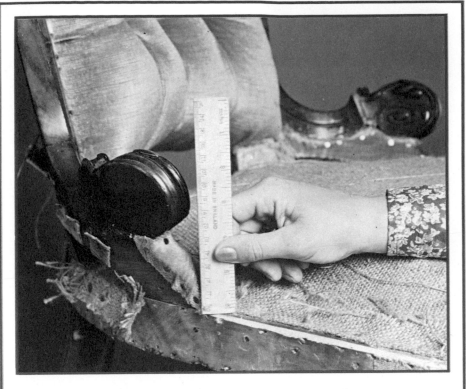

Measuring to check required height of stuffing.

Applying the stuffing

It is essential to take time and care over applying the first layer of stuffing and attaching the scrim because if this stage is well done the stitching of the roll will be easy.

Attach the webbing, springs (if any) and hessian canvas. (The section on dining chairs has these techniques.) Work the bridle ties into the hessian.

Chamfered edge. The scrim covering the first layer of stuffing is always tacked to a chamfered edge—a narrow angled surface between the top and side faces of the frame. This is because the tacks have to be put near the edge and if they were not placed into the chamfered edge they might split the wood.

☐ After stripping the old upholstery check that the chamfered edge is strong enough to support more tacks. If there are many holes, fill with Plastic Wood and sand smooth when dry.

☐ If your chair does not have a chamfer, you can make one with a file. The edge should be at 45° to the top and sides of the frame and equal in width to an improved tack head. If your frame has horns—a small raised section of wood at the front corners—make the chamfer round these too (fig.4).

Shaping the stuffing. Insert the stuffing in the bridle ties to the desired depth (see box), compressing it lightly with the flat of your hand to gauge it.

☐ Add the scrim, making sure that the centre marks are correctly aligned.

The stuffing depth

Always make a note of the original stuffing depth before you strip off the old upholstery. Then, because the stuffing will probably have become compressed, cross-check the depth against any guiding features the frame may have. On the chair in the photographs, for example, the stuffing depth should equal the height from the seat frame to the tack bar at the back and also from the seat frame to the show-wood at the sides.

Corners. Pay particular attention to corners. For square corners at the front of a frame, pack in plenty of stuffing and fold the scrim into a square pleat (fig.6). At uprights fold the scrim back diagonally and cut into the edge just up to the fold. Pull the scrim down over the stuffing on each side of the upright and tuck in the pointed corner between the stuffing and the upright. Fold down the remainder in a neat square pleat. Check that the stuffing on each side of the upright is firm and not sloping away from the edge.

Tacking down. When you are satisfied with the shape of the roll, tack the scrim to the chamfered edge. Make sure that the outer edges of the tack heads do not protrude over the edge of the chamfer or they will spoil the line of the final cover.

Check that the line of the roll follows the frame exactly by tilting up the frame and looking at it from below. Adjust if necessary.

6. *Folding scrim into a square pleat at front corners. Notice tack heads placed well within chamfered edge.*

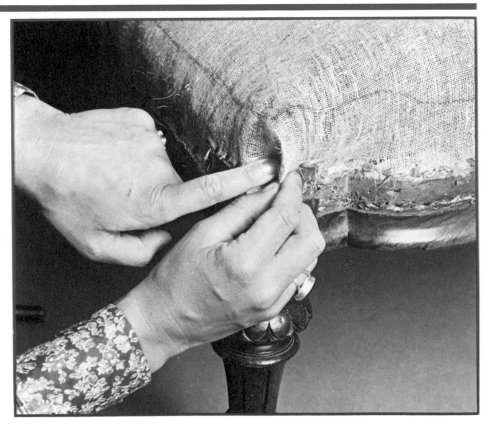

Traditional armchairs

Traditional armchairs are more difficult to re-upholster than dining chairs, but they will give you the basic skills to try even larger pieces. The wing armchair featured in this section uses the techniques of webbing, springing, stuffing and stitching used in the earlier upholstery sections, so if you have gained some confidence in these, you can probably tackle a larger piece like an armchair successfully. However, be prepared to allow plenty of time.

Planning your work

It takes a professional upholsterer two to three days to strip down and rebuild a fully padded armchair by traditional methods so it will certainly take the amateur longer. Find somewhere convenient to work like a spare room or garage, where you will not have to clear up after each session. If possible use a pair of trestles on which the chair can stand while you are working. You can convert woodworking trestles by attaching narrow fillets of wood round the top edge to prevent the chair from slipping off.

Preparing the chair

Start by stripping off the old cover, making sure first whether it has been attached by slip stitches or tacks. Remove any extra wadding and the calico undercover if there is one. You can then examine the upholstery underneath. Look carefully at the webbing and hessian supporting the stuffing on the arms and back; look at the

Above: wing armchair, before re-upholstering has begun.

scrim covering them. If they are torn and the stuffing is lumpy or falling out, they probably need replacement. Test the rigidity of any stitched roll edges—if these are flabby but still in good shape and the materials are sound they can usually be repaired without being completely stripped. However, if the edge has completely fallen back, it is wiser to strip and replace it. Examine the seat webbing and springing underneath. If the webbing is broken but the springing is sound, the webbing can be replaced without disturbing the rest of the seat. However, if the springs are out of shape or the cord lashing them is broken, you should strip out the seat completely.

If the chair seems a borderline case, it is still worth stripping it back to the frame to be on the safe side. With the cost of the covering fabric and the amount of work involved it is essential that the innards are in good order. If you do strip off the upholstery completely, make notes and sketches at each stage about the number and position of webbing strands, edges which are stitched into rolls and other design details which affect the shape.

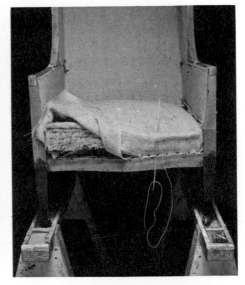

1. *When replacing webbing where you are not removing the springs, lay the strands between the springs (rather than over them) for tightness. The springs can then be pushed inside the webbing.*

2. *Leave the back edge open when attaching the hessian to the wings so that successive layers can be pulled through. Notice how the original stitched roll at the top has been re-used.*

3. *The original padding was removed in one piece from each section so that it could be re-used. It was then covered with new scrim and top stitch worked along any roll edges.*

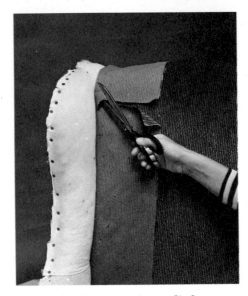

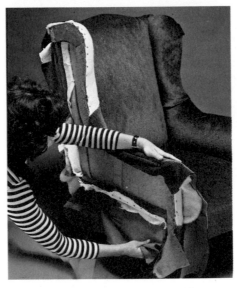

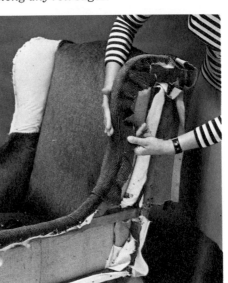

5. *The main cover is applied over a layer of polyester wadding for softness. To fit the fabric round the frame, the edge is folded back and cut in an elongated Y shape.*

6. *To ensure there are no gaps between the arms and seat, the fabric covering the inside arms is pulled through under the tack bar and tacked to the side face of the seat frame.*

7. *The edge of the fabric is clipped to give enough ease for fitting the cover over the lower wings. At the top it must be pulled firmly and evenly so no fullness is left on the front edge.*

Order of work

Generally, the best order of work is to complete the seat first, then the back followed by the arms and finally the wings, if any. The photographs show the re-upholstery of a traditional wing armchair which will probably be similar in many respects to your own chair even if it does not have wings.

One major difference, where you may encounter difficulty, is if your chair has an independent sprung edge. This is where the springs have been placed along the front edge of the frame instead of a short distance back from it. The lashing of these front springs is done separately and in a different way

from normal as shown in the box opposite. If you have scroll arms, pad and stitch them as for seats.

The cover

Although it may seem complicated, the method for covering traditionally upholstered armchairs is more time-consuming than difficult.

If you are simply re-covering the chair without touching the upholstery, tease out the top stuffing on each section and add more if necessary. Place new wadding over the calico cover. It is always worth applying a calico under-cover—even if this was not on the original—because it will help shape

the top stuffing and it will give you practice at fitting and cutting.

The most usual mistakes in applying the cover are the incorrect alignment of the grain, incomplete pulling of the sections over the stuffing to make the cover smooth and taut, and inaccurate cutting round upright parts of the frame.

The grain must always be square on the frame with the selvedge (warp) threads running perpendicular to the floor at the centre of the relevant section, although it can be pulled out of square at the edges where the stuffing tapers off.

Tautness is essential on each section

4. *To enable the main cover to be pulled through, the back edge on the wings of the calico cover is left open and the inside arm panel is tacked to the outside face of the tack bar.*

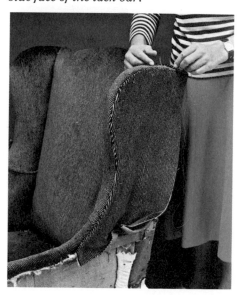

8. *Slip stitching the top and front edges of the outside wing fabric. The back and bottom edges can be tacked to the frame because they will be covered by the remaining panels.*

and each piece must be pulled as smooth as possible without over-straining the fabric. To test whether you have pulled it tight enough, run the palm of your hand over the surface —there should be no wrinkles. Always pull the fabric with the grain—if you pull with the bias, it will stretch.

Cutting. To fit the fabric round upright sections of the frame, turn it back so that the fold is level with the frame. Cut from the edge in a line which is at right angles to the fold and pointing to the centre of the upright to within 1.5cm (½") of the fold. Then cut at an angle to each corner of the upright of the frame.

Independent sprung edges

These were devised to make the front edges of seats more comfortable. The front rail of the frame is higher than the remaining three rails of the seat and the springs used are 7.5cm-10cm (3"-4") lower and also softer than the other seat springs.

☐ Start by attaching the main seat springs in rows on the seat in the usual way. (See section on dining chairs, page 50). On some you may find it easier to make two strands of lashing across the rows, one tying the middle rungs of the springs and the other across the tops (fig.A).

☐ Place the edge springs in position on the front rail. Use netting staples to fix them to the rail.

☐ Cut a strip of webbing to the length of the rail and pass it through the springs over the bottom rungs and tack it to the rail between the springs. This prevents the springs from squeaking when they are compressed and touch the rail.

☐ Cut a 15cm (6") length of webbing in half lengthwise for each pair of edge springs. Tack one end of a strip to the left of the first spring on the front rail as shown in fig.B, pass the other end up and round the middle rung, pulling the spring forward. Tack down to the right of the spring. Repeat for the remaining springs.

☐ To form a firm edge, a piece of cane or heavy wire is lashed along the top at the front of the springs (figs.B and C). If you have to make a wire, bend the ends to the shape as shown.

☐ Lash each front spring from the back at the bottom, over the top to the front edge (see fig.B).

The hessian. Cut a piece of hessian large enough to cover the top and front of the seat plus 20cm (8") for a gutter. This gutter is made behind the edge springs to allow them to move freely from the other springs. The gutter is held down with laid cord stitches which are pulled down to the front rail and held with improved tacks between each spring (fig.D). Tack hessian in place and stitch to springs and wire.

Stuffing. Apply the first stuffing over the hessian, tucking plenty into the gutter.

☐ Apply the scrim over the stuffing, making a roll at the front. Because of the edge springs you cannot tack the edge of the roll to the frame; instead, stitch it to the hessian with twine and a curved needle (see fig.D). Then stitch the edge into a roll in the usual way.

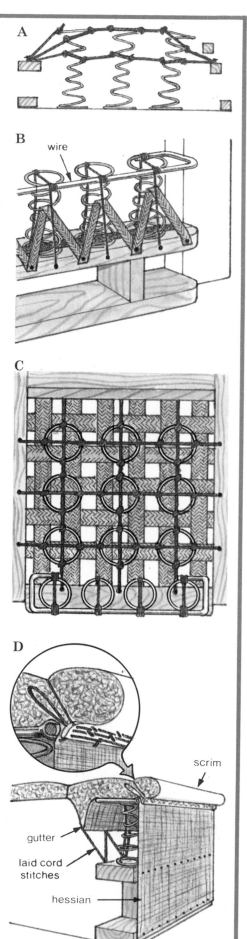

cane, rush & seagrass

Rush plaiting for seats

Rush seating is probably the ultimate in rush work, but plenty of practice is needed on weaving and plaiting rushes before starting to do rush seating. Plaiting mats will give the necessary experience in handling rush, before beginning rush seating. Choose thick rushes for floor matting and fine for table mats. Start with some plaiting to get the feel of stroking and twisting the rushes.

Preparing the rushes

Prepare the rushes first by wetting them for about five minutes, either by sprinkling with a hose or watering can, or by dipping them in a bath of cold water. Then wrap the rushes in a wet blanket, flannelette sheet or sacking and leave overnight.

Before use each rush must be prepared. First test for strength by holding a rush in both hands about 15cm (6″) down from the thin end and pull it apart with a gentle tug. Discard any broken bits and try again until the rush is firm and does not snap. Then 'wipe' each rush, to clean and remove all air and water from the stem. Hold the stem in one hand at the thin end and wipe along the rush with a damp cloth, pressing it flat at the same time so that the water runs out. If this is not done the work will shrink too much after weaving, leaving it loose with gaps showing.

Rush plaiting

☐ Select 3 rushes and tie them together somewhere in the middle, but not in half or the ends will all run out at the same time and make the joining of new rushes difficult.

Fine strong string or linen thread is used to tie the rushes. Always leave the ends of the string long enough to allow for sewing later on.

☐ Loop the rushes, at the point where they are tied together, round a hook or a nail in the wall. Bring the six ends together and divide them into three pairs so that each pair has a thick and a thin end. This will keep the thickness of the plait constant.

Although the plaiting looks just the same as braided hair, in rush work only the right hand is used for actually plaiting; the left hand merely holds the material.

☐ Hold two of the pairs in the left hand. Using the right hand twist the other pair, two or three times to the right, stroking and pulling the rushes at the same time, so that the two rushes look like one and are quite firm.

☐ Place the right-hand pair over the top of the centre pair and hold under the left thumb. Pass the left-hand pair over the top of the twisted rushes. The original right-hand pair is now the left-hand pair, the left-hand pair is in the centre and the centre pair is now the right-hand pair.

This pair is now ready to be worked by the right hand. Continue twisting the right-hand rushes, as before, with the right hand and then placing the rushes in the left hand by taking them over the centre pair. The left-hand pair is then placed over it so that the centre pair is on the right.

Keep the width of the plait even. A marker can be used by slipping a ring of the required size over the plait. If the plait gets thicker the ring will not slip down along the plait and if the plait gets thinner the ring will become too loose.

To join in a new rush, wait until the end to be replaced is about 10cm (4″) long and in the centre of the plait. Lay the new rush against the old so that the top end of the new rush protrudes 7cm (3″). When it is their turn twist all three together working with the old and the new. Continue plaiting until the short end of the old rush is lost in the plait.

Generally, a thick end should be replaced by a thick end and a thin end by a thin end in order to keep the plait even. At all times aim to keep the combined thickness of the six rushes even.

☐ After plaiting a length cut off all the ends of the new rushes as close as possible to the plait as well as any old ends which may be showing. Short lengths of plaiting are suitable for table mats but floor mats will require a much longer plait.

Round mats

For a small round table mat, about 20cm (8″) in diameter, plait for about 4.6m (5yd). Make the plait 13mm (½″) thick. Do not finish off the ends.

Press the plait flat by either passing it through a wringer or by pressing.

Stitching. Thread the string at the beginning of the plait on to a needle. Make a tight coil with the flat part of the plait forming the thickness of the mat. Stitch in position (fig.1).

Do not worry if the plait is not long

1. *Stitching the plait to form a mat.*

enough for your requirements; re-wet the ends of the plait and continue with the rope for as long as you wish. Many rushworkers make the mats by plaiting a length and then stitching the plaiting before continuing.

To join in a new thread, tie the old and the new threads together with a reef knot and continue to sew, pulling the knot through the rushes until the old thread is used.

To finish off a plaited mat, cut off the underneath rush from each pair and weave the remaining three rushes into the plait of the previous row.

Stitch into place.

Oval mats

To make an oval mat about 25cm x 35cm (10″x 14″) plait for 11m (12yd). Begin the coil by doubling back the end and stitching into position. The piece doubled back should equal the difference between the width and the length required—in this case 10cm (4″). Continue to stitch the plait round this elongated coil which will form an oval.

Coils

The mats can be made more interesting by adding a series of coils.

For coils make a length of plait and mark the centre. Coil and stitch from one end towards the centre. Stitch in the usual way. Bind the other end with the thread and then stitch towards the centre so that the two coils are opposite to each other (fig.2).

It is usual to have an odd number of

2. *Double coil used for decorating.*

coils so that the end of the last one is continued to form the plaiting round the outside. In this way a sudden start is avoided.

Table mats made from lengths of plaited rush which have been coiled and stitched. Designed by Barbara Maynard.

Re-seating a chair

Antique chairs are very often sold cheaply because the rush seats need replacing—if you can repair them yourself it is well worth the effort. An average chair takes about three-quarters of a bolt to re-seat. No special equipment is necessary and, apart from rushes, the only other material required is string.

Strip off all the old rushes and make sure that the joints of the wood are secure.

A square chair or stool is started by tying two rushes—one thick end and one thin end—to a corner on the left-side rail, with string (fig.3). Make sure

3. *Starting the rush seating.*

that they are tied very securely.

Take the two rushes in the right hand and twist them to the right, stroking and pulling them quite firmly at the same time so that the two rushes look like one. Take the twisted rushes over and down the front rail at the corner (see fig.3). Now the rushes pass under the front rail and up through the chair untwisted.

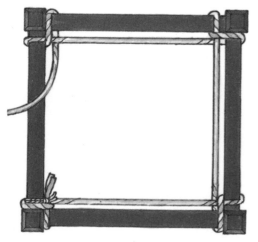

4. *Each corner is worked in turn.*

Left: rush seating is suitable for a variety of chairs—this chair is wider at the front than the back.

Twist the rushes to the left this time, stroke pull and twist, and then take them over the first twist, over and down the left-side rail. Pass under the left-side rail and all the way to the right-side rail untwisted.

Turn the chair round so that you can now repeat the looping process in this corner. Work each corner in this way (fig.4). The first twist in each corner is always to the right and the second one to the left. You may prefer to think of it as always twisting away from the corners. Try to use your right hand to do the right twist and your left hand to do the left twist. (So for once it does not matter whether you are left- or right-handed.)

Keep the diagonal lines of the pattern at 45° from each corner and make sure each twisted pair is parallel to the side rails.

Join in a new rush by tying the old end and the new end together with a reef knot. Try to keep all the knots on the untwisted section between the rails where they will be covered and so hidden. At first this is easy but becomes increasingly difficult as the work progresses. At the end the knots will show underneath the chair so keep them as neat as possible and turn the ends into the work.

Packing. When you have made about twelve rounds it is time to start 'packing' the chair. This is to make the rush work quite firm and even, and prevents the rails cutting the rushes.

Turn the chair upside-down. Use any leftover oddments of dry rush for padding; the ends that have been trimmed, weak pieces, spotted rushes etc are all used up at this point. Cut them into short lengths and stuff them into the eight pockets (two at each corner) formed by the pattern of the work. Push them right into the corners and make the padding quite firm and tight. Use a knife handle or something similar to help push the packing into the work.

Continue to rush the seat but do not attempt to do the whole chair in one session. The rushes should be allowed to dry and can be pushed up closer when starting to rush again. If you do it all at once the finished seat will be quite loose. Pad every dozen or so rounds and try to keep the rushes very tight. When the centre is reached tie the last rush on to the one opposite, underneath the chair.

Oblong shapes are started in the same way as a square chair. Work until the short side is filled up. Then continue to fill the long sides with a figure of eight pattern between the two long sides (fig.5).

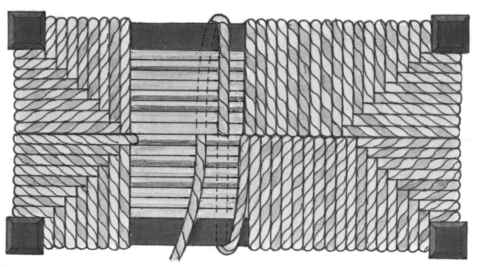

5. *Completing an oblong shape.*

For a chair that has the front rail longer than the back rail (that is wider in the front) start as before (round the two front corners only), then tie the ends firmly against the right-hand rail. Now start all over again at the left side and weave only round the front two corners and tie off. Continue in this way until the area still to be rushed is exactly square (fig.6). Pad the corners if necessary. Then continue as before and work over the tie in pieces.

6. *Rushes tied with string and worked round frame to form a square.*

seagrass seating

Most households have the odd chair that is useless because the seat is worn out. But whether the seat was originally upholstered or caned it can be repaired quickly and easily with seagrass. Seagrass is both inexpensive and quick to work with and this makes it a useful alternative to cane or upholstery. Most four-sided frames without arms, or with open arms, can be covered with seagrass; this includes square and rectangular frames and chair frames wider at the front than at the back. Even circular chairs are suitable providing they have four legs. The only unsuitable type of frame is one where the pieces vary sharply in thickness, for example if decorated with deeply cut carving or turning.

Seagrass is a tough, natural fibrous material, shiny and pale green or beige in colour. It is bought woven into a continuous cord, like string. It is generally sold in hanks and two will be required to cover the seat of a large chair.

Seagrass is stronger, more flexible and cleaner to use than the rushes described in the previous section.

Alternatives to seagrass are thick brown string, seating cord and macramé twine.

Thick brown string is just as strong as seagrass and it is easier to work with but is not so attractive.

Seating cord is strong and tightly twisted to give it a fine texture. It is available in bright colours although natural colours are usually preferred. Macramé twine is finer and smoother than other types of seating cord but it is more difficult to handle.

Tools

No special tools or equipment are needed for the job. There are, however, some that will make working a lot easier.

As seagrass comes in continuous lengths it will speed up the work if you make some wooden 'shuttles' on which to wind the seagrass.

Shuttles can be used to pass through the chair frame, gradually unwinding the seagrass as work progresses. Make a shuttle out of very thin wood (such as from orange crates) or 3mm (⅛″) plywood, cut into a rectangle 23cm x 7.5cm (9″ x 3″) with V-shaped notches in each short end (fig.1) so that the seagrass can be wound on lengthwise.

A screwdriver is useful for pushing the loops of seagrass along the chair frame to tighten them.

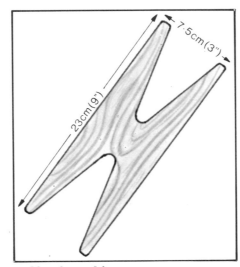

1. *Shuttle used for seagrass.*

Preparation

Seagrass must be soaked in water to make it pliable. This should be done after winding it on the shuttles to prevent it from shrinking. Place a weight on the seagrass to keep it under water and leave it for half an hour. Once the seagrass is removed from the water, cover it with a wet towel to keep it damp.

To prepare a chair, simply remove all traces of the old covering to expose the frame. Polish or varnish the chair before starting the seating.

Seating

The basic method is for a perfectly square frame with all four sides the same length. It must be modified slightly for rectangular frames or frames with sides of unequal length.

The technique is the same as rush seating, except you do not have to twist the seagrass or tie in new lengths as shown in the previous section.

Typical seagrass seating includes a pattern which interlocks to form a neat X-shape with arms running towards the four corners. Alternative patterns have a more woven appearance.

Stools with seats made from seagrass and seating cord, in various patterns make a colourful addition to children playroom.

The pattern forms automatically as you work round the frame. A very simple loop secures the end at one corner. Following fig.2, continue to make loops round the frame working towards the centre of the seat.

Pull the seagrass as tightly as you can and, using the screwdriver, push the rows of loops together.

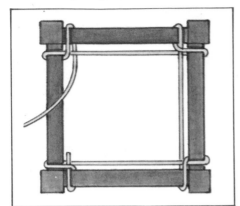

2. *Loops are repeated at each corner.*

When you have gone round the frame four or five times, passing the shuttle through the frame, you will notice the formation of the pattern. Push the seagrass around with your fingers to make the arms of the X-shape straight. Continue doing this as you work and keep each successive round as close as possible to the previous round.

When you have completely covered the chair seat with seagrass (you will find it easier to do the last few rounds without the shuttle) stop at a point which leaves the loose end in the middle of the chair pointing downwards. Tie the loose end to any of the strands on the underside of the seat.

Rectangular frames are started in exactly the same way as square frames. When the shorter sides have been filled with seagrass continue along the longer sides with a series of figure-8 loops (fig.3). Tie the loose ends as for a square seat.

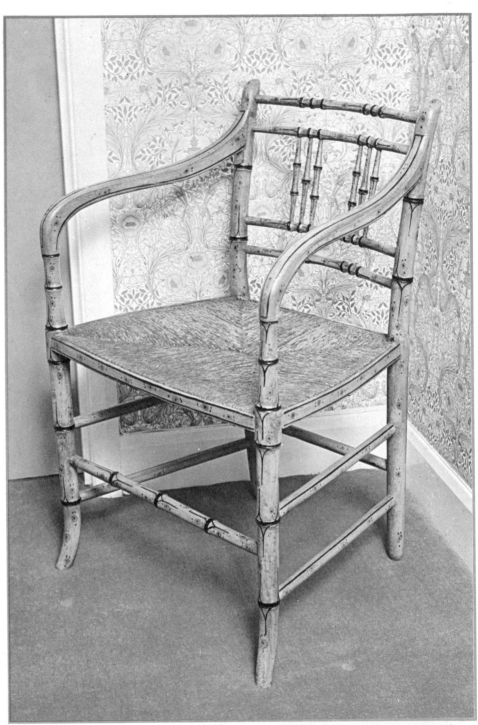

Above: chair with varnished seagrass.

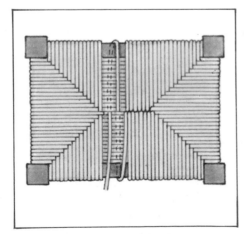

3. *Finishing a rectangular frame.*

Odd shapes, such as a chair with a wide front and a narrow back, are worked in a slightly different way. To broaden the row of loops along the front, the seagrass is looped round twice on every alternate round (fig.4). Start as usual at a corner, and take the seagrass round the frame and over to the other side. On the second round, instead of looping the rush under the frame and immediately passing it to the next side, loop it round twice and then pass it on. (Note: this is only done on the front half of the frame.)

As soon as this alternate double looping

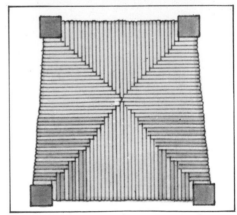

4. *Double loops on alternate rounds.*

68

Above: detail of one of the most popular seagrass patterns.
Below: alternative pattern worked with natural and coloured seagrass.

has compensated for the slant, and the area left to be covered is square or rectangular, continue without the double loop. Tie off on the underside of the work.

Most chairs that are not square can be worked in this way. For example, a chair with the front and back rails curved slightly downwards will not have a level seat, but the seating is still worked as described above. As long as the seagrass is pulled tight and pushed close together the end result will be perfect.

The seagrass can be coated with polyurethane varnish. Do a test patch to see if you like the effect.

Alternate patterns

A different pattern can be used and varied if desired on square frames. You will need a length of dowelling 12mm ($\frac{1}{2}$″) in diameter and slightly longer than the length of the chair frame.

You will find it easier to work the second stage with the seagrass threaded through a large needle (or one fashioned out of a wire coat-hanger).

First stage—mark the centre of each side of the frame and make sure that you weave the same number of rounds on either side of the marks.

Tie the end of the seagrass, on the underside, to the frame. Place the dowelling across the centre of the frame at right angles to the direction in which you are working.

Loop the seagrass (on the shuttle) up and round the front rail twice. Take it across to the opposite side on the underside of the frame and wind it around the frame twice. Return to the front on top of the frame.

Take the next four rounds straight round the frame, without the double rounds, going from front to back on the underside and back to front on the top.

Repeat the two wraps or double loops on each side and then repeat the four straight rounds etc (fig.5). Proceed in this way across the frame remembering to check that you have the same number of strands on either side of the half-way marks. End the weaving with double loops at front and back.

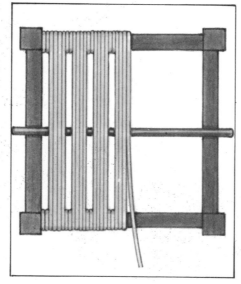

5. Top view only of pattern.

If there is a long length of seagrass left take it round to the adjacent side, on the inside of the frame, to begin the second stage, otherwise tie it in on the underside of the frame and start a new length of seagrass for the second stage. Remove the length of dowelling from between the seagrass.

Second stage—this is worked similarly to the first stage but the seagrass should be threaded on a needle. (The shuttle could be used initially but, as the weaving progresses, a needle will be more suitable.)

Make two double rounds to start, then weave under the first four strands and over the next four etc, and repeat the double loops at the opposite rail. Return on the underside, weaving under and over as before. Weave four straight rounds and then repeat the double loops etc.

When weaving the top you will find it easier if you use the dowelling to raise the alternate four strands going in the opposite direction so that you can pass the needle through easily to the other end (fig.6).

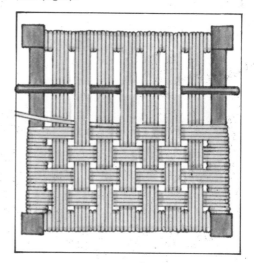

6. Dowelling lifts alternate sections.

Joining in, should it be necessary, must be done on the underside. Tie the old end and the new end together so that the knot (fig.7) will be hidden on the underside of the frame.

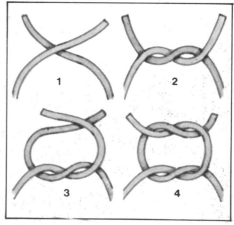

7. Reef knot used for joining.

Adjusting the pattern. The pattern is simple to alter; instead of two double loops and four straight rounds you can do various combinations, such as one and three or two and five etc.

cane chair seating

Caned chair seating dates back to ancient Egypt and, although nothing was written about the technique until this century, early artefacts such as Tutankhamun's day bed show that the method has changed very little.

Caned furniture has been fashionable over the centuries, but especially during the past three hundred years. In the 18th century finer cane than was previously used became available in

Europe, and elegant cane-bottomed chairs by cabinetmakers, such as Adam and Hepplewhite, were the result.

Caning reached its greatest popularity in the 19th century with the development of bent-wood furniture, and in Vienna one factory produced 400,000 bent-wood chairs in a year. Bent-wood furniture is popular again and pieces which need re-caning can often be bought cheaply. For this reason, as well as the innate pleasure of working with cane, it is a craft worth pursuing. Do not be too ambitious in the early stages however—leave antique chairs alone until you become experienced at handling and weaving cane. Start with a square or oblong shape before attempting more complicated ones.

Materials

The materials required are readily available and apart from the cane very little else is required.

Cane. Chair seating cane comes from a creeper which grows in South East Asia. It is a member of the rattan family and grows to enormous lengths. The bark has sharp barbs; but this outer bark is discarded. Underneath is a hard, shiny inner bark and it is this which is used for caning chairs.

The cane comes in two qualities and various sizes. Blue tie is the best quality cane and is used for antique chairs, but red tie is suitable for most other chairs.

The cane is available in six sizes which are numbered from 1 to 6. The thinner the cane the smaller the number. Two different sizes of cane are often used on one chair; the most common sizes are No.2 and No.4. The size of the cane required depends on the distance between the holes on the chair frame. The usual distance between holes is 12mm ($\frac{1}{2}$") making the frame suitable for the ever-popular seven-step pattern illustrated in the photograph.

If the holes in a frame are closer together than 12mm ($\frac{1}{2}$") the cane will become crowded, making it difficult to work, and No.2 and No.3 must be used instead. For very fine work use No.1 and No.2. If you are re-caning a chair, take a sample if possible and purchase a similar-sized cane.

Although two sizes of cane are traditional, most people—for reasons of economy—will prefer to use only one size of cane (unless a large number of chairs are being re-caned). This is because one bundle of cane will be more than sufficient for caning one chair; working with different sizes will mean left-over material unless several chairs are being caned.

Pegs are required for chair seating.

Left: chairs caned in the ever-popular seven-step pattern.

They are used to hold the cane temporarily during the weaving although some are left permanently to secure odd ends or to plug 'blind' holes. Any pointed 5cm (2") sticks are suitable, as is thick cane if you have it. Alternatives, for temporary pegs, are golf tees and Rawlplugs.

Tools

There can be few crafts that require less tools and most of the tools are part of any household, or can be improvised.

Scissors—to cut the cane. Any size will do as long as they make a clean cut.
Knife—also to cut the cane where the scissors cannot reach; can also be used to make and point the pegs.
Clearer—this is used to clear the holes. A 7.5cm (3") nail is suitable if the pointed end is cut off. Similarly a metal knitting needle or a screwdriver can be used—the diameter of the tool should not be more than 3mm ($\frac{1}{8}$").
Bodkin—a small fine bodkin is very useful to help the cane through tight spaces, but you can make do with a hat pin or a large rugging needle.
Small hammer—for rapping the knots flat at the finish and for tapping the pegs into holes.

Preparing the chair

A chair must be stripped of all its old cane and any repairs to the frame must be done before re-caning is started. The frame must be sanded and varnished or painted, as this is not possible once the weaving is started.

The old cane can be cut away close to the frame and kept for reference—this is especially useful if the shape is irregular. Alternatively, before removing the old cane make a sketch of the frame, marking the holes and the number of canes from each hole and their direction—this is particularly useful for round and oval shapes.

Remove all the old cane from the holes and underneath the seat. If the caning has been pegged, knock all the pegs out of the holes using the clearer. If the pegs are very stubborn and will not come out with gentle tapping, it is less strain on the frame if you drill a hole in the peg—use a drill bit the same size as the existing holes.

Sometimes corner holes are 'blind', ie they do not go right through the wood. In these cases the pegs must be drilled out to clear the original hole. Once all the old cane is stripped, the holes cleared and the frame painted or varnished, you can start weaving.

Seven-step pattern

If you are working on a square or oblong frame this pattern is simple.
Preparation. The cane must be prepared before it is used. You will find it

easy to handle the cane if you dip it in hot water for a moment before using it. Keep the cane wet while working by passing it through a bowl of water. The cane will also absorb enough water if you dip your fingers in the water and stroke the underside of the cane (not the glossy side) occasionally. While dry cane is very brittle, and cracks and splits easily, you should never soak the cane or it will become discoloured, nor should you wrap it up in a damp cloth for later use—it's so easy to dip each piece just before using it.

One word of warning—be careful not to tread on the cane (the lengths of the cane make this very easy). The cane will split lengthways and a split, once started, has a nasty tendency to creep up the length. Discard split pieces—they will spoil the appearance of the chair. Prepare the cane as you need it.

Step 1—the first setting. Starting at

The first step of the pattern.

the back, on the left, insert one end of the cane (if weaving with two sizes, use the thinner one) into the hole next to the back left corner hole.

Allow 10cm (4") to protrude underneath the frame and place the cane so that the glossy surface is facing up when the cane is placed across the frame. Peg the cane in the hole so that the cane is held firmly (fig.1).

Take the long end of the cane down

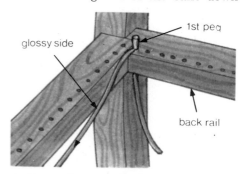

1. *Peg end to start the first step.*

through the hole at the front next to the corner hole. Make sure that the glossy side of the cane remains up and that there are no twists in the cane. Also make sure that the cane is not

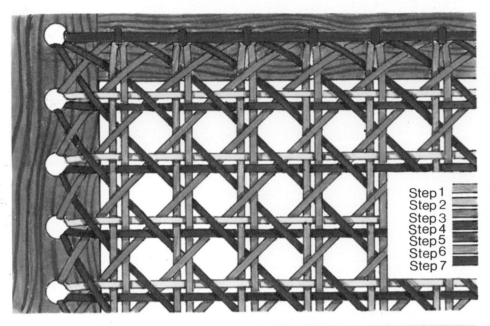

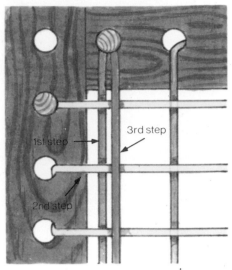

to the right of the first step, especially at the holes (fig.4).

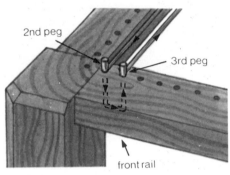

2. *Top: detail of seven-step pattern.*
3. *Bottom: Cane temporarily pegged.*

twisted as it goes through the hole. Pull the cane fairly tightly and peg it. (For detail of pattern, see fig.2).

The cane is now brought up through the next hole, untwisted, glossy side always facing—even on the underside of the frame. Pull tight and secure with another peg (fig.3).

The cane is now passed to the opposite side to the hole next to the starting one. Take the third peg (or remove second peg) and use it to peg this hole.

The first peg is holding the cane end but each successive peg is taken from a hole to 'travel' with the weaving. Continue going backwards and forwards until the end is reached.

If the cane runs out, leave the end protruding from the underside and leave a peg in the hole to hold the cane securely until the ends are finished off. Then start a new length of cane in the next hole just as you started the first cane. Always leave 10cm (4″) protruding from the underside, for old and new lengths of cane.

Keep the tension fairly tight and even. Do not make it too tight—each successive stage tightens the work—but do not make it too loose either; the work must never sag of its own accord.

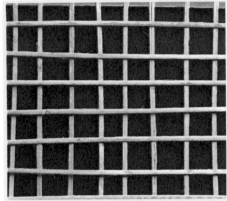

The second step of the pattern.

Step 2—this is worked exactly the same as the first stage but going over the first step at right angles.

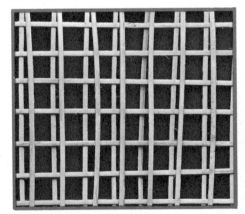

The third step of the pattern.

Step 3—the second setting. The first step is repeated on top of the previous two steps.

The next step will be made easier by positioning the cane in this step so that it does not lie directly on top of the first step but is parallel to it—keep

4. *Step 3 is parallel to first step.*

Try to plan the work so that you use the spaces on the underside of the frame that were not covered the first time.

Tying in the ends—see also Finishing ends. You can tie in the ends, if you wish, as you work. Pass the new end untwisted twice over the short strands on underside between holes (fig.5).

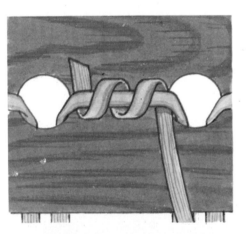

5. *Tying in on the underside of chair.*

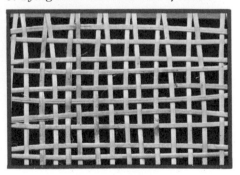

The fourth step of the pattern.

Step 4—is a repetition of step 2 but, unlike step 2, the cane must be woven under then over the vertical pieces (not over and under). This step takes longer than any of the other steps. Run your fingers along a length of cane in both directions, and then use the cane so that it will be woven in the direction which feels smoother.

Start as in step 2 and peg one end. The cane must now be kept untwisted and the right way up. Starting from the fixed end, run the cane through your fingers, keeping it untwisted all the way to the working end. This is very important as there is no way of un-twisting it once it is woven unless you unpick it.

Having untwisted the cane, thread the end underneath the cane of the first setting (the one on the left) up between the two vertical canes and over the second setting.

Repeat with each pair of canes as you reach them. Do not pull the whole length of cane through until you have passed six pairs. As you pull the cane through it will flatten, straighten and tighten the work. Continue, backwards and forwards, joining in as required and pegging protruding ends.

Keep the pattern correct—remember that in this step the weaver always goes under the first setting and over the second.

Don't worry too much about making the lines neat and tidy with close little squares—the next two steps will do this.

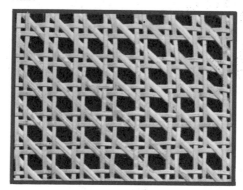

The fifth step of the pattern.

Step 5—the first diagonal. If you have been using thin cane now is the time to change to the next size (otherwise continue with No.4).

Peg the cane end in the back left-hand corner. Start weaving over the first pair (horizontals), move over to the right by going under the vertical pair then over the next horizontal pair etc. The weaving appears to be done in 'steps' but once it is pulled through tightly it forms a diagonal line (see fig.2).

If the chair frame is square you will end in the opposite corner, otherwise thread it into whichever hole that has been reached.

Bring the untwisted cane up through the next hole in front to the left and weave back. Keep the pattern correct —*over* horizontals and *under* the verticals.

Weave like this until you finish off in the corner by passing straight across from one hole to the other.

Go back to the starting hole and start another cane (the corner holes are used twice) to fill the remainder of first diagonals. Go under the verticals, over horizontals, as before.

Complete this weaving then check and make sure that the pattern is correct. Remember the only way to correct errors is to unpick the weaving.

The weaving is usually easy, not needing tugging and pulling—if you find that you are having trouble check again that the pattern is correct.

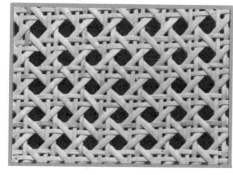

The sixth step of the pattern.

Step 6—the second diagonal. This is exactly the opposite to step 5. Start in another corner and weave at right angles to the previous diagonals. Corner holes are used twice again. This time the weavers go *under* the horizontals and *over* the verticals.

Finishing ends. By now the frame will have quite a lot of pegs holding various lengths of cane. These can now be tied if you have not done so already.

Dampen the ends to make them pliable. Cut each end to a point. Thread the end twice under a loop that is lying adjacent to it—use the bodkin if necessary to gently ease the cane into position. Keep the ends untwisted, glossy side outwards. Tap the 'coil' gently with a hammer to flatten it and cut the end off close.

If you have three or four ends coming out of the same hole, tying in can be awkward. Pass the cane to be tied under an adjacent loop then take it back under itself and cut off the end.

Pegs are used in blind corners and in holes which hold loose ends which cannot be tied in position. The pegs must fit tightly and once tapped in position they must be flush with the chair frame. If you are going to cover the frame holes with a cane beading, don't do this pegging until the beading is in position.

Beading—the seventh step.

Step 7—beading is a fairly modern addition and is an optional extra—it is a length of cane positioned around the outline of the weaving. It can be put on with two different-sized canes, usually No.2 and No.6 although there is no set rule and No.4 can be used.

The thicker cane is laid over the top of the holes and so hides them. The thick cane is couched down with the thinner cane. Beading is combined with either pegging or tying in. Tie in before starting the beading.

Start the beading by inserting a length of No.2 cane into a hole next to a corner. Allow the end to protrude 3cm (1½″) towards the top. Bend this end down into the next hole and bring the long end up through the same hole. This method will secure the short end. Insert a length of No.6 cane down into the same hole and position it so that it lies over the holes along that side of the chair frame.

Pass the thinner cane over the thick cane and take it down the same hole. Pass this thin cane to the next hole on the underside—always untwisted, glossy side facing—and up through that hole. Take it over the thick cane and then down the same hole (fig.6).

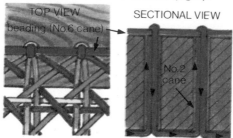

6. *Couching beading into position.*

Continue to the corner hole and insert the thick and the thin cane into this hole. Start the two canes for the beading along the adjacent side before pegging the ends finally. Repeat this all round to complete the beading.

Finally trim all the ends underneath. Make sure that all ends are tied or pegged before doing this.

If the holes are very close together you will find it easier to do the beading with No.4 cane, otherwise couch the thick cane down through alternate holes instead.

74

Rugs & mats

Mats from plaited scraps

Plaits are simple enough for children to make, and may have been the first textile process mastered by primitive man. The ancient Egyptians and Peruvians braided fabrics, some as wide as 46cm (18"). Much later, American settlers in New England found it a thrifty way of recycling worn-out clothes. Plaiting with scrap material is still an economical and rewarding way of creating fabric. It is a means of producing practical and attractive articles from discarded clothing, scraps of yarn, stockings and tights, old blankets, curtains and covers using all these materials as a form of yarn. Knee rugs, floor coverings, table mats and cushion covers are just a few of the items that can be made from the contents of a rag bag.

Construction. A plait is formed by interlacing 3 or more strands of yarn just as hair is plaited. It is the first step on the road to weaving: later chapters go on to finger weaving which is virtually a form of plaiting with numbers of threads. This in turn leads on to building up a warp and weft using rigid heddles and then to working with various types of loom.

Choosing the materials

Bear in mind how you want the finished article to look and what it will be used for. Avoid fabrics that unravel and shed their pile, such as fur fabric, and also scratchy ones that contain metallic threads. Velvets, woollen fabrics and linens tend to fray, so the edges must be turned in carefully to make sure that they don't escape. Felt is useful where a smooth look is wanted as it does not fray but, not being washable, it is unsuitable for items that are likely to get stained. Fluff and dust can be shaken out, or removed by vacuum cleaner. Cotton is suitable for most purposes and is easy and pleasant to plait.

Nylon stockings, tights and jersey fabrics are ideal, especially for making cosy and comfortable rugs. Rugs, of course, take a lot of material, so if you are planning a special colour scheme you will need whole garments. You can, however, quite successfully blend different types of fabric of toning or contrasting colours, as long as the thickness and weight are the same. When making table mats, choose a washable fabric thick enough to take a hot plate.

Colour and design

Completely different effects can be achieved depending on the number of

An excellent idea for recycling old nylons—the muted colours and original texture of this rug are obtained by plaiting together old or discarded nylons. Designed by Hilary Dukes

76

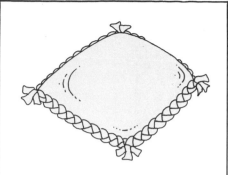

Use plaits to trim a cushion

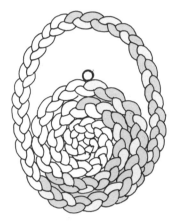

Make a handbag with two mats.

Join two lengths to make a belt.

Revamp last year's clothes with beautiful, bold braids

different fabric colours and patterns available. For example, if you have a lot of a particular shade, with just a few scraps of other colours, make a feature of them. Alternatively, scatter them at random throughout the entire piece of work. Or if you have equal amounts of various colours, give strength to each by plaiting a couple of coils in each colour. Again, if there is more of one colour than another,

either work a whole band from the smaller amount, or split it up into sections and stagger them to form a definite design. With a variety of different fabrics and colours you can create a handsome and unique article.

Basic working method

Preparing the strips. Cut or tear fabrics of similar thickness into strips, as long as possible. The width depends on the thickness of the material and what you are making. For rugs, work with 5cm-7.5cm (2″-3″) wide strips; for table mats, about 2.5cm-5cm (1″-2″). If they are cut too narrow it is difficult to turn under the edges neatly.

Fold the strips so that the raw edges meet in the middle of the wrong side of the fabric, then bring the folded edges together to make a flat strip with all raw edges enclosed (fig.1). You can

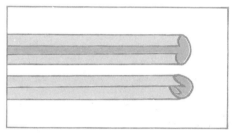

1. Fold edges of strip to centre and fold strip in half, enclosing edges

do this as you plait, but beginners are advised to press the fabric into its proper folds before plaiting together. Keep the strips folded either by pinning, or by winding them around pieces of cardboard.

Plaiting. To begin a 3-strand plait, unfold the raw edges of 2 strips and sew the ends together with a bias seam. Trim off corner (fig.2). Refold

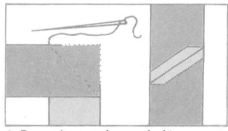

2. Sew strips together on the bias

with the raw edges of the bias seam hidden inside. Attach the 3rd folded strip with a few stitches, to form a T (fig.3).

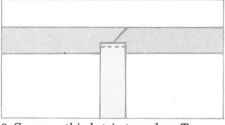

3. Sew on a third strip to make a T.

It is best to work with all the strips held taut. Secure the T end to a hook or door handle so that both hands are free for plaiting.

Start by bringing the left-hand strip over the centre strip and then the right-hand strip over that (fig. 4). Continue

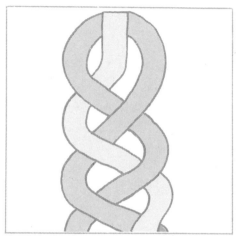

4. Plait the three strips together.

plaiting, making sure that the folded edges are always towards the centre of the plait. Keep the tension even, neither too tight nor too loose, and push the work up against the already plaited end.

As you finish a strip, join on a new one with a bias seam.

If the lengths to be plaited are very long, keep them wound around a piece of card to prevent them tangling and twisting. Make a slit in the edge of the card to hold the working end; as the work progresses, small amounts can be released as required.

It is an advantage if the strips are uneven in length, so the joins will not be all in one place. Try to plait over a join so that it is hidden in the finished work. When introducing a new colour, secure the completed plait with a safety pin to prevent it unravelling, then turn in the ends of both the new and old plaits and sew them together edge to edge (fig.5). Make sure you keep the butted ends flat when sewing together.

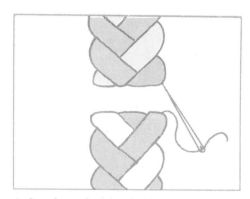

5. Sew butted ends of plaited strips

Make a charming and colourful set of table mats from scraps of toning fabrics. You can use any pieces of material that you have around the house that go well together. Choose complementary designs and colours.

Making up. As soon as you have plaited about 60cm-90cm (2'-3'), begin sewing together. Lacing is the easiest and strongest method of connecting plaits. Thread a blunt tapestry needle or bodkin (flat needle used for threading elastic) with either carpet thread or strong waxed cotton. Draw it through the loop of one plait, then thread through the corresponding loop of the plait opposite (fig.6).

When making a circular rug, wind the plait round and round, keeping it flat. This requires a little practice; if wound too tightly it will buckle, but it must not be too loose or the work will look rough and untidy. Ease in the fullness on the curves to keep the work flat.

When lacing together, it may be necessary to pass the needle through one loop on the inner plait and through two on the outer one.

To make an oval rug, begin with a long plait folded in half and laced together to give a long, shaped centre. Wind round it, easing in the fullness where necessary.

Finishing. As you approach the end of the rug, start to taper the strips (fig.7). This will diminish the size of

the plait so that it will gradually blend into the last plaited row of the rug. Weave the remaining ends of the plait into the outer ring of the work—you may find a crochet hook helpful here. Slipstitch the ends invisibly to secure in place.

Backing. You may wish to line, or back the finished work. Choose a non-slip fabric if backing a rug or table mat. Place the finished article flat on the lining and cut to shape, allowing 1.5cm-2cm ($\frac{1}{2}$"-$\frac{3}{4}$") all round for turnings. Turn in the edges of the lining and slipstitch to the back of the work.

Round nylon rug

Most women get through dozens of pairs of stockings or tights every year. Instead of throwing them away once they are ruined, keep them—and ask all your friends to do so as well—then make them up into a tough, smart rug for the kitchen or bathroom.

Tights are better to use than stockings as they are longer and therefore need fewer joins. Discard any that are very badly damaged as the runs will show in the finished rug.

To make a rug 90cm (3') in diameter:
You will need:
About 150 prs of tights or stockings
Nylon sewing thread
Sewing needle and bodkin

☐ Cut off and discard feet and reinforced tops from tights and stockings.

☐ If the nylons are all of a similar colour, bleach some of the legs in a weak solution of ordinary household bleach or proprietary nylon bleach. Dye others dark brown.

☐ Sew the legs into strips, then plait them, taking care to mix the various shades effectively. Try to work 2 or 3 rounds that are predominantly pale and to finish with 2 or 3 rounds that are predominantly dark.

☐ Finish the rug in the usual way.

Round table mats

Worn or out-of-date cotton clothes are ideal for making table mats.

To make a set of 4 mats 40cm (16") in diameter:
You will need:
A total of 3m (3yd) of cotton fabric 90cm (36") wide—a set of 4 mats as shown uses about 1m (1yd) each of red, pink and orange sprigged cotton
Cotton thread
Sewing needle and bodkin

☐ Cut each colourway into strips 2.5cm (1") wide and fold.

☐ Divide the colours equally into 4 mixed piles.

☐ Working with one pile, start by plaiting 2 strands of one colour to emphasize it, then mix all the colours, then make another colour predominate. This will create strong, interesting

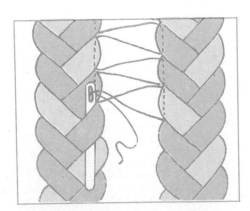

6. Lace coils together with a bodkin.

7. Weave away ends into last coil.

This attractive, cosy rag rug is made from long tweedy strips, plaited together in subtle combinations and coiled into an oval

bands of colour in the completed mat.
☐Finish in the usual way.
☐Make up the other 3 mats in the same way, but do not attempt to make the varying bands of colour identical in each mat. Part of their charm is that each has its own unique qualities.

Oval tweed rug

A warm oval rug of this type would look good in front of the fire, by the bed or inside the front door.

You may be able to get hold of some bags of scraps from a garment manu-facturer—otherwise it's worth looking through shapeless, unloved tweed and woollen clothes at second-hand sales for rock-bottom bargains.

To make this oval, multi-coloured rug 90cm x 60cm (3′ x 2′):

You will need:
Tweed and woollen scraps adding up to about 7m (8yd) x 90cm (36″).
Thread, sewing needle and bodkin
☐Cut fabric into strips 7.5cm (3″) wide.
☐Turn under the edges and fold.
☐Join and plait the strips. If the

colours are predominantly muted, with only the occasional bright touch, try to space out the bright pieces. Other-wise, work all the colourful pieces together to make a band a little way in from the edge.
☐Make the first plaited length 30cm (12″) long, before coiling and sewing it up into an oval.

Pattern variations
You can go on to develop intricate rug patterns on the lines of decorative rush matting. For example, work an oval centre, surround it with round panels sewn on firmly, then sew 2 or 3 rows of plaiting all round the outside.

Latch-hooked rugs

Rugs can be woven, knotted, hooked, stitched and even plaited, knitted and crocheted. With all the methods you can use new materials or you can recycle old fabrics and yarns to make hard-wearing and attractive floor coverings.

In one traditional method of rug-making the foundation is woven on a loom and the pile threads are knotted on to it by hand. A variation of this method, which is simple to do at home, is to buy a woven canvas foundation and insert the pile into it with a latch-hook.

Equipment

Latch-hooks look like crochet hooks but have a wooden handle and a hinged latch which closes round the hook to prevent it from being caught in the canvas as the knot is formed. Latch-hooks are not expensive and can be bought from most handicraft shops. They are easy to use and once you get into a rhythm the rug grows quite quickly. For extra speed, you could buy a second hook so that two people can work on the rug at the same time, by working from opposite ends of the canvas.

The yarn. For making a short-pile rug you can buy a special coarse 6-ply rug wool—often called Turkey wool—or a 3-ply acrylic yarn. Both types of yarn are available in skeins which you cut to the length you want or they can be bought in packs of 320 pre-cut pieces, 7cm (2¾″) long. Each piece makes one knot with two strands of pile about 2cm (¾″) long and one pack of wool covers just over three 7.5cm (3″) square blocks on standard rug canvas.

The advantage of buying the cut packs is, of course, that you are saved the trouble of cutting the pieces yourself. On the other hand, you are restricted to the same length of pile throughout and some of the most unusual designs include areas of different pile height. You will in any case have to buy some skeins of uncut yarn in order to finish the edges of the canvas.

Cutting your own pile. When calculating the length of each strand, remember that each strand forms two lengths of pile and the knot uses up about 3cm (1¼″) of yarn. Therefore for a

Latch-hooking equipment—the latch-hook, Turkey canvas and cut yarn. The 7.5cm (3″) grid is marked by the coloured weft and warp threads which divide the canvas into 10-hole blocks.

5cm (2″) length of pile, for example, you should cut the pieces 13cm (5¼″) long.

To cut the pieces in this case, use a piece of firm cardboard 6.5cm (2⅝″) wide and wind the yarn round it. Cut yarn along one edge of the card.

Canvas with holes large enough to take the thick rug wool is often known as Turkey or Smyrna canvas. It is woven with double threads for strength and has 10 holes to 7.5cm (3″). It can be bought in different widths from 30.5cm-122cm (12″-48″).

To make counting individual squares easier, the canvas is divided into blocks of 7.5cm (3″), marked by different-coloured thread, usually red or brown. If you are making a rectangular or square rug you should buy the exact width you want by 10cm (4″) longer than the required length. For round rugs and cushions of any shape you should buy an amount which is at least 10cm (4″) more than the required diameter.

Re-cycling materials. The latch-hook method can also be used for re-cycling strips of old fabrics and yarn. Before you start work you should experiment to see how wide the fabric strips should be cut or how many strands of yarn you would need in each knot in order to cover the canvas satisfactorily. With a double-knitting yarn, for example, you would probably need three or four strands in each knot.

The design

Short-pile, latch-hooked rugs lend themselves well to pictorial and oriental designs, and other attractive rugs can be based simply on geometric patterns or subtle blends of colour which may not form a definite pattern.

In the same way as for needlepoint, it is possible to buy the canvas already printed with the design together with the necessary amount of yarn.

Alternatively you can choose a design printed on a chart or you could adapt a chart designed for needlepoint on a finer canvas, but you should avoid those with very fine detail as they lose their subtlety because of the thickness

of the yarn and the pile. Or, if you are more ambitious, you could make up your own design.

Making your own design. Whether you choose an elaborate theme or prefer a more random effect it is advisable to work out your design to scale to give you the chance to adapt and improve your design before you start work. You will also be able to work out how much of each colour yarn to buy, so that you do not run the risk of having to use yarn from different dye lots, and you will be able to work the knots across the rug in straight lines from one end of the canvas.

If instead you work areas of colour and then fill in the background, the result is likely to be uneven and you might miss squares because they are hidden by other knots. The exception to this is with geometric designs where you could work the basic outline first and then fill in the areas enclosed by it.

Transferring the design. Intricate designs can be transferred directly on to the canvas by placing the design underneath and 'tracing' with acrylic or oil paint. For less complicated designs which have bold outlines or large areas of one colour, you can trace the design on to the canvas with felt-tipped pen.

Calculating the amount of yarn.
The only sure way of calculating the amount of yarn for each different colour in an intricate design is to count the number of knots to be worked. Draw out the design on graph paper and draw on your design to scale so that each square represents one hole on the canvas.

For less intricate designs where you are working large areas in one colour, it is normally possible to gauge the amount of yarn required by measuring each area.

Basic knots

Four-movement knot
The quickest knot consists of four movements.
Fig.1 Fold the cut length of wool in half and loop it round the neck of the hook below the crook and latch.
Fig.2 Holding the ends of the wool between the thumb and index finger of your left hand, insert the hook under the first of the weft threads (those running from left to right, across the canvas).
Fig.3 Turn the hook a little to the right, open the latch and place the ends of the wool into the hook.
Fig.4 Pull the hook under the thread and through the loop of wool. As you pull, the latch will close to prevent the hook from getting caught in the canvas.
Fig.5 Pull the ends of the wool tightly to make the knot firm.

Five-movement knot
When two people are working from opposite ends, one person should use the five-movement knot so the pile will lie in the same direction.
Fig.6 Insert the hook under the first weft thread. Fold the cut length of wool in half and, holding the ends between your thumb and index finger, loop it over the hook.

Sunflower wall-hanging
For a first project in rug-hooking this simple flower motif provides the necessary practice. The diagram on the left gives a working chart for the sunflower with one square equalling one knot. The photograph on the right shows the back of the completed rug and the positions of each colour area.

Once you have grasped the basic idea of the pattern, you can alter it to fit your own canvas, arranging several flowers and leaves to make a circular rug or one with a patchwork look.

One flower, two leaves and a stalk takes 4 units of coloured wool to cover 1018 holes. Work out the total number of holes in the canvas (width holes multiplied by length holes) and subtract from it the number for each complete flower motif (1018 holes). This will give you the background number. Divide this number by 320 (the number of pieces of wool in a unit) to give the number of wool units you need for the background colour. The main

Above *Colour plan for sunflower motif*
Left *Chart for rug – 1 square = 1 knot*

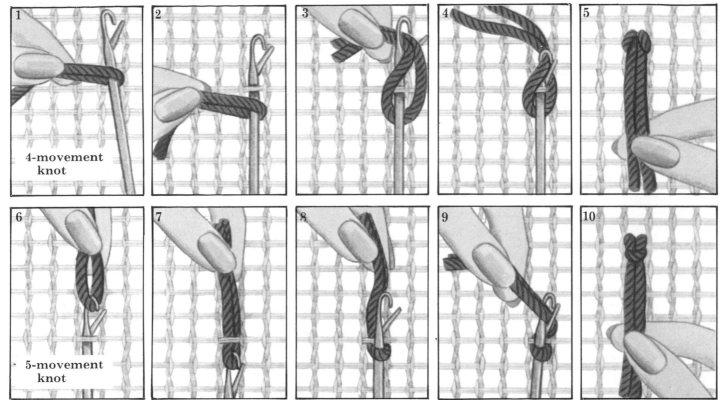

4-movement knot (Fig.1 area)

5-movement knot (Fig.6 area)

Fig.7 Pull the hook back through the canvas.

Fig.8 Push the hook through the loop of wool until the latch is clear and the loop is on the neck of the hook.

Fig.9 Place the cut ends of wool into the crook of the hook from below, so they are enclosed by the latch.

Pull the hook back firmly through the loop of wool until the ends are clear.

Fig.10 Pull the ends of the wool tightly to secure the knot.

thing to remember is to subtract from the total number of holes however many flower motifs you decide to work on your canvas. To determine background wool requirements if you use only one element of the design, see the 'You will need' section for the number of holes covered by each colour.

You will need
These instructions are for a rug 61cm (24″) square.
Canvas 61cm (24″) wide, 68cm (27″) long, to allow an extra 3.5cm (1½″) at each end for turnings.
Yarn to cover a total of 6400 holes (80 × 80):
red – 1 unit (231 holes)
yellow – 1 unit (294 holes)
green – 2 units (493 holes)
cream – 17 units (5382 holes)
Extra cream rug wool in a hank, not cut, for binding the edges of the finished rug.
Latch-hook.
Very large blunt needle (a large-eyed tapestry needle is ideal) for binding and making up.

Preparing the canvas
Fold a 3.5cm (1½″) turning to the right side of the canvas on one of the raw edges, matching the holes and threads exactly with those of the canvas below. The outer rows of

knots can then be made through the two layers of this fold.
To bind the turned edge, lay a strand of hank wool along it and oversew with blanket stitch. Oversew the opposite raw edge roughly to prevent fraying; the 3.5cm (1½″) hem at this edge should be turned as the rug nears completion and oversew neatly as before.
Bind the outer selvedge with matching carpet braid.

Working the motif
To obtain an even finish, work horizontally along the rows using the four movement method of hooking shown on page 83 across the canvas from left to right or right to left if you are left-handed, from selvedge to selvedge beginning in the lower left-hand corner.

needlepoint rugs

Rug making with a needle on a canvas foundation is a natural development of needlepoint. Many of the same techniques and principles apply, although even a small rug is an ambitious project since the amount of work involved and the cost of the materials exceed those of many of the items normally undertaken in needlepoint.

Needlepoint rugs may be made with stitches which give a smooth-faced finish as described in this chapter or they can be made with a pile finish as described in the following needlepoint chapter. Sometimes the two techniques are combined where the main interest of the rug is intended to be in its texture rather than its pattern. The basic materials, however, are similar for both methods.

Canvas

In order to produce a good heavy surface which will be hard wearing, the rug should be worked on a heavy gauge canvas or a special jute backing so that the surface can be stitched in a thick yarn. This has the extra advantage as far as the working is concerned of being quicker and easier than on finer gauge canvas.

Suitable double mesh canvases are those with 3½, 4, 5 or 7 holes per 2.5cm (1″). Single mesh canvases can be used for some needlepoint rugs although they are not suitable for all stitches.

The canvases are available in a variety of widths from 30cm (12″) up to 90cm (36″) or even 115cm (45″). You will often find that a mail order supplier will stock a wider range than a small retailer who may not have space for all the different widths and gauges.

Jute backing. This can be used as an alternative to a canvas background fabric and it is preferred by many experienced needlepoint rug makers because the finished rugs feel more substantial and more like woven rugs. Jute backing fabric (sometimes known as jute embroidery canvas) is available in 90cm (36″) or 122cm (48″) widths.

Except for the edging which should be worked over two threads, the stitches on jute are always worked over four threads. To make counting easier, the threads are woven in blocks of four (fig.2a, overleaf) or in pairs (fig.2b), with 16 threads per 2.5cm (1″).

Amount of background fabric. If the desired width of the rug corresponds with an available width of background fabric, buy a piece of the desired length plus 10cm (4″) for turnings. If the background fabric is not available in the exact width required, buy the next

This simple, bold design was worked in cross stitch in six-ply wool on a heavy-gauge rug canvas.

Amount of yarn for canvas			
Double mesh canvas— No. holes per 2.5cm (1″)	Yarn—No. strands	Types of stitch	Approx. weight of yarn per 30cm (12″) sq
3½	1 strand 6-ply or 3 strands 2-ply	short pile smooth-faced	300gm (11oz) 225gm (8oz)
4	3-4 strands 2-ply	long pile	325gm (12oz)
	2-3 strands 2-ply	short pile	225gm (8oz)
		smooth-faced	200gm (7oz)
5	1-2 strands 2-ply	short pile	175gm (6oz)
		smooth-faced	
7	1 strand 2-ply	short pile	160gm (5½oz)
		smooth-faced	
Jute: 16 threads per 2.5cm (1″)	2 strands 2-ply	short pile	225gm (8oz)
		smooth-faced	200gm (7oz)

width up and cut it to size, allowing 5cm (2″) all round. When doing this, halve the amount of background fabric to be removed from the width and cut this amount from each side.

Yarn
Essential factors when selecting yarn for needlepoint rugs are that it must be hard wearing and it must cover the background fabric satisfactorily to give good wear, yet it should not be so thick that it distorts the background.

Six-ply wool is sold specially for home rug making and is easily available although it is fairly expensive and can be used only on the heaviest gauge canvas unless it is split. It is available in a fairly wide colour range and is sold in hanks of 50gm (2oz) each.

Two-ply Axminster wool of the type used in carpet manufacture is the most economical yarn to use although it is usually available by mail order only. It can be used on jute and all gauges of canvas by threading two, three or even four lengths in the needle to make the required thickness.

It is available in a wide range of colours, in continuous lengths in hanks or as broken lengths in thrums.

Thrums are the cheapest way of obtaining yarn for making rugs. They are the ends of the warp cut from the loom after a length of carpet has been woven industrially. They are sold off from carpet mills in bundles of mixed colours and, if you order 'long thrums', they are in good working lengths for stitching.

Usually it is possible to specify the types of colours you would like— autumnal or floral shades for example —but it is advisable to over-estimate the amount you will need because the colours are dyed for a particular run of carpet and are seldom repeated.

Other yarns. Where you want an interesting texture it is possible to use fancy weaving yarns, such as bouclé. These are fairly expensive and are usually only available through special-ist shops.

Amount of yarn. This varies accord-ing to the type of stitch and the gauge of canvas. For example, a pile stitch will usually take more yarn than a smooth-faced rug, and double cross stitch will take more than single cross stitch. The chart shown here gives a general, generous guide to the amount required for jute and each type of canvas. Always buy more than the minimum amount you expect to use— any colours remaining can usually be incorporated into another project.

The needle
Use a large-sized tapestry needle which can easily be threaded with the yarn. A No.14 size is suitable for most yarns. When making a multi-coloured rug, you will save time by having several needles, each threaded in a different colour.

Frames
Unlike many other forms of needle-point it is not essential to mount the background fabric on to a frame and, in many cases, it is not possible to find a frame large enough unless you work the rug in sections. Small, smooth-faced rugs, however, can be mounted on a frame with rollers, although this type of frame should not be used for pile rugs. If you are not using a frame it is quite comfortable to work with the rug across the knees or with it on a table.

Working on a frame with the spare canvas wound on to the rollers.

Preparing canvas

To form a neat, firm edge, the cut edge at the top of the canvas—where the needlepoint will be started—should be turned over for about 5cm (2″) and the first few rows of stitching worked through the double thickness. Unlike pile rugs—where the canvas should be turned up on to the right side—with smooth-faced rugs it is better to make the turning on to the wrong side to avoid the danger of forming a ridge which would show through the needlepoint.

Canvas with selvedges. Make the fold about 5cm (2″) from the top edge along one of the canvas threads so that the holes in the turning correspond exactly with those above or below.

☐ Stitch down with cross stitch using ordinary sewing cotton double or button thread.

☐ Prepare the bottom edge by overcasting over the single thickness, passing the stitches over one complete hole. Do not turn the edge until you are within about 7.5cm (3″) of completing the design so that you can check the exact number of rows required and the turning can be made accordingly.

Four cut edges. On canvas where you have cut off the selvedges, fold over the top edge as described above. Count the threads across the width to check you have the required number for the design and fold over the side edges along the next thread. Crease well with your fingers.

☐ To mitre the corners, open out the folds and turn under the corners diagonally where the crease lines meet, matching the squares (fig.1). Crease the folds firmly and overcast to hold the squares in place.

☐ Turn under the edges again along the same creases and secure by working cross stitch in ordinary sewing cotton, double or button thread. Start 10cm (4″) from the bottom of the rug, work up one side, along top and down the opposite side to within 10cm (4″) of the bottom. Work overcasting along the bottom edge as described for canvas with selvedges.

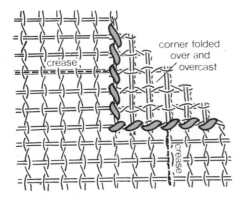

corner folded over and overcast

crease

crease

1. *Folding the corner diagonally.*

Preparing jute

Fold over the selvedges for 1.5cm (½″) and secure by herringbone stitch (see Embroidery chapter 6, page 802). Fold over the top and bottom edges for 5cm (2″)—there is no need to mitre the corners—and herringbone in the same way.

☐ Work the rug to within 7.5cm (3″) of the complete design, check the number of rows needed to complete the pattern and adjust the depth of the turning if necessary.

a

b

2a, b. *Herringboned edges of jute backing. Notice how the edges are turned to the right side for pile stitches (2a) and to the wrong side for smooth-faced stitches (2b).*

The edging

The strongest and most attractive type of edging is formed by the plaited stitch described in Latch-hooking chapter 2, page 1132.

On smooth-faced rugs worked on heavy gauge canvas it is often advisable to oversew the edges in matching yarn before the plaited stitch is worked so that none of the canvas shows through. Work the edging along the top edge and along both sides to within 15cm (6″) of the bottom edge. Complete the sides and work along the bottom edge when this is turned up.

Stitches for smooth-faced rugs

The stitches which cover the background fabric effectively, thereby giving maximum wear, are those which cross the fabric threads diagonally.

The best stitches include tent stitch, cross stitch and its variations, double cross stitch and rice stitch. (These can be found in any good embroidery book). Another good stitch is a long-legged cross stitch (fig. 3).

In a rug where the design is pictorial or oriental, it is usually better to work in one stitch throughout. On a rug where the design is a simple geometric pattern or where texture and colour are the main features the stitches may be mixed, thus adding to the textural effect.

Working the stitching. If you are doubtful about how many strands of yarn to use work a sampler of the stitches you plan to use so that you can see the effect.

When working with several strands, use the fingers of your left hand to keep them flat so they lie side by side without twisting.

If you are not using a frame, work the stitching with the top edge of the rug towards you and with the bulk of the unworked fabric stretching away from you. If you are using a frame it is a matter of personal preference whether you work from the top down or vice versa, but still mount the canvas with the selvedges to the left and right.

The stitching may be worked in horizontal, vertical or diagonal rows, or motif by motif, according to the nature of the pattern. Where a geometric pattern is based on a grid, as shown in the blue and beige rug in the photograph, work this first and then fill the spaces in between.

If you are making a multi-coloured rug try to work as many stitches as possible at one time from the length of yarn in your needle—even if it means passing behind the canvas for a few squares—to avoid the wastage which comes from continual fastening on and off. To ensure neatness on the wrong side of the rug, either work subsequent stitching over these long stitches or pass the thread through the backs of previously worked stitches, as appropriate.

Stretching the rug

Both smooth-faced and pile rugs benefit from being stretched and dampened after the needlepoint has been worked.

Tack the rug, right side up, to a wooden surface, pinning through the unworked edge, and checking the corners are square. (Place a cloth, such as an old sheet, underneath the rug to prevent the work from becoming marked.) Cover it with several sheets of clean blotting paper and soak the paper with as much water as possible.

Cover the wet blotting paper with an old dry towel or blanket and leave to dry—this will probably take a week. Fluff up the pile with your fingers.

This kind of naïve pictorial design is fun to plan and work.

Basic stitches

Long-legged cross stitch. This stitch must be worked in alternate directions across the fabric to prevent the rug from going out of shape. Notice how the long leg connecting each stitch is worked in the direction in which you are travelling. Start and finish each row and each block of stitches worked in one colour within each row with a regular cross stitch.

☐ Start by working a regular cross stitch between holes A-B-C-D (fig. 3a) and return the needle to hole A (fig.3b). Pass to hole E and work a cross stitch between holes E-F-B and bring out the needle at C (fig.3c). Continue like this along the row, finishing as shown in fig.3d.

☐ To start the second row, pass the needle vertically on the wrong side of the canvas to emerge at the first hole of the row (fig.3d, point A). Continue as shown in figs.3e-g. The tops of the stitches in this row should be worked into the bottoms of the stitches in the previous row.

Deep long-legged cross stitch. This is worked in a similar way but over two double bars of weft instead of one double bar (fig.4).

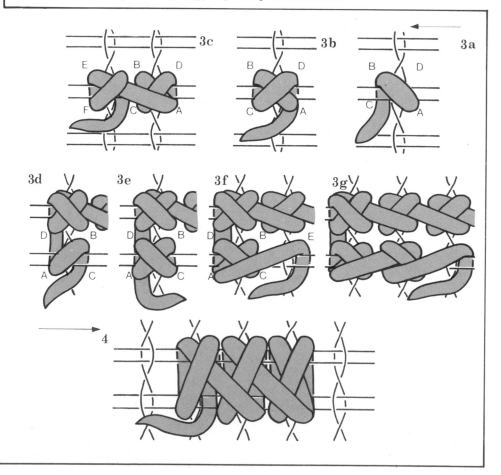

Hooked rag rugs

Hooked rugs are made by holding a strip of fabric against the underside of a piece of hessian and pulling the strip through to the right side of the hessian in loops to form a pile (fig.1). This type of rug was first made in America in the early 19th century on coarse linen and sacking, and the craft became more popular among country people when hessian became the common material for sacking and provision bags. (The animal motifs printed on the sacks as trade marks were often included in the design.)

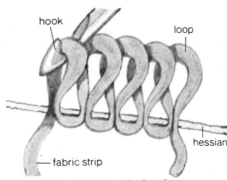

1. *How the pile is hooked in loops.*

In Britain hooked rugs appeared in the mid 19th century when homespun fabrics were being superseded by cheap, commercially produced cloths. When garments made from these wore out, much of the material in them could be re-cycled in a rug. (York has a tradition of making scarlet rugs, made from military uniforms, for example.)

Many rugs were designed to celebrate special occasions such as jubilees, birthdays, sporting events, weddings and their dates: pictures of folk heroes were also common.

Materials and equipment

Rags of all kinds can be used to make a rug although it is best to use one type of fabric within a specific rug if it is to be used as a floor covering. For wall hangings, however, different types of fabric may be combined. You should allow about 50gm (2oz) mixed fabrics per 12cm (5″) square.

Old nylon tights and stockings and yarn unravelled from knitted garments may also be used for hooked rugs.

Hessian sacks for the foundation are rarely obtainable these days but hessian is available in various widths by the metre (yard) from craft and furnishing shops. Choose the width to fit your rug frame and buy a piece 10cm (4″) longer and wider than the desired size of the rug.

If you are making the rug as a floor covering, it is advisable to back it with a second piece of hessian of the same size to give extra strength.

Rug frame. The hessian must be stretched over a frame so that the strips can be hooked through easily. Although the rug can be longer than the frame (the excess length is wound round the stretchers), it cannot be wider than the frame, unless you make it in sections. You can make a rug of the same width as the frame providing you turn under the raw edges before mounting the hessian on the frame. If you have a large needlepoint frame with rollers you could use this or you could buy a special frame.

The top and bottom sections (the stretchers) of these frames are morticed at each end and have strips of webbing fitted along the section in between. The ends of the hessian are sewn on to the webbing so that when the 'swords' or side pieces are pushed into the mortises and wooden pegs are pushed through holes in the swords, the hessian is held taut. The hessian

Left: narrow strips of tweed form the close looped pile of this hooked rug.

Right: subtle shading of the fabrics contributes to the beauty of this hooked rug designed by Dennis Barker.

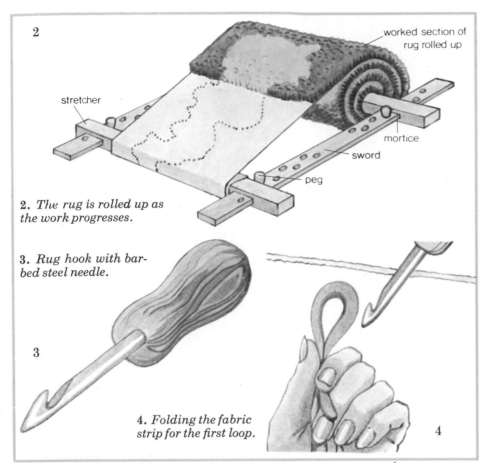

2

stretcher

worked section of rug rolled up

mortice

sword

peg

2. The rug is rolled up as the work progresses.

3. Rug hook with barbed steel needle.

3

4. Folding the fabric strip for the first loop.

4

may be rolled up over the top and bottom pieces of the frame as the work progresses (fig.2).

Rug hooks are barbed steel needles fitted with handles (fig.3). The barbs are designed to make holes in the hessian through which the fabric strips can be pulled. Hooks for use with wide strips of 2.5cm (1") and more should be made from heavier metal so that the initial hole is larger and the fabric can be hooked through it without difficulty.

Preparing the strips

Rags. Cut the strips on the straight grain as long as possible from the available fabric. Do not cut the strips on the bias—they tend to disintegrate when pulled through the hessian.

For a neat, tightly hooked floor rug cut the strips 1.2cm ($\frac{1}{2}$") wide if you are using medium-weight fabrics. If you are combining fabrics of different weight, cut those from the lighter weights wider and fold them to provide the same width and bulk as the heavier weights.

Tights and stockings. These can be cut into strips or, for a heavier effect, sheer tights and stockings can be used as they are (but with the feet and body sections removed).

Unravelled yarn. Several strands should be held together to make the same thickness as a fabric strip 1.2cm ($\frac{1}{2}$") wide.

Designing

Hooked rugs can be effective when made in a randon mixture of colours and patterned fabrics or you could work them in a simple geometric or pictorial design.

More ambitious designs can be drawn straight on to the hessian in chalk or felt-tipped pen.

Often the types of fabric available may inspire a design. White or cream bouclé wool, for example, could be used for a poodle or polar bear or even a snow scene; yellow might suggest the sun, moon or an animal such as a lion or cockerel.

You will often find that multi-coloured fabrics—such as tweeds—make livelier designs than plain flat colours.

Pile length. Choose your pile length to suit the type of design and the type of wear to which the rug will be put. Designs with elaborate detail and subtle modulated colour should be worked with small loops of about 1.2cm ($\frac{1}{2}$") long. These are less hard wearing and should be kept for wall hangings. Random geometric designs can be worked with longer pile from 2.5cm (1") long for a pebble or mosaic effect to about 10cm (4") long for a luxurious finish.

Making a rug

You will need:

Hessian 10cm (4") larger all round than the desired finished size of rug, plus a second piece of the same size if you are backing the rug.

Prepared rags.

Hook.

Frame.

Sacking needle and carpet thread.

☐ Turn under and tack down the edges of the hessian or leave them until the hooking is complete and turn them under then.

☐ Mount the hessian on to the frame by stitching the ends to the webbing.

Finished lobster rug, being worked opposite. Design by Dennis Barker.

Wind any surplus length on to one of the stretchers, insert the swords into the mortises and put in the pegs so that the hessian is held taut.

Lay the frame horizontally for hooking the rags. If it is supported across two tables or a table and chair it is possible for two or more people to work together on the rug.

The hooking. The design may be worked in horizontal rows across the hessian or you could work the main motifs first and then fill in the background.

☐ Loop the end of the first strip over for about 2.5cm (1″) and hold the loop below the hessian in the required position. With your free hand push the hook through the hessian from above (fig.4) and insert the hook into the loop. Pull it back through the hessian and draw up the loop to the desired length.

☐ Still holding the fabric strip under the hessian, make another loop, push the hook through in the required position—about 5-10mm (¼″-⅜″) away—and repeat the process (see fig.1).

☐ Continue in this way using strips of appropriate colours for your design. Leave the ends of strips on the underside to be trimmed later to about 1.5cm (½″). If you intend to cut the loops on the right side, the ends may be pulled through.

☐ Remove the rug from the frame. Turn under the raw edges if you have left them until now, and hem in place.

Backing the rug. Fold under the turnings on the backing piece and place it

Hooking the last loops in the border of the lobster rug. The hessian was mounted on a needlepoint floor frame.

on the wrong side of the rug. Pin and hem firmly with the carpet thread and sacking needle.

Quilting. For extra strength it is advisable to quilt the backing to the rug. This has the added advantage of holding the backing firmly in place when the rug is washed and hung on a line.

☐ Pass the needle from the back of the rug to the front, make a tiny stitch in the hessian (which will be hidden by the loops) and pass the needle to the back again. Tie the threads ends in a firm knot and cut off.

☐ Repeat at 15cm (6″) intervals over the whole surface.

Lampshades

paper lampshades

Making card lampshades is an agreeable craft and it is not very difficult to achieve professional-looking results. Moreover, the advantages of making your own lampshades are considerable. Home-made shades show an enormous cost saving over shop-bought lampshades and allow you maximum freedom of choice as regards colour, pattern, size and shape. Ready-made shades available in the shops are restricted, inevitably, to a limited number of variations. (How often have you found a lampshade in just the colour you were after but too large or too small to suit your purposes?) Selecting your own paper, light fitting and rings enables you to tailor a lampshade precisely to meet your requirements.

Rings and frames

Essentially, a paper lampshade is made by gluing paper on to two rings, one of which incorporates a light bulb fitting. These rings can be bought singly or already incorporated into a lampshade frame and are to be found in handicraft shops and the haberdashery section of some department stores.

Lampshade frames, which consist of two rings joined at intervals by struts, are available in a series of predetermined shapes and sizes. These frames are much favoured by some people but the extra support given by side struts is, in fact, designed for and only necessary when making silk and other flimsy fabric lampshades.

Lampshade rings are cheaper than frames. They provide all the support required for paper shades, they are easier to fit, and are additionally advantageous in that they allow you total flexibility in deciding exactly how tall and how flared your lampshade will be.

Types of lampshade

Whether you decide to make a large or small lampshade—irrespective of whether the shade is to be round or oval, for a table, wall bracket, standard or hanging lamp—a home-made paper lampshade should be one of the following three basic types:

Drum lampshades (sometimes called cylinder lampshades) are distinguished by the fact that they have parallel sides—ie the circumference at top and bottom is the same.

Coolie lampshades are so called because of their similarity to coolie hats, very narrow at the top and very wide at the bottom.

Empire lampshades are a less exaggerated version of the coolie shade, the circumference of the top being slightly smaller than the bottom to give a gently flared effect.

Making a pattern

A drum lampshade is quite straightforward but even so it is advisable to make a pattern first, using rough paper, rather than run the risk of cutting your chosen lampshade paper inaccurately. The pattern can, of course, be used as a template for cutting the chosen paper. Measure the circumference of your rings adding 1.2cm ($\frac{1}{2}$") for overlap, and decide on the finished height of the shade. Draw up a rectangle accordingly using a set square for accurate right angles (fig.1). Cut out, join the overlap at top and bottom with paper clips or clothes pegs and slip over the rings to test for size.

Empire or coolie lampshade. The pattern for a flared or tapered shade is slightly more complicated, and should be done on squared graph paper.

You will need:
A large sheet of squared graph paper.
Clothes pegs or paper clips.
A pair of compasses, a piece of string, a drawing pin and sharp scissors.
Tape measure, ruler and pencil.

☐ As shown in fig.2, near the bottom left-hand corner of the paper, draw a horizontal line (A-B) equal in length to the diameter of the bottom ring.

☐ From the centre of this line (C) draw a perpendicular line upwards equal to the required height of the finished shade (D).

☐ Using D as centre, draw another horizontal line (E-F) equal in length to the diameter of the top ring.

☐ Join A-E and B-F and extend these

Decorative frieze cut from gift paper was used for this small drum shade.

lines upwards until they intersect (G).

□ Using G-E as the radius, draw an arc from E equal to the circumference of the top ring. Use a compass or a piece of string tied to a pencil at one end and anchored at point G with a drawing pin (thumb tack).

□ Using G-A as the radius, draw an arc from A, equal to the circumference of the bottom ring.

□ Add 1.2cm ($\frac{1}{2}$") to the length of each arc, then join them (H-I).

□ Cut out round A-E-H-I for your lampshade pattern, join the overlap at top and bottom with paper clips or clothes pegs and slip over the rings to test for accuracy.

Suitable papers

Theoretically, only very stiff paper or card is suitable for paper lampshade making but, in practice, a light-weight, limp paper can prove equally satisfactory—providing it is mounted on to a firm backing paper or card to give necessary rigidity to the finished shade. **Pulpboard, indexboard and cover-board** are all available in 250g/m²-300g/m². This means the papers weigh between 250gm-300gm per square metre —an ideal weight and thickness for lampshade making.

Because they can be used alone without a backing paper, these materials are probably the easiest to use for lampshade making. Orbit Ivory board is a pulpboard which comes in a good range of colours; it is available in sheets measuring 640mm x 900mm (25"x 36") and 520mm x 650mm (20"x 25$\frac{1}{2}$").

Light-weight papers. The choice of colours and patterns in light-weight papers is, of course, far greater,

Above: elegant coolie shade and base in natural colours.

offering temptingly pretty designs and enormous scope to the lampshade maker intent on unique and personal results. Decorative gift wrapping paper, shelf lining paper and wall-papers come in literally thousands of designs, plain or patterned and sometimes with textured finishes. A lampshade that matches your walls not only looks charming but makes good use of leftovers too!

It should be noted, however, that it is inadvisable to make a very tapered shade with a large floral, striped, checked or otherwise very distinctively patterned paper. Choose a simple drum shade instead because the curved cut-out shape of a tapered shade makes pattern matching impossible and may well distort the design in an extremely unsightly way. Small designs with frequent pattern repeats present a lesser problem as do muted designs and random patterned papers (such as marbled papers)—but, even so, a drum lampshade makes for neater looking results and is easier to handle.

Silver kitchen foil looks gleaming and exotic yet is relatively cheap. Even throw-away materials, such as yesterday's newspaper or brown parcel wrapping paper, can be used for highly decorative and original lampshades.

Self-adhesive card. Some papers are tricky to mount successfully on to card —because liquid adhesive, however carefully applied, is liable to be absorbed into, and leave disfiguring marks on, the paper. The problem of

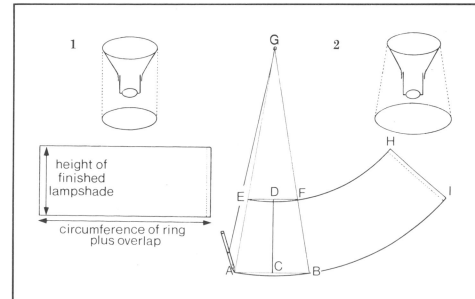

1. *A drum lampshade pattern is a simple rectangle.*
2. *Patterns for tapered (empire or coolie) lampshades need to be carefully calculated on graph paper. Use string to measure circumferences. To draw an arc, anchor the string with a drawing pin and tie a pencil to the other end.*

staining can be overcome by using a self-adhesive card, such as Selapar, which can be bought from handicraft shops. Self-adhesive card can be used for backing close-weave fabrics as well as paper lampshades and is simple to use.

First prepare your decorative paper, using a cool iron to remove any fold marks if necessary. Lay the paper, reverse side facing upwards, on a firm flat board and pin taut with drawing pins. Use one hand to unroll a few inches of backing paper. With the other hand, press the adhesive surface of the card down on to the back of the decorative paper, carefully aligning the edges of both papers. Work slowly and carefully, smoothing the adhesive thoroughly to avoid any trapped air bubbles or wrinkles (fig.3). Gradually peel away the remaining backing paper and stick the card into position.

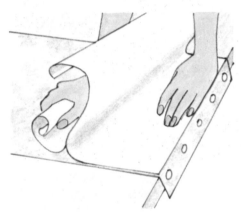

3. Self-adhesive card is useful for mounting light-weight papers. Pin decorative paper, wrong side up, to a work table. Peel backing paper from adhesive card and press into position.

To make a lampshade

These instructions apply to any paper lampshade—whether drum, coolie or empire shaped—made with two round rings.

You will need:
A set of rings.
Adhesive cotton tape.
Paper pattern.
Coloured card, or decorative paper mounted on self-adhesive card.
Ruler, soft pencil, scalpel or sharp knife and scissors.
General-purpose clear adhesive, such as Bostik 1 or UHU.
Blotting paper or other thick clean paper.
Clothes pegs.
Decorative braid (optional).
☐ Check that rings are clean and grease-free. Then cut a piece of adhesive tape (available from craft shops) long enough to cover the circumference of one ring and allow a 1.2cm (½″) overlap.

☐ Press the edge of the tape into position along the outside of the ring (fig.4).

4. Top edge of adhesive cotton tape is pressed around outside of ring.

☐ Wrap the tape under the ring, making cuts into the tape where necessary to avoid the lamp fitting (fig.5).

5. Curve the tape under the ring and up inside, snipping where necessary to avoid the lamp fitting.

☐ Bring the tape over the top of the ring and stick down on itself with an overlap on outside of ring (fig.6).

6. Tape is finally stuck back on itself with overlap on outside of ring.

☐ Cover the second ring with adhesive cotton tape in the same way.
☐ Lay the lampshade card, reverse side facing upwards, on the work table. Place the prepared pattern on top and trace its shape on to the card with a soft pencil.
☐ Cut out the card accordingly, making clean decisive cuts.
☐ Curl the cut-out lampshade card into shape. Hold the overlap in position temporarily by placing a clothes peg at top and bottom and slip the shade over the prepared rings. Then tightly peg all the way round the top ring, pulling the card quite taut so that it fits the ring exactly (fig.7).

pencil line

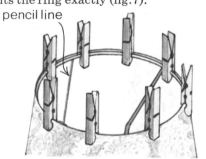

7. Cut-out paper shade is tightly pegged round the rings. Exact overlap line is marked on the inside of the shade with a soft pencil.

☐ Repeat this procedure round the bottom ring, then pencil mark the overlapping seam point along the inside of the lampshade as shown.
☐ Remove the pegs and lay the lampshade card, reverse side facing upwards, on a sheet of clean blotting paper or other clean thick paper. Place a second strip of protective blotting paper against the pencilled seam and gently spread a thin, even coat of adhesive along the lampshade overlap area (fig.8).

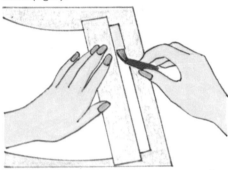

8. Sandwich lampshade card, wrong side up, between protective wads of thick, clean paper. Spread glue over the whole of the overlap area.

☐ Carefully remove both pieces of blotting paper to avoid the possibility of any surplus adhesive spoiling the shade. Then lift the other end of the shade and curl it over the top. Lay the edge along the pencilled seam mark and press down on to the glued area (fig.9). Place a ruler or piece of wood and a weight on top of the seam and leave for 1 hour or more until the adhesive is set firm.

9. Curl the lampshade card over, carefully abut unglued edge against pencil line and press down to stick seam.

☐ If you are making a drum-shaped lampshade, insert both rings now, placing them about 1.2cm (½″) from the top and bottom edges of the shade and using a few pegs to hold the top ring in position.
☐ Spread a ring of adhesive about 3mm (⅛″) wide and about 3mm (⅛″) from the inside bottom edge of the shade. Then use your ruler to push the bottom ring gently down inside the shade until it

meets the glue line (fig.10). Leave for 1 hour to set firm.

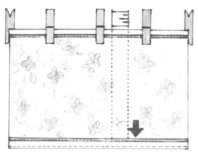

10. *Inside section of drum shade. Top ring with lamp fitting is temporarily pegged in place while bottom ring is fixed. Use a ruler to push bottom ring down to glue line (shown by dots).*

☐ Then turn the shade upside down and stick the second ring in place in the same manner.

☐ If you are making a coolie or empire lampshade, spread a ring of glue about 3mm ($\frac{1}{8}$″) wide and about 3mm ($\frac{1}{8}$″) from the inside top (narrow) edge of the shade and place the shade, narrow end downwards, on the work table.

☐ Insert the bottom (large) ring, placing it about ($\frac{1}{4}$″) from the edge of the shade. Then insert and gently push the top ring with lamp fitting down the inside of the shade until it meets the glue line. The side wires of swing gimbal fittings should be positioned at right angles to the side seam of the shade (fig.11). Leave for 1 hour to set dry.

11. *X-ray view of fitting narrow ring inside tapered shade. Shade is upside down with large ring pegged in place. Keep swing gimbal side wires at right angles to seam and gently push narrow ring down on to glue line.*

☐ Remove the bottom ring. Spread a line of glue 3mm ($\frac{1}{8}$″) from the bottom edge of the shade and replace the ring. Leave for 1 hour to dry.

☐ Cut a length of braid equal to the circumference of the top of the shade plus a little extra to allow for turning under the ends of the braid. Glue carefully round the outside top of the shade and press the braid into position, placing the braid join at the side seam and turning under the ends.

☐ Braid the bottom of the shade in the same way.

Colour co-ordinated wallpaper and shade by Designers' Guild.

Fabric Tiffany lampshades

Careful preparation of the frame is essential for lampshade making because it determines the final appearance and long-lasting wear of the shade. The preparation is done in two stages: cleaning and painting the frame to ensure that it does not tear the fabric and stain it through rusting when the lampshade is washed, and binding it with tape to give a foundation to which the fabric can be pinned and stitched.

To prepare the frame
You will need:
Metal file, wire wool, old newspapers.
Paint in white or to match your cover fabric. Use a quick-drying cellulose paint (such as is sold for touching up car bodywork) or an enamel (such as Humbrol).
Small soft brush.
White cotton tape, 1.5cm ($\frac{1}{2}$") wide. Use a loosely-woven tape sold for the purpose (this can be dyed to match your cover fabric). You can use bias binding (with one crease opened out) but it is not recommended because its edges tend to fray and it is more bulky than the special tape.
Needle and sewing thread to match the binding.
□ Examine the frame carefully and use the file to remove any sharp points where the struts are joined to the rings. Clean the frame by rubbing with the wire wool.
□ Stand the frame on newspaper and paint it. You may have to do this in two or more stages so that you can reach all sides of the rings without smudging. The paint is usually touch dry quite quickly but leave the frame for 24 hours so that it can harden before you bind it.
Binding the frame. This is the most important stage of the preparation. The binding must be very tight or it will slip and the fabric will not be tautly stretched over the frame however much time you spend on the fitting. For most styles of lampshade the rings and two struts, on opposite sides of the frame, are bound so that the fabric can be pinned and fitted on to them.
The binding on the struts is then removed because it is no longer needed but it is kept on the rings so that the cover can be stitched in place. This is

a modern development of lampshade making: traditionally all the struts were bound and the binding remained on the finished lampshade, which sometimes had the disadvantage of showing through as ridges.
The main exceptions to this are square and other panelled styles where the fabric is fitted and stitched to each side of the frame individually, in which case all the struts must be bound. A neater effect is achieved if the struts are bound before the rings.
□ To bind the top ring cut a piece of tape equal to twice the length of the circumference. Place one end of the tape under the ring at the top of a strut, bring the tape over the joint and bind over the end of the tape. Continue binding the ring as tightly as possible, keeping the tape at an acute angle and overlapping the previous wrap slightly (fig.1).
□ At each strut, wrap the binding around the ring an extra time before you reach the strut and then go on to the next section on the other side of the strut (fig.2). To finish, stitch down the end of the tape on the outside of the ring.
□ Turn the frame upside down and bind the bottom ring in the same way.
□ To bind the struts, cut a piece of tape twice the length. Start at the top and loop the end round the T-joint (fig.3). Bind over the end and continue winding tightly down the strut. Finish by winding round the ring on both sides of the strut and pull the end through a previous loop (fig.4). There is no need to trim off the excess tape unless the binding is to remain on the finished lampshade.

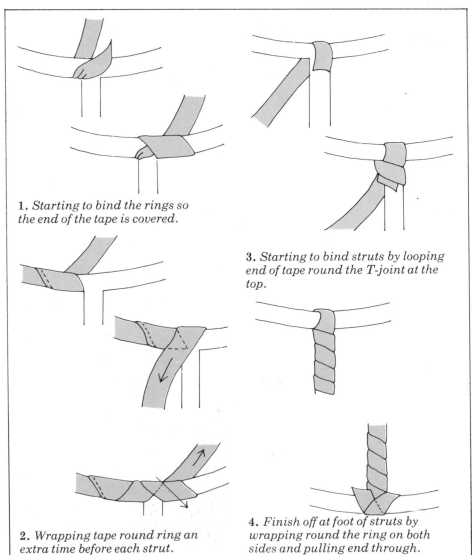

1. *Starting to bind the rings so the end of the tape is covered.*

2. *Wrapping tape round ring an extra time before each strut.*

3. *Starting to bind struts by looping end of tape round the T-joint at the top.*

4. *Finish off at foot of struts by wrapping round the ring on both sides and pulling end through.*

Tiffany lampshades

These are the simplest kinds of lamp-shade to cover because they do not require the elaborate fitting of a fully tailored style.

The frame is traditionally bow-shaped and has twelve struts. The cover is semi-fitted so that it fits the bottom tightly but is gathered to fit the much narrower top, and it looks prettiest in a light cotton or broderie anglaise fabric. It is often trimmed with a heavy fringe which gives it its distinctive character or a scalloped or lace trimming could be added for a lighter effect.

You will need:
Prepared frame.
Fabric (see below).
Sewing thread.
Scissors, lills pins, 'betweens' needles.
Adhesive such as Bostik 1.
Trimming (see below),.

Fabric requirements. Measure the frame at its widest part (this is not necessarily the bottom ring). If the measurement is less than the width of the fabric, the cover can be made in one piece. If it is more than the width of the fabric, the cover should be made in two halves.

☐ Measure the length of the struts and add 9cm (3½"). If you are making the cover from one piece of fabric, allow enough to cut one piece on the straight grain to the length of the struts plus 9cm (3½") x the measurement of the circumference of the widest part plus 2.5cm (1"). If you are making it in two halves, allow enough to cut two pieces on the straight grain to the length of the struts plus 9cm (3½") x the measurement of half the circumference plus 2.5cm (1"). If you are making a scalloped fabric trimming, allow enough to cut a strip of the measurement of the circumference of the bottom ring plus 2.5cm (1") x 12.5cm (5").

Fitting the cover. Cut out the fabric

Broderie anglaise makes a pretty cover for a Tiffany lampshade. When cutting the trimming place the edge along the scalloped selvedge of the fabric to give a neat finish.

to the measurements given. If you are using one piece, fold it in half with the shorter edges together and mark the fold with tacking. If you are using two pieces join them using one of the methods given overleaf.

☐ Place the fabric with the right side facing out on to the frame so that the seam or line of tacking is level with one of the bound struts. Centre the fabric on the length of the strut so that 4.5cm (1¾") extends at the top and bottom. Pin the seam or tacking line to the bound strut in one or two places in the middle.

☐ Wrap the fabric round the frame and pin the edges together in line with the opposite bound strut so that the cover fits tightly at the widest part of the frame but does not distort the fabric (fig.5). Remove the fabric from the frame and tack along the straight grain level with the pin.

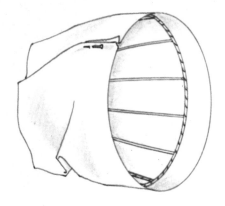

5. Pinning the fabric round the frame.

Joining the fabric. The fabric may be joined in one of three ways, depending on your own preference and the fabric you are using.

The two main methods are either to use a plain seam and trim the turnings to 3mm ($\frac{1}{8}''$) and neaten the edges together by overbasting or a machine zigzag stitch; or you could use a French seam. Alternatively, if you are using broderie anglaise with a scalloped edge, you could overlap the scalloped edge over the plain edge by 6mm ($\frac{1}{4}''$) and machine stitch.

Stitching the fabric to the frame. Place the cover on the frame as before, with the right side facing out, and pin it to the binding along the bottom ring. Place the pins so that the points face into the body of the lampshade so that you are less likely to scratch yourself. Smooth cover up the line of the struts, keeping the grain straight, and pin at the top of each strut.

☐ Fold away the fullness between the struts into tiny pleats and pin them. Repeat along the bottom ring if this is narrower than the widest part of the frame (fig.6).

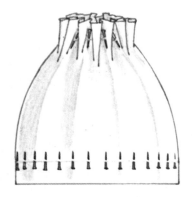

6. Folding the fullness into pleats.

100

☐ Start stitching the fabric to the binding on the outside of the rings using a small oversewing or hemming stitch. Work in a clockwise direction around the ring, making sure that you catch the gathers firmly in position. Use doubled thread and begin and fasten off securely, using several small back stitches (fig.7).

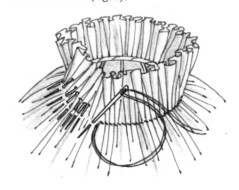

7. Stitching round the top ring.

☐ Turn the surplus fabric back over the stitching so that the fold is level with the edge of the rings, and stitch through all thicknesses. Trim surplus fabric close to stitching (fig.8). To finish, see scalloped or fringe edging.

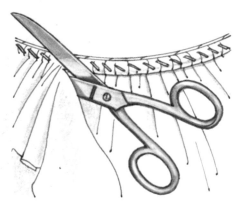

8. Trimming away the surplus fabric.

Scalloped edging

You will need:
Fabric, 12.5cm (5″) wide x the measurement of the circumference of the bottom ring plus 2.5cm (1″).
Strip of paper, 10cm (4″) wide x the measurement of the circumference of the bottom ring.
Compasses, ruler, pencil.
Velvet ribbon, the measurement of the circumference of both rings plus 1.5cm ($\frac{1}{2}''$) for turnings.
Clear adhesive (such as Bostik 1).

☐ Measure the distance between the struts on the bottom ring and divide the paper into sections of this measurement. Draw another line half this measurement away from one long edge of the paper.

☐ Using a radius of the same half measurement, place the point of the compasses on the long line in the centre of each division and draw a semi-circle (fig.9). Repeat along the length of the paper.

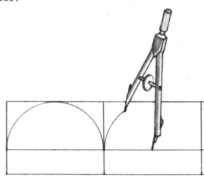

9. Drawing the scallop pattern.

☐ Place the fabric strip around the bottom ring with the wrong side facing out and pin the short edges together so that the strip fits the ring exactly. Remove the strip and machine stitch along this line. Press the turnings open.

☐ Fold the circle of fabric along the length to make it 6.25cm ($2\frac{1}{2}''$) deep with the wrong side facing out. Place on the paper pattern so that the edge with the curves is 5mm ($\frac{1}{4}''$) from the fold and the short edges of the paper meet on the seam line. Tack the paper to the fabric along each edge (fig.10).

10. Tacking the pattern to the fabric.

☐ Machine stitch along the curves through all thicknesses, following the drawn line. Tear away the paper carefully and trim the fabric to within 3mm ($\frac{1}{8}''$) of the stitching. Clip into the angle between each scallop.

☐ Turn right side out and tack along the curved edge so that the seam is exactly on the edge. Press.

☐ Place the trimming on to the lampshade so that the raw edges are in line with the turned-up edges of the cover. Stitch in the same way as the cover.

☐ Fold under one edge of the ribbon for 6mm ($\frac{1}{4}''$) and place in line with the seam of the cover so that it covers the raw edge and stitching of the trimming. Smear some adhesive along the underside of the ribbon and smooth the ribbon down on to the ring, keeping it as straight as possible. At the end, fold under to meet the first fold and press firmly to make sure that it is securely fixed.

☐ Place the ribbon around the top ring to cover the raw edges and stitching in the same way.

Fringe edging
You will need:
Fringe, the measurement of the circumference of the bottom ring plus 1.5cm ($\frac{1}{2}$″) for turnings.
Co-ordinating braid, the measurement of the circumference of the top ring, plus 1.5cm ($\frac{1}{2}$″) for turnings.
Clear adhesive (such as Bostik 1).

☐ Fold under one end of the fringe for 6mm ($\frac{1}{4}$″) and stick down with a spot of adhesive. Place the fold on to the bottom ring so that it is level with a seam and the top edge of the fringed section is level with the edge of the ring. The braided or solid section along the top edge of the fringe must cover the binding on the ring, the raw edges and stitching of the fabric.

☐ Apply adhesive for about 10cm (4″) along the underside of the braided section and place it in position on the ring, stretching it slightly. Secure with a pin. Apply adhesive to the next 10cm (4″) and stick down as before. Keep checking that the braid is level with the rings as you progress. When you reach the other end, fold it under to meet the first fold exactly and stick down. Secure with a pin.

☐ The braid is attached to the top ring in a similar way but the outer edge should be pinched up slightly with your fingers so that the inner edge will lie flat.

Frilled edging
You will need:
Fabric, 10cm (4″) wide x 1½ times the circumference of the bottom ring.
Ribbon, the measurement of the circumference of both rings plus 1.5cm ($\frac{1}{2}$″)—optional.

☐ Place the short ends of the fabric strip together with right sides facing and machine stitch taking 5mm ($\frac{1}{4}$″) turnings. Press open the turnings.

☐ Fold under the edges of the fabric circle on to the wrong side for 5mm ($\frac{1}{4}$″), tack and press. Fold the circle in half along the length with the right side facing out. Work a row of gathering stitches through all thicknesses 5mm ($\frac{1}{4}$″) from the open edge of the circle and pull up the gathers to fit the bottom ring. Pin and stitch round the ring and cover the stitching with ribbon. Cover the raw edges at the top with ribbon as for a scalloped edging.

Removable Tiffany cover is easy to sew.

Easy Tiffany cover
One of the easiest and quickest ways of covering a Tiffany frame is to make a detachable cover. This method has the extra advantage in that the cover can easily be removed for washing, and you do not need to bind the frame because the cover is not fitted or stitched directly to it. It is, however, advisable to paint the frame.

You will need:
Fabric (for the amount, see Fabric requirements, Tiffany lampshades).
Elastic, 6mm ($\frac{1}{4}$″) wide x the circumference of the bottom ring.
Cotton tape, 6mm ($\frac{1}{4}$″) wide x the circumference of the top ring, plus about 10cm (4″).
Bodkin, needle, sewing thread, pins.
Edging, as already described.

☐ Start as if you were making a semi-fitted cover and join the fabric so that

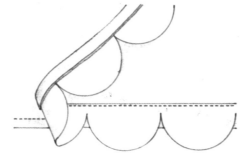

11. *Top stitching the edging.*

it fits the widest part of the frame.

☐ Fold over 5mm ($\frac{1}{4}$″) on to the wrong side along both the edges of the fabric and press. Fold over 1.5cm ($\frac{1}{2}$″) again to make casings and tack and machine stitch, leaving openings in the stitching of about 1.5cm ($\frac{1}{2}$″).

☐ Pin and machine stitch the trimming 2.5cm (1″) above the lower edge of the cover (if you have a scalloped trimming, fold under the raw edges and topstitch them to the cover as in fig.11 —it is not necessary to use ribbon to cover the stitching).

☐ Thread the elastic through the casing along the lower edge of the cover, draw up the elastic and pin the ends together.

☐ Thread the tape through the casing along the upper edge of the cover.

☐ Place the cover on the frame so that the trimming is positioned on the lower ring. Draw up the elastic tightly to draw the margin of fabric under the frame. Pin and stitch the elastic at the required place and trim off the excess. Arrange the gathers of fabric neatly.

☐ Arrange the fabric neatly on the frame at the top and draw up the tape so that the cover is firmly held over the frame making sure the trimming is still correctly positioned. Tie the tape neatly and trim off the excess length. Stitch up the openings in the casings.

panelled shades

A panelled cover for a lampshade is made from sections which are fitted and stitched to the frame individually. It is the best type of cover to use on square or hexagonal frames, some half frames, and on covers where you are using a fabric which has almost no flexibility, such as glazed chintz. It is also a good method to use where you are using a sheer fabric—such as lace, chiffon or voile—which needs to be backed, where you are using a piece of embroidery or appliqué for one or two of the panels, or where you want to combine two different fabrics of different flexibility.

The lining
These types of lampshades are usually difficult to fit with an internal lining (one which is placed on the inside of the frame to hide the struts), but they can be 'lined externally'. This type of lining is really a secondary cover because it is fitted on the outside of the frame in the same way as the cover. It is attached to the frame before the cover, which is stitched over it. External linings are also useful for dark-coloured lampshades where you need a white lining to help reflect the light up and down.

Choose a lining which enhances the cover fabric. Jap silk or crepe-backed satin (which can be used with either side facing into the frame) are both suitable for velvet and silky sheer fabrics, whereas a light cotton fabric is a better choice for a cotton voile, broderie anglaise or chunky lace. Allow the same amount of lining as for the cover fabric. (You should have enough to cut each panel on the straight of the grain, plus 7.5cm (3″) all round for fitting.)

The binding
Because the binding shows inside the finished lampshade, it is often a good idea to dye it to match the lining if you are using any colour other than white. Use a permanent cold water dye, then rinse the tape carefully so that all the excess dye is removed to prevent the possibility of it running later on when the lampshade is washed. Buy enough binding to cover all the struts and both rings. (For preparing and binding the frame, see Lampshades chapter 2, page 1184.)

The trimming
As well as the normal trimming round the rings of the frame, the stitching on the struts is also neatened by a trimming. Choose a neat unobtrusive trimming such as velvet ribbon or, if you have any spare fabric, you could cut bias strips for a self-trimming.

Measure the length of the struts and buy enough to cover each one, plus the circumference of each ring. Allow about 7.5cm (3″) extra for turnings.

Fitting the fabric
Although the lining and cover fabrics are fitted in a similar way, each piece should be attached to the frame separately because one of the fabrics may stretch more than the other which would cause wrinkling or sagging if they were fitted together.

Start by fitting the lining, remove the lining from frame and fit the cover.

☐ Measure the section of the frame to be fitted first (it does not matter which one you choose), over its widest and longest part. Cut a rectangle of fabric on the straight grain to the same dimensions, plus 5cm (2″) all round. Mark the centre of each side of the rectangle with tailor's chalk.

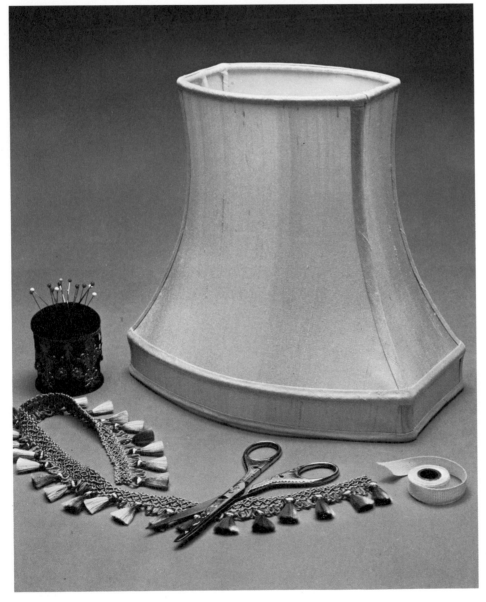

Covering a square, sectional frame with separate panels of fabric. All the struts are bound with tape because the fabric is stitched to them as well as to the rings.

Mark the centres of the corresponding section on the top and bottom rings and on both struts on the frame.

☐ Place the fabric, right side out, on to the section so that the centres are aligned. Pin the fabric to the rings and struts at these points (fig.1).

On frames with straight or convex rings, tighten the fabric between the centre points on the struts, keeping the grain absolutely straight between them. Working upwards, pin the fabric to the struts so that it is quite taut. Pin down to the bottom in the same way (fig.2).

☐ Starting from the centre and working outwards, pin the fabric to the rings along the top and bottom, tightening just enough to remove any wrinkles and to obtain a smooth curve along the edges.

Frames with concave rings. In order to maintain the correct shape of the panel pin and tighten the cover between the rings first and then pin it to the struts (fig.3).

Marking the panels. Using a sharp pencil or tailor's chalk mark the line of the rings and struts on the fabric (fig.4). Remove the fabric from the frame.

☐ Place the marked panel on to a rectangle of fabric cut to the same size, matching the grain and with wrong sides together. Pin all round just outside the marked lines. Work tailor's tacks at 1.5cm (½″) intervals along the marked lines, remove the pins and cut through the tailor's tacks (fig.5).

Cut as many panels to this size as needed and then fit and cut any panels of different size in the same way.

Stitching the fabric

Stitch the lining panels to the frame first and then stitch the cover. If the shade is unlined follow the instructions for stitching the lining.

Stitching the lining. Replace one of the lining panels on the frame and pin in position so that the tailor's tacks are in line with the struts and rings. Tighten the fabric if necessary to remove any wrinkles and check that the straight of grain is quite vertical and horizontal.

☐ Oversew the panel to the bound frame all round the edges, keeping the stitches as small and close as possible and placing them on the outside of the struts and rings. Trim the excess fabric close to the stitching along the struts but leave it along the rings (fig.6).

☐ Fit the corresponding panel on the opposite side of the frame in the same way, then fit the side panels.

Stitching the cover. Replace the panels on the frame and stitch as for the lining. Trim off the excess cover fabric only as close to the stitching as possible all round.

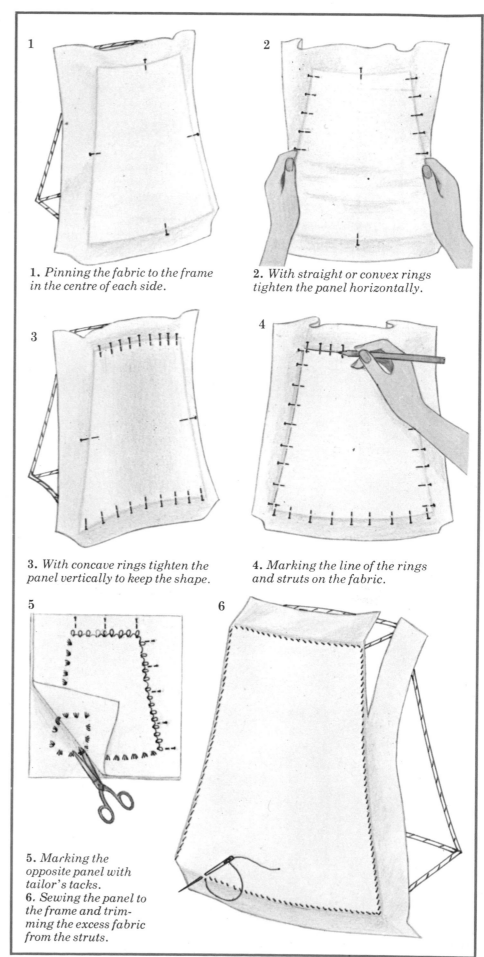

1. *Pinning the fabric to the frame in the centre of each side.*

2. *With straight or convex rings tighten the panel horizontally.*

3. *With concave rings tighten the panel vertically to keep the shape.*

4. *Marking the line of the rings and struts on the fabric.*

5. *Marking the opposite panel with tailor's tacks.*
6. *Sewing the panel to the frame and trimming the excess fabric from the struts.*

Attaching the trimming

Fold back the excess lining (or cover) fabric over the stitching along the rings and stitch down. Trim off excess fabric close to stitching (fig.7).

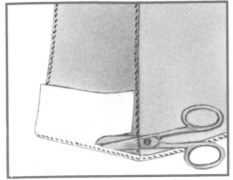

7. *Trimming excess fabric from the top and bottom rings.*

Velvet or braid trimmings. Trim the struts first by cutting a length of trimming equal to the length of the struts and sticking on with adhesive (see Tiffany Lampshades, page 103).

Trim the rings in a similar way. If you would rather sew the trimming on, follow the instructions for stitching the self-trimming on the struts below.

Self-trimmings. For the struts cut 1.5cm ($\frac{1}{2}$") wide bias strips of fabric equal in length to the struts. With the right side facing out, fold over the raw edges of the strip to meet at the centre and press carefully with an iron (fig.8). Be careful not to stretch the strip.

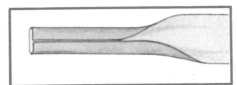

8. *Folding the bias strip.*

☐ Place the strip centrally on to the strut so that it covers all the stitching and raw edges of fabric and pin at the top and bottom so that it is quite taut.

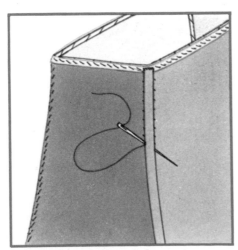

9. *Stitch bias strip over the struts.*

☐ Starting at one of the rings, stitch one end of the strip to the ring.

Pass the needle a little way along the fold down one long edge of the strip and pull out. Make a small stitch into the cover fabric at the edge of the fold, return the needle to the fold so that it forms a very small stitch and pass the needle through the strip to the opposite edge in a diagonal movement (fig.9).

☐ Make another small stitch into the fabric on that side, being careful not to pull the thread too tightly or the strip will pucker. Continue like this along the length of the strut and stitch along the other end.

☐ For the rings cut 3cm (1¼") wide bias strip equal in length to the circumference of each ring plus 1.5cm ($\frac{1}{2}$") for turnings.

☐ Fold each strip in half lengthwise with the wrong side facing out. Place the strip round the appropriate ring so that the raw edges are level with the turned back edges of the fabric and the bulk of the strip extends beyond the frame. Stretch the strip round the ring slightly if the struts bow inwards. Pin the short ends together along the straight grain so that the strip fits tightly (fig.10). Remove the strip, open it out and stitch, with right sides together, along the pinned line. Press the seam open.

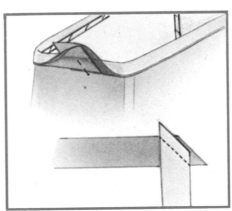

10. *Join the bias strip for trimming top and bottom rings by overlapping the ends and pinning. Tiny holes mark the seam line when the strip is re-pinned with right sides facing.*

☐ Refold the strip with the right side facing out and place it on the frame as before. Oversew the double strip in place firmly all round, making sure that the outer edges of the stitches come to the outer edge of the ring. Fasten off securely and turn back the strip on to the frame so that the fold is level with the rings and the stitches and raw edges are covered. If the strip is sitting well, leave it and do not stitch the inner edge. If you feel it necessary, however, press it lightly with your fingers and slip stitch neatly along the inner edge.

Shades with square, oblong and hexagonal top and bottom rings are made with panelled covers where the fabric is fitted in sections to each side. On the cream shade the fabric is fitted in one piece to the panel and bottom gallery.

colourcraft

Hard edge design with paint

Hard edge painting is one of the easiest and most effective techniques for decorative painting. It is achieved by painting against strips of masking tape. When the tape is removed, a perfectly straight, hard edge remains. This process is excellent for all kinds of striped or abstract patterns. It is primarily useful for decorating walls, but the same technique can be used for applying designs to furniture, floors — even on suitcases.

Preparing the surface. It is vital to have the right surface to work on — it must be smooth, free from old flaking paint and solid, not papered, as the tape might peel the paper when it is removed. It is best to cover the surface first with a good quality emulsion or latex paint.

One important note: before masking out your design, stick a small piece of tape on to the surface in an inconspicuous place. Press it firmly, wait a moment, and peel it off. It should come away cleanly without ripping the paint. There are special low-tack tapes for paint masking which you should use. Ordinary masking tape is more likely to damage the paint. *Never use transparent tape:* it's particularly damaging to a painted surface.

Basic principles

Use a ruler and a pencil to mark all the design lines. A carpenter's square will be useful for marking right angles and a spirit level for horizontal lines.

Stick the masking tape carefully along these lines, leaving any areas of light colour unmasked so that they can be painted first.

Angled corners. Lay the masking tape from one side of the corner over that from the other side and trim if necessary. Make sure there is no gap.

Travel-worn luggage can be given a new ticket to fashion with a few carefully placed and coloured stripes, using the principles of hard edge design and techniques described here.

Rounded corners. Build up a solid square of tape over the whole corner. Using compasses, or string and pencil, draw the arc wanted (fig.1a). Cut carefully along this arc with a sharp blade and peel away the tape from the area you want to paint (fig.1b).

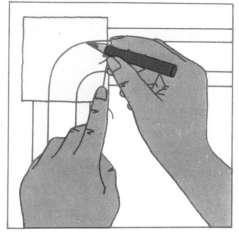

1a. *For rounded corners, draw an arc over the masking tape on either side of the stripe you are going to paint.*

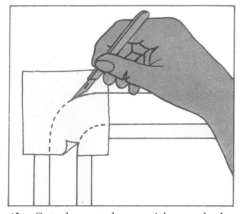

1b. *Cut along each arc with a scalpel or sharp knife and peel off the tape covering where the stripe runs.*

From these basic principles you can create many different motifs. You can also use lines to accentuate an attractive window or break up a large wall.

Lighten your journey upstairs with broad bands of colour that follow each bend and curve of the way.

A window that won't take curtains can be neatly covered in masked-off squares painted with gloss paint—and it won't cut off the daylight!

When you have finished masking, go over the whole area with a small wallpaper roller, or something similar, to make certain that the edges are firmly stuck so the paint cannot seep underneath. The longer you leave the tape the harder it sets, so paint as soon as you have fixed it. When the paint is touch-dry, carefully and slowly peel the tape off, lifting up the edge with a razor or sharp knife.

Suitable paints and brushes. If possible use sable brushes of a size appropriate to your design. For walls, a non-drip matt or eggshell emulsion paint is recommended as it should require only one coat. Use special floor paints, eg Liquid Lino, for floors.

Painting the design. Remember that you paint the areas between the strips of tape and that sometimes, as with checks, you may need to wait for certain areas to dry before you can continue taping and painting adjacent areas.

Now that you know the basics of hard edge painting you could go the whole way and paint a complete wall with a tartan pattern!

Paint any areas of light colour first and paint from top to bottom wherever possible. Make sure that this paint is absolutely dry before masking the edges to paint adjacent areas and always use fresh tape on a new area.

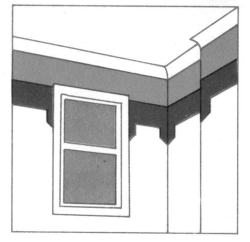

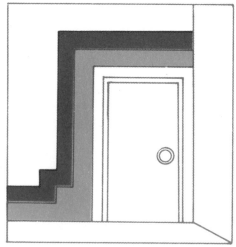

Lower a high ceiling and detail a door with hard edge stripes of colour that tone in with your decor.

Bathrooms need not be boring if there is a clever use of colour and shapes, not only in the ornaments you use but also in what you paint on the walls.

Pyramid frieze

Before starting to make this design based on an equilateral triangle (where each side is equal to the base), measure the width of your wall or the surface to be painted, and decide how many triangles you want and what size they should be. In the design illustrated there are 3 complete triangles across

the width, with a ½-triangle at each end. Each of their sides is ¼ the width of the wall. If you want 5 triangles, counting the 2 ½-triangles as one, their sides should be 1/5 the width of the wall, and so on.

☐ To make the basic shape of the design, draw an equilateral triangle whatever size you have decided. Do this on a piece of paper first before attempting to draw it on the wall.

☐ Divide the base of the triangle into 6 equal parts. Using these points, construct two more equilateral triangles

as shown (fig.2).

☐ Begin marking the front series of triangles on the wall, starting with the ½-triangle at one end (fig.3 ABC). The bases of the triangles should just touch to form a straight line, ending with another ½-triangle at the other end to complete the front row.

☐ To draw the back series of triangles follow exactly the same principle, only terminate the sides of the triangles where they meet the sides of the front series. Therefore, draw an equilateral triangle (fig.3 GBD), but don't draw in the dotted lines. The mid-point of the base of this triangle is where the front triangles touch.

Continue marking off points along the bases of the triangles and drawing in lines as in Fig.2. Repeat throughout the design.

☐ When you have drawn the whole design in this way, use masking tape to mask off each area of colour in turn, as described above. Make sure when painting that each colour is completely dry before you start to paint the colour next to it.

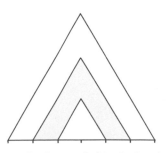

2. *The basic shape of this design is three equilateral triangles.*

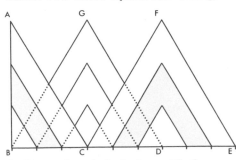

3. *Draw the whole design with the triangular motif repeated.*

Chevron design

When painting patterns such as this, where bands of different colours overlap, arrange the work so that you begin by painting the lightest colours. Draw the design on paper first to decide on your colour scheme—experiment with different colours and shapes to make a variety of designs.

☐ To make the design illustrated, draw a square to the size required. This forms the outer boundary of the design. Divide each side into 16 equal segments. Draw an inner square as shown

4. Mark off the boundary square.

(fig.4). All the diagonal lines of this design stop at the inner square. As this boundary will be black, do not paint it yet—it will cover any imperfections at the ends of the coloured bands.

☐ To draw the white stripes, draw lines connecting the points marked on the outer square (fig.5). The dotted lines need not be drawn in.

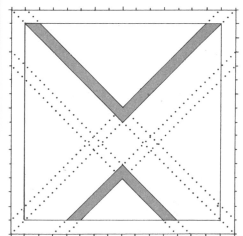

5. Connect the outside points to give the white stripes (shaded grey).

☐ Paint the shaded areas in white at this stage. If you have a friend to help you, you can check the positions of the stripes with string held taut between the marked points, and then lay the masking tape straight down. Check the position of the tape before you start to

paint—and remember to make sure that the edges are well stuck.

☐ To draw the light grey stripes, connect the points marked as before (fig.6). Where the lines intersect a stripe you have already painted, remember to lay masking tape over it. Paint in the shaded areas.

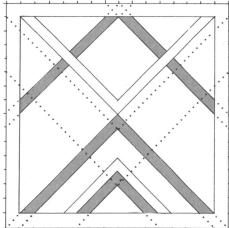

6. Draw in the light grey stripes, which are shaded grey.

☐ Draw the dark grey stripes following fig.7, and paint in the shaded areas. Where the stripes overlap a previously painted area, make sure you completely cover it. Use an extra coat of paint if necessary.

☐ Draw the black stripes following fig.8 and paint in the shaded areas.

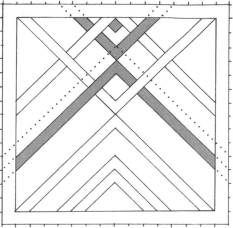

7. Draw in the dark grey stripes.

8. Black stripes complete the design.

Paint a rug on your floor if you're not fond of carpets or plain boards.

111

Gaily painted chests

Painted whitewood furniture is both inexpensive and useful. With a little paint and patience you can make it decorative too. The ideas for chests shown here are full of imagination yet they are easy to do. They also give some indication of the range of possibilities—from bright easy-to-draw motifs like the tree design to the more complex jungle pattern overleaf.

All the designs shown can be adapted to chests of different dimensions. They were created with unpainted or whitewood chests in mind, since these can be bought in most department stores, but they are equally suitable for reviving old furniture. Chests without knobs, on the whole, tend to be best suited but chests with knobs can also be used, and the knobs incorporated in the design.

Preparing the surface

Whether you are decorating an unpainted chest or an old one with several coats of paint already on it, you must sand the surface with fine glasspaper and wipe it down with white spirit. Unpainted furniture should be given a coat of leadless white primer.

If you are re-painting a chest make sure that the surface is smooth and in condition to receive the paint. Some old chests require considerable attention before they are ready for re-decoration.

Paint

All the designs shown are painted with oil-based enamel paints available from hardware shops. At least two and sometimes three coats of each colour are normally required and when there is a background colour, as in the jungle chest, then the entire surface must be given two coats of enamel *before* the design is applied.

Since enamel paint tends to run and form drips when applied vertically, you should paint each side in a horizontal position. This is time-consuming because enamel paints take several hours to dry properly and the chest must be rotated on to the dry areas in order to paint and re-paint each side. You must therefore expect the entire process to take a few days. The effort is worth it, however. Your finished surface will be smooth and hard wearing.

You may, in some cases, want to sand lightly with fine glasspaper between coats if dust has accumulated while the paint was drying, for example.

Tree pattern

This charming design has a naive, spontaneous quality and can be drawn freehand. Observe that the tree is the same on the front and sides of the chest. The ingenuity of the design is that each view represents the tree at a different time of day. The top is a bird's eye view (complete with bird) of the tree from above.

You will need:

Soft lead pencil.

Masking tape.

Plates or washing-up bowl for guide lines.

Sheets of tracing paper sufficient to cover front of chest if making a pattern.

Stiff paper for star pattern (optional).

Enamel paint in 8 colours: yellow, orange, lime, a bright green, sky blue, white, tan, dark blue, black.

Selection of natural bristle paint brushes.

White spirit for cleaning up.

Leadless white primer.

Long ruler.

Protractor (optional).

Before you begin, sand and prime the chest as described above.

To make the outline: first mark the ground line all round the front and sides of the chest by drawing a line 10cm (4″) from the bottom.

☐ Next, make a pattern for the green tree shape by drawing a rounded design using plates and saucers for guidelines. Cut out the pattern so it can be traced round and transferred on to the chest. When tracing, take care to centre the free shape and when copying the pattern on the front of the chest let it hang straight and then connect the gaps between the edge of the drawers and the recessed frame.

☐ The tree trunk is made by drawing two straight lines perpendicular to the base or ground line and 7cm (2¾″) apart. Make these in the centre of each side.

☐ The sunrise background can be made by tracing the outline of a large plate or a washing-up bowl just above the ground line while the sun rays

must be measured using a long ruler (or other guide). A protractor will help to get the rays at the best angle.

☐ In the midday sky on the front of the chest the clouds are drawn freehand using plates to make the contours. Take care to match up the drawers with the support frames between them.

☐ The stars in the evening sky are drawn freehand on the chest shown but if you prefer to have them uniform then draw a star on stiff paper using a ruler, cut it out and trace round its outline at the places on the chest.

☐ Use plates to make the tree top shape on the top of the chest and transfer the bird design from pattern given (fig.1).

To paint. Before you begin spread a thick layer of newspapers on the floor around the chest, remove the drawers and place them, face side up, on the paper in the same relative positions they occupy in the chest.

Begin with the background and paint the sky on the top of the chest first. Then lay the chest on its back on newspapers and paint the sky on the front, avoiding the white cloud areas. Paint the sky areas on the drawers at this stage too.

☐ Roll the chest carefully on to its left side so that the sunrise background is exposed. Paint the yellow disc and rays next, using masking tape on the outside of the rays to get a good straight line.

☐ Allow the paint to dry.

☐ Roll the chest on to the sunburst side and expose the evening sky. Paint the dark blue areas, taking care to avoid the stars.

☐ Gently turn the chest on its back and apply a second coat of sky blue to the front and to the drawers.

☐ Then turn the chest back on its side and apply a second coat to the evening sky. Allow to dry.

☐ Paint the second yellow coat of sun rays and allow this to dry.

☐ You are now ready to paint the orange rays but you must first remove the masking tape from the sun ray areas you have already painted and

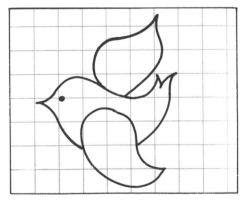

1. Graph pattern of bird motif.

The progress of a day is delightfully recorded in this simple design showing a tree at different times—first at sunrise, at midday and finally by starlight. The top is quite literally a bird's eye view. Designed by Lorraine Johnson.

2. The jungle motif above is painted over an enamelled background. *4. The pattern on the right is by Lorraine Johnson.*

apply new masking tape along the outline of orange rays.

☐ Continue rotating the chest, painting the clouds next and, when the sunburst is dry, the stars. For a crisp delineation you can mask the star outlines.

☐ When all this is dry it is a good time to check your drawers to make sure the design is properly aligned. Replace the drawers temporarily and correct any discrepancy by marking it with chalk and re-painting where necessary.

☐ Apply a second coat to the clouds and stars. The ground colour and the tree leaves can be painted at the same time. Mask the ground line first and paint the front and one side. Allow to dry and paint the other side.

☐ When the green areas are completely dry and have received two coats of paint you are ready to paint the trunk. Make sure, however, that the surface is absolutely dry. You must mask the outside lines of the trunk to be assured of a straight line and the tape may pull up some of the green paint if it is not completely dry.

☐ When the trunk has been painted by the rotation method already described return the chest to its original vertical position and complete the top.

3. Jungle motif incorporating both a chest and the surrounding wall.

Jungle chest

This pattern (fig.2) is a more complex design which requires careful tracing and more delicate painting. The result is a more sophisticated decoration that could also be continued on to the surrounding wall (fig.3).

The design shown here has a white enamel background but the pattern might look even more dramatic on a dark background, navy blue for instance. Bear in mind however, that if you choose a dark background it will mean more coats of paint since the design must completely cover the en-amelled background.

To paint the design, first enlarge the design from the pattern (fig.4) and trace the pattern carefully on to the enamelled surface making sure to link up the spaces between the drawers with those in between. On a dark background use dressmakers' carbon paper in a pale shade for tracing the design. Choose three or four basic colours such as lime, emerald green, tan and bright yellow and mix the co-ordinating hues yourself.

Paint by rotation as described in the tree motif chest above.

114

cutting simple stencils

Stencilling has been successfully used to decorate everything from manuscripts and fabrics to walls and floors, more or less since the beginning of civilized history.

Janet Waring, in her fine book 'Early American Stencils on Walls and Furniture', says that the English term 'stencil' probably comes from the Old French *estanceler*—to cover with stars —because in early churches, walls and ceilings were often painted blue and then gold stars were stencilled all over them.

The craft of stencilling was brought to a fine art in New England at the end of the 18th century and beginning of the 19th century.

Stencils are a quick and easy way of reproducing patterns by hand and can be used to give an individual touch to most homes or to create original, personal greetings cards, letter headings or (using fabric dyes) to hand-print lengths of material for clothes. Stencilling isn't a difficult craft to learn, though it needs care and thought in the preparation stages.

Stencil paper

Thick stencil paper, especially treated to withstand repeated applications of paint, can be bought from art supply shops but there are cheaper alternatives. In 18th-century America, a great deal of decorative stencilling took the place of wallpaper and floor coverings. The craftsmen used leather stencils or, more often, heavy paper stiffened with oil and paint, with a bevelled edge to ensure a sharp outline.

Modern stencillists can use heavy brown paper coated with lacquer, thick aluminium foil, or cardboard, rendered non-porous by the use of a commercial sealer, PVA glue or several coats of varnish. If you are only going to make one or two stencils, you can use thick, untreated cardboard, though this will not last for much longer than two impressions.

You can also use thick acetate film. Because this is transparent, it can be placed over the pattern and cut without first tracing, which is a great time saver.

Beginners are advised to use stencil paper or thick acetate film.

Tools

Cutting tools. Depending on the material which you are using, you will need either a light scalpel or a heavy-duty trimming knife. Both are available from craft shops and have removable, replaceable blades.

These blades are all lethally sharp and have to be used with great care. Always keep them away from children.

The scalpel has a thin, flexible, usually very pointed blade which is quite difficult to change and which should be stuck into a rubber when not being used.

The heavy-duty trimming knife has a standard blade for general cutting but for cutting card and paper you need a blade with a sharp edge that points downwards. You can buy a blade for lino cutting—an angled blade for slitting and trimming and a convex blade for scoring and cutting.

One very good type of cutting tool has a long, multi-edged blade, the tip of which can be snapped off when it has become blunt.

Metal ruler. Another tool needed is a metal ruler for cutting straight lines— a wooden edge soon becomes chipped and therefore inaccurate, and you should in any case cut straight lines against a metal rule or the cutting tool may slide off and cut you.

Tracing paper to transfer designs on to the stencil paper.

A wooden board to cut on.

Stencil brush. This should be a round one with a flat-cut surface but not too big because, if it is, it will hold too much paint which will seep under the stencil edges. Clean brushes well after use.

To make a stencil

Before starting work, make sure the working surface is firm. Tape the cutting board to a table, then tape the stencil paper to the board. Then you can begin to cut.

When cutting any stencil, make sure that the outside edges of the stencil are square and even, as this will help with

With stencils it is easy to reproduce original designs on most surfaces.

the spacing and placing if you want to repeat your pattern over a large area.

How to cut straight lines. Place the metal ruler along the line you wish to cut. Hold the ruler firmly in place with one hand, keeping fingers well out of the path of the knife. Hold the knife in the other hand, either like a pencil or a table knife, whichever is the most comfortable.

Keeping your arm rigid, draw the knife against the ruler without angling the blade but keeping it absolutely straight on the line, leaning down on the knife and drawing it backwards towards you. Don't try to cut right through all in one go but cut lightly at first, then more and more firmly until the line is cut through. It is usually easier to cut a long line a little at a time.

Cutting circles and curves. Again, never angle the knife to the left or right but lean it backwards towards you. Hold the paper firmly, keeping the fingers well away from the path of the blade. Untape the paper from the board, cut a little of the stencil at a time, then turn the paper and cut a little more until the circle or curve is complete.

Planning designs for stencils

Except on thin paper or on card that is being used, perhaps, for one or two repeats, even the sharpest knife will have difficulty in cutting very intricate designs, so keep your stencil patterns simple to begin with.

When cutting out a shape of any kind from a stencil, it must be attached to the outside border of the design or the cut shape will simply fall out.

There are two ways of attaching the shape. Either leave linking tags (or stays) attached to the outside border (fig.1), or make the shape large enough

1. *Victorian design with linking tags.*

Originally based on a piece of patchwork, this abstract flower design is ideal for a repeat pattern (see page 124). Stencils designed by Joanna Ball.

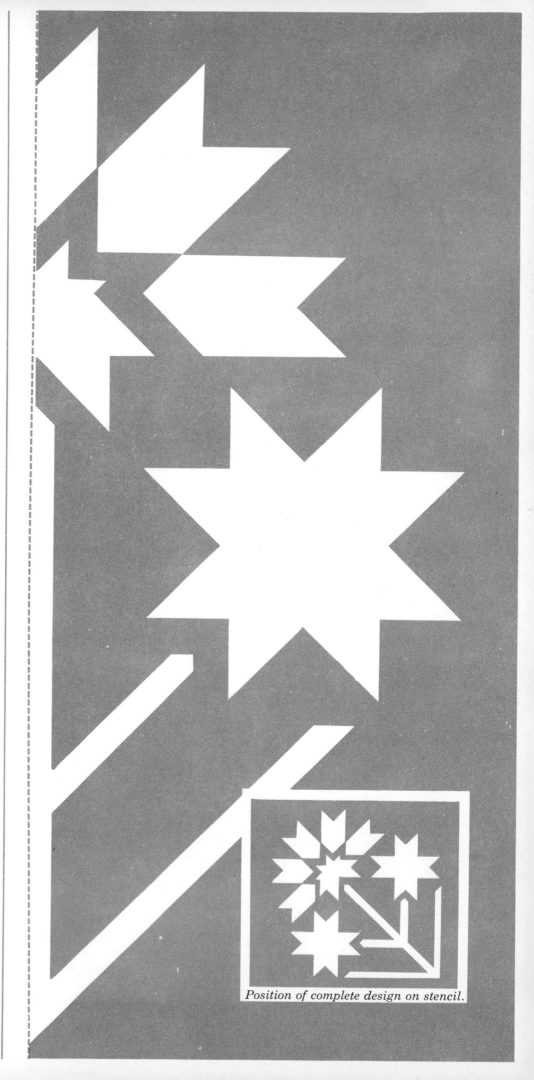

Position of complete design on stencil.

to touch the frame at various points, which will hold it in place (fig.2).

2. *Design touching the frame.*

Stencils can either be negative—ie the background is cut away to form the design (fig.3) or positive, when the actual design is cut away (fig.4).

3. *Result of negative stencil.*

4. *Result of positive stencil.*

So from one design you can get two completely different-looking stencils. Stencil patterns can also be varied by colouring different areas in different colours, adding strong colour on top of pale colours at a later stage.

It is also possible to cut two-part stencils that fit on top of each other, so that first one colour is printed and, when that is dry, another design in another colour is placed on top. When doing this, cut register marks (fig.5) on both stencils so the designs will fit accurately over each other.

This charming pattern has been stencilled on to a trunk, pictured on page 121. The design would be equally attractive on fabric.

5. *Two-part stencil with register marks.*

This flower stencil can be used with the trellis design as a border as shown on page 123. Trace the patterns given below.

119

Decorating with stencils

The American colonists were among the first to exploit the marvellous ways stencils could be used in home decoration. In 18th-century America wallpaper was a luxury only the very wealthy could afford, but the colonists soon found that with a little imagination and patience they could simulate the elegance of imported, handblocked paper by cutting out designs in stencils. Using stencils they found they could repeat the same motif again and again and get a uniform overall pattern just like that produced by fine printing techniques.

For their designs the colonists turned to the natural world around them—willows, oak leaves, fruits—and to patriotic motifs like the American eagle. They did not stop at walls but stencilled floors to resemble floor coverings and other artifacts to look like items difficult to get in the New World. The result was a fresh, original style.

Like all good design these early ones are still popular but, just as the colonists adapted European styles to suit

Delicately stencilled 18*th-century room from the American Museum in Britain.*

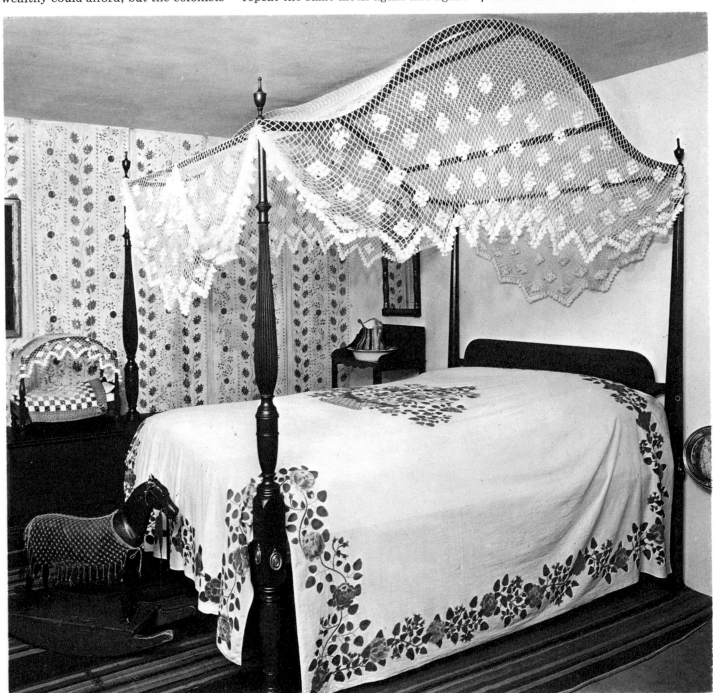

120

their needs and environment, their designs in turn can be adapted to modern tastes. The trunk in the photograph, for example, has a motif adapted from the copy of an 18th century wallpaper which lines it.

General rules

When stencilling a surface it is important that it is properly cleaned or the paint will not adhere.

Wax must be removed from floors and furniture and sometimes an old surface, such as a wall or trunk, must be repainted. If you are stencilling on an old, solid-coloured wallpaper or wall, scrub it before you begin.

Choosing the right paint. The sort of paint you use will depend on the surface upon which you are working. Many experts recommend poster colours, which can be sealed when dry with clear lacquer, but high-gloss surfaces such as mirrors or tiles should be sprayed with spray-on enamel. There is no reason why modern oil, emulsion or vinyl paints should not be used on walls. Acrylic polymer paint is hardwearing and recommended for floors. Gold and silver paints can look most effective too.

If you are using a mixed paint be sure that you have prepared enough for the entire surface. It is difficult to mix and match a colour in the middle of a job, since a paint that is dry is never the same shade as when it is wet. Stencilling a wall can take a long time and mixed paint can be stored in a tightly lidded container between sessions.

Finally, when choosing your colour scheme, remember that it is difficult to stencil a light colour over a dark one as several coats may be required.

Stencilled trunk adapted from the paper lining it. A copy of an 18th-century paper by Sibyl Colefax and John Fowler (trace pattern on page 228).

A beautifully stencilled chair from The American Museum in Britain.

121

Floor border inspired from a patch-work quilt motif. Designed by Joanna Ball.

Decorating ideas

Once you know how to make a stencil the possibilities of stencil design are infinite. Ideas can come from many sources: the repetition or adaptation of earlier designs is one.

Designs can be traced from natural objects like leaves or based on existing motifs, as are the blue birds on the child's cot in the photograph, which have been taken from the quilt fabric. Positioning depends on personal fancy. Tin and glassware, such as bread bins and canisters, can be decorated or lettered with stencils, and suitcases, which all look so much alike, can be made identifiable by stencilling on initials or other personal motifs.

To stencil a floor

You can stencil floor boards or cork tiles in all-over designs like the American colonists or you can stencil a border pattern round the edge. The latter can be especially useful when moving into a new house if your old carpet doesn't quite cover your new floor. By stencilling with colours related to the carpet you can turn a misfortune into a successfully integrated design.

Before you cut your stencil, measure the size of the floor space to be filled. The design you choose must be able to fit an exact number of times into the strip or strips to be stencilled, so the size of your motif depends partly on this.

You will need:
Oil bound or waterbased paint or (recommended) acrylic polymer paint.
Clear gloss polyurethane wood finish.
Stencil cut to size.
Stencil brushes or plastic sponge.
Chalk.
Sharp point, eg skewer.
To work a border. First chalk the

outline of the carpet on the floor (AB in fig.1). Decide how far from the edge of the carpet you want the design and chalk a second line (CD) which will mark the base line of the pattern. Extend this line at each corner (EF and GH). The first stencilled motif will be in the top left hand corner.

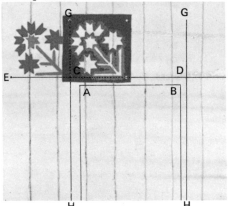

1. *How to align stencils.*

☐ When you have decided on your repeat distance, mark it on your stencil by making four holes as illustrated. These can be made with a compass point, skewer or other sharp instrument. The two holes at the bottom should be along the base line. These and the equidistant ones at the top, will keep the design straight.

☐ Starting at the top left corner, fasten the stencil down with masking tape and mark the floor through the holes with pencil or coloured chalk. Be sure the bottom holes are along your base line.

☐ Now paint in the motif with either a stencil brush or a piece of plastic sponge. When finished, lift the stencil carefully and move it to the next place, taking care to align it again with the base line and to place the left side holes over the previous right side dots. This automatically gives you the right spacing.

☐ If your design has more than one

colour and the different coloured areas are fairly far apart you can stencil both colours as you go. If not, mask out the second colour and do all one colour first. Before you begin the second colour you must let the first dry completely. When you do begin, remember to use the original chalk dots for lining up your stencil.

☐ Any blobs or mistakes can be scraped off with a sharp knife or razor blade.

☐ Before finishing with polyurethane, remove all chalk marks and allow at least two days for paint to dry.

☐ Give three coats of polyurethane finish, allowing it to dry well between each coat.

Using two or more stencils

The variation in wall sizes and the fact that some are not quite square can cause special problems, but by careful measurement these can be overcome. Don't just start at one end and hope for the best.

Give yourself lightly pencilled guide lines, which can be removed later, and first work out the number of times your design must be repeated.

☐ To place a border accurately use the hole and dot method described above. When working round a window or door calculate the exact number of times the design can be repeated and decide whether you should have a centralized motif at either end of the central point, to even out the design.

If the motif will not quite fit in you might cut an auxiliary design such as a dot pattern (fig.2) or other motif to fill in the gaps.

2. *Dot motifs can fill border gaps.*

Secondary stencil motifs can also be used to point up the corners of a border by accentuating them, yet filling in gaps at the same time. The wall border illustrated was stencilled with three complementary stencils—a trellis, vine and a flower. This allows latitude for dealing with difficult corners and other areas where the design must be adjusted.

If the second stencil pattern overlaps the first in any way, make certain the first pattern is dry before you apply the second.

Above: trace pattern for stylized bird stencil.
Left: stencil motifs can come from a number of sources.
This one is taken from the fabric designed by Shirley Liger.
Below: stencils make handsome borders, as shown by this
trellis design by Janet Allen.

stencilling on fabric

Stencilling on cloth gives anyone with an eye for colour and an urge for creativity wide-ranging opportunities for making changes in their home or wardrobe.

A single stencilled motif such as a sailing ship or a palm tree, for example, is easy to cut out and can be stencilled on to a tee shirt or a table mat, the pocket of a blouse or the front of a laundry bag.

Alternatively, stencilled motifs can be repeated over and over again to make a border or an all-over design. Delicate flower borders on sheets and pillowcases or on the hem of a child's dress can be very effective, while all-over patterns can be used on a number of items, such as tablecloths, scarfs and shirts.

Straw hats and baskets, satin shoes and canvas awnings can all be sten-

cilled and more ambitious designers can even stencil lengths of cloth. Beginners however, may prefer to stencil ribbons and tapes for trimming clothing or household items, since mistakes are not so disastrous as when made on the object itself.

Choosing a design

Design requires careful consideration and, when stencilling on cloth, the use the fabric will be put to is important both in the choice of motif and in the positioning of decoration.

When choosing a motif be sure its size and subject suit the item you are stencilling. For example, a large, single motif like a tree may be used on a table mat or tee shirt, but would not be suitable on a handkerchief unless reduced in size and printed in one corner or repeated in a tiny all-over pattern.

Decide whether you want a bold design or a delicate one, which colours will be suitable for the item you are stencilling on, the motif you are using and the surrounding colour scheme. Should you use a multi-coloured design? All these are important considerations since the final result depends as much on getting the design colour scheme right as on its correct execution.

Materials you will need

Stencils can be bought or you can make them yourself in the size and shape you require (see the section on cutting stencils on page 118).

You will also need masking tape, an old blanket or other padding material, newspaper, drawing pins or tacks and dressmaking pins.

It is advisable to have two stencil

Stencils look well printed in a grid pattern on cotton cushion covers.

Materials for stencilling are not expensive: all you need are special flat headed brushes, paste fabric dye, stencils and cloth to print on. Below: stencil trace patterns.

brushes if you are painting with more than one colour—one for light and one for dark shades. These are obtainable at art shops.

Fabric dye. Although cloth can be stencilled with fabric paint, the best medium to work with is fabric dye in paste form. Liquid dyes tend to be too runny and fabric paint leaves a stiffness on the areas of cloth to which it is applied.

Another advantage of dye is that it can be mixed, so only the basic colours need be bought.

Fabric paste dyes are colour fast and can be used on natural fibres such as cotton, silk, wool or linen and viscose rayon. If you are not sure of the fibre content of the item you wish to stencil, test a sample with the dye to find out if it 'takes'. Remember also that dyes blend, so if you are stencilling blue on to yellow, the end result will be green. Obviously the same rules apply to red and blue (purple), and red and yellow (orange).

In addition to coloured dyes you can also buy 'medium' to make colours lighter and more transparent. 'Medium' is the colourless substance in which the dyes are suspended. When mixing medium with dye colours, always add the dye gradually to the medium until you reach the right shade.

Acrylic polymer paint, which is waterproof, is the most suitable colouring for woven straw.

Preparation

Before you start make sure the fabric is free of creases. Iron it, dampening if

Star stencils can be cut out in many sizes and printed singly or in 'milky way' clusters on denim or canvas.

Below: The trellis design (see page 119) makes a handsome border for a cotton tablecloth.

necessary. If the cloth contains starch or dressing, you should wash it thoroughly before printing.

Secure the blanket or padding material to the table top, stretching it taut. This can be done by wrapping it round the table ends and taping it to the underside or fastening it with drawing pins or tacks.

Put several sheets of newspaper on top of the secured blanket to soak up any excess dye that may go through. If the fabric you are stencilling is very fine, put some blotting paper on top of the newspaper for added absorption.

Stretch out the fabric you intend to print and attach it to the blanket with pins.

If you are stencilling something double-sided like a pillow-case or shirt, slip some paper inside to prevent the dye from going through and marking the other side.

If your design involves a repeated pattern, it is wise to pencil guide lines very faintly on the cloth. Small holes in the corners of the stencil paper can be useful for this purpose (see earlier, page 122). For dark fabric use tailor's chalk which can be brushed off easily.

To stencil

Fasten the stencil to the fabric with pieces of masking tape and put some of the dye into a shallow container.

Do not overcharge the brush with paint but take enough to allow you to work with ease and in control of the brush.

Using white dye or a very light colour mixture may make it necessary to stencil the image twice. If so, let the first coat dry before applying the second and line the stencil up carefully using punched holes in the stencil paper corners.

When working multi-coloured designs

stencil the first colour and let this dry before proceeding with further colours. In such cases it is often helpful to mask out the areas to be coloured with a second colour while applying the first and vice versa. This way you avoid getting the dye in unwanted places and it is also less confusing.

When the finished item is thoroughly dry, iron it from the back, according to the dye manufacturer's instructions, to fix the dye.

When washing later on, use care and do not wring.

Reverse stencilling

With reverse stencilling a mask or template of the shape of the design is used to prevent the paint from reaching the surface to be decorated, so that the design is painted round the outside of

The lamb is a 'reverse' stencil using a template from a child's drawing set.

the shape. This technique can be used on any sort of surface from walls to fabric. Use double sided tape to fix the template to the surface. Then, if the colour is to reach right to the edge of the surface, apply colour in the usual way.

Or the area of colour can be contained by making a larger, square mask to frame the colour.

Otherwise fade out the colour gradually by stippling, ie by varying the pressure of the brush when you apply dye or paint. For walls or furniture, aerosol spray paint is also effective.

You can use the cut-out part of any ordinary stencil to build up an alternating 'positive/negative' design with the stencil.

Straw hats can be stencilled to match the print on a summer frock.

simple gilding

Gilding is an old and distinguished craft which has long been practised for royalty, the aristocracy and the rich. At one stage it was so popular in Europe that almost anything within reach of a palace ladder was deemed eligible for enhancement by a thin layer of gold leaf and it was doubtless at this time that the metaphor for overdoing things, 'gilding the lily', originated.

The frame is rubbed down thoroughly with steel wool.

Gold paste is rubbed on the surface and into crevices.

Finally the surface is burnished with a soft cloth.

The result is evident in this 'before and after' picture.

The application of gold leaf is still practised today by the same methods developed generations ago, but with the advent of new materials special paints and powders have also been developed which, although not true gold, give remarkably effective finishes. These, being inexpensive, considerably widen the scope of the craft. The relatively simple techniques of using imitation gold are described in this chapter while the art of true gilding, using real gold, is discussed later on.

Suitable surfaces

The new mediums on the market allow almost anything to be gilded with the simplest procedures and gilded objects such as old frames which have become

Richly gilded frames have the patina of gold leaf but much more simple and inexpensive techniques have been used.

tarnished or worn can be quickly and effectively rejuvenated. It is not advisable, however, to use these materials on fine ormolu (gilded metal) since ormolu is a special process which cannot be accomplished in the home. Not-so-fine metal work can be painted or re-gilded, however, as can wood and plastic—almost any surface, in fact, including bizarre, unlikely objects such as the flower pots and shells shown overleaf.

Choosing the material

There is more than one material available for gilding and a selection can usually be purchased in art supply shops. One product is a liquid (Liquid Leaf) which automatically puts on an undercoat and gilds at the same time; the liquid contains golden particles which rise and cover the surface. Also available is a paste (Treasure Gold)

which is rubbed on the surface and then polished to a shine. In appearance, the paste looks a little more authentic. The liquid has a deeper, duller, finish. Both materials come in several non-gold metallic tones such as brass, copper and pewter, as well as gold, and these may be mixed to give highlights or an antique effect.

Application

Preparation. It is necessary to clean the surface to be gilded thoroughly with an abrasive material such as steel wool or glasspaper before attempting to apply the gold finish. In the case of an ornate frame this is rather a painstaking operation but old, flaking finishes and grime must be removed to assure adherence of the new coating. Protect your working surface before beginning by putting down newspaper.
Applying paste. Apply a small amount

to one area and start working it into the surface with a small piece of cloth or your fingers. (Fingers work much better.) Gradually work the paste into the surface, covering it slowly and thoroughly. Do not be afraid to put on a little too much in order to fill tiny cracks and crevices, as the excess paste will be removed by polishing. Finally, polish the paste with a clean cloth just as you would polish a newly waxed surface. This produces an even, glossy sheen.

Applying liquid. If you choose to use the liquid medium, this is also extremely simple. Follow manufacturer's instructions regarding thinning and take care to apply the paint as evenly as possible to eliminate brush strokes.

Sealing. A special sealer designed for protecting both paste and liquid gilding products is also available. This prevents tarnishing and is particularly recommended in a humid climate.

Flower pots

Most DIY shops stock ornate plastic mouldings used for decorating door panels and walls. These are inexpensive and can readily be cut to size and applied to plastic flower pots.

To apply mouldings to the rounded surface of the pot lay the cut mouldings in a warm oven for a minute or so. When removed they will be quite hot but they will also be pliable.

☐ Gently bend them to fit the contours of the pot, then leave them to cool. They should stay in their newly moulded forms.

Above: golden sea treasure produced with Midas-like simplicity by painting natural forms. The shells can be displayed singly or together.

☐ All that is required now is to fix them to the pot with an epoxy glue—preferably a rapid setting one like Araldite Rapid.

☐ Once the glue has dried apply the gilding liquid or paste to the exterior of the pot and to the insides of the rim. It is also possible to highlight the moulding slightly by applying a different tone of paint or paste here and there along the moulding edges.

Right: empire-style flower pots make elegant decorations and belie their inexpensive origins. By Neil Lorimer.

Moulding is made malleable by heating.

Moulding is glued to plastic flower pot.

Liquid 'gold' is painted on the surface.

Traditional gilding

Traditional gilding falls into two main categories: oil gilding and water gilding. Oil gilding, which involves gilding on an oil size base, is the simpler of the two and, unlike water gilding, can be used on both exterior and interior surfaces. It cannot, however, be burnished and for this reason the more complicated technique of water gilding is preferred for fine interior decoration.

This chapter is an introduction to the principles and materials of traditional gilding and deals with the step-by-step technique of oil gilding with leaf.

Leaf

Leaf, refers to thin slivers of metal—pure gold or silver or alloys—which are used to decorate a prepared surface either entirely or along portions such as the moulding of a door. (This partial gilding is known as 'parcel' gilding.)

Common leaf refers to leaf which is made from alloys and there are several types. These are comparatively inexpensive and are heavier and therefore easier than precious leaf to handle. Common leaf makes a fine material for beginners to work with before investing in precious leaf, and also produces a handsome finish.

Perhaps the best type of common leaf is an alloy of copper and zinc called Dutch metal which gives a gold leaf effect. An aluminium leaf, while darker than silver, gives an effective pewter-like appearance.

Common leaf is generally available in 14cm (5½″) square sheets or leaves which are pressed in a book of 25 leaves; 20 books make a package and will cover about 8 sq m (9 sq yd).

Precious leaf. True gold leaf is 23¼ carat gold which has been cut into leaves 9.5cm (3¾″) square. It is so thin it almost crumbles at touch and so wispy that it floats on the air like a feather.

Silver leaf is slightly heavier than gold and therefore somewhat easier to handle but, unlike gold, it tarnishes and so must be varnished immediately following application.

Precious leaf can be bought either in a book in which each leaf is attached to tissue paper backing (this is called transfer leaf) or in a book of detached sheets (loose leaf). In either case each book contains 25 leaves and a book should cover about 45cm square (1½ feet square).

Transfer leaf is applied rather like Letraset by pressing it against the surface and rubbing, and is especially useful for outdoor gilding since it will not blow about. Transfer leaf is not advisable for fine finishes since it may result in gaps where sticking is uneven.

Gilding tools

Simple, though special, tools are required to handle leaf and these can be purchased at art supply shops or improvised at home.

A gilder's knife is something like a kitchen knife and it often has a diagonal shape at the end. The cutting edge must be kept sharp enough to cut the leaf cleanly and the surface must always be kept free from grease and dirt. This can be done by wiping the blade with cotton wool and methylated spirit, then with emery paper.

Although it is better to have a proper knife, it is possible to use an old steel kitchen knife. You can change the tip; making it diagonal if preferred.

Cush. This special cushion or palette for handling wispy gold leaf consists of a wooden base 15cm x 25cm (6″x 10″) softened by cotton padding and covered with chamois on the top and calf on the bottom (fig.1). A shield of parchment or buckram about 15cm (6″) high protects the leaf from disturbance by draughts. A leather strap is usually added to the base so the gilder can hold the cush in his left hand while cutting, lifting and applying the leaf. A cush is not required for applying common or transfer leaf.

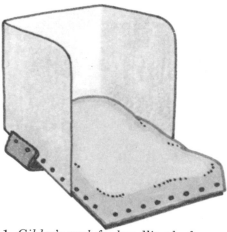

1. Gilder's cush for handling leaf.

Gilder's tip. This is a thin, flat short-handled brush used to lay precious loose leaf and it can be purchased along with other gilding equipment. Experienced gilders have several sizes for manipulating different sizes of leaf.

Mop. A tiny mop is used for patting the leaf into position.

Brushes. You will need a selection of brushes for applying undercoating to objects. Ox-hair brushes are particularly useful for this.

Gilder's tools include cush, tips, knife, paintbrushes and a mop or similarly shaped brush.

Left: this old clock, retrieved from a junk shop has been elegantly rejuvenated by Michael Baker.

Oil gilding

Oil gilding is a straightforward process which can be used on many different surfaces—wood, plaster, metal, paper and papier mâché—either covering them entirely in gold or highlighting edges or relief surfaces. Both carved and flat surfaces may be gilded. On a flat surface the leaf must be laid absolutely flat and smooth, whereas, on a carved surface the leaf can crinkle slightly without marring the result.

Oil gilding is also recommended for exterior gilding since it will withstand weather.

Remember that leaf laid by oil gilding cannot be burnished because of the undercoat and will produce a matt or soft glow rather than a polished finish.

Preparation of the surface

This is one of the most important steps in the gilding process and attention to its thoroughness cannot be over emphasized. The smoother the surface, the better the luminosity of the gold finish.

First, clean the surface thoroughly. If it has been previously painted, make sure any flaking paint or plaster is removed.

On new materials always prime the surface with the appropriate primer to ensure adhesion of the new finish.

Where there are imperfections such as unevenness caused by flaking, fill in the chips to make a smooth surface using, for example, putty on wood, Polyfilla on plaster.

Painted or varnished surfaces should be rubbed over with alcohol and sanded with fine glasspaper. Newly filled areas should be shellacked or primed.

New wood should be sanded and shellacked also, while plaster should be given two coats of shellac.

Metal must be stripped and coated with metal oil primer.

If parcel gilt is to be applied to a painted piece, paint the entire surface before gilding.

Applying size

Oil or gold size with different drying times is available at art suppliers. In a dust-free atmosphere paint the size on the object to be gilded—or part of it if it is a big area—with an ox-hair brush. Lay a fine even coat and re-stroke the surface without applying more size to the brush in order to ensure complete coverage. The leaf will not hold at uncovered spots.

Remember to confine the area sized to an area which can be covered in one session with leaf.

A tall object is sized from the bottom up so that particles will not fall on any exposed sized surface.

Size a four-sided object on opposite sides first. If there is a lid, size the inside closing edge first. Do the sides next and finally the top.

When the size is ready you should be able to touch it and feel a slight resistance when you remove your finger. If it is sticky it is too wet and if there is no resistance then it is too hard.

Applying leaf

Loose leaf and transfer leaf are each applied by slightly different methods but all leaf is laid down in the same overlapping pattern.

Start at the top left if you are right handed and overlay by about 2mm ($\frac{1}{8}$") (fig.2). Note that overlaps must be made both vertically and horizontally. Although each piece of leaf can be cut to desired size, do not worry about small gaps that occur when you are

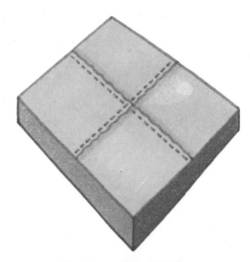

2. Leaf should overlap slightly.

laying it. These are put right later on by 'skewing'.

Skewings are tiny fragments of leaf that crumble from the edges of the overlaps and these must be 'skewed' or brushed away with a fine ox-hair or camel-hair brush. Always sweep in the direction of the overlaps not against them, which would cause them to lift up.

The faults which are less than about 5mm ($\frac{1}{4}$") in size can have particles brushed into them and pressed down with a finger. Excess particles can be collected in an improvised paper cone. The whole surface is tapped down with a mop and smoothed over lightly with cotton wool.

Transfer and common leaf are the easiest materials to begin laying. Common leaf can be worked with your fingers.

Cut sheets and attached leaves into strips or squares suitable for covering the particular surface, then press each leaf to the surface, gold side up.

Press with cotton wool or a mop and remove the tissue backing. The leaf should remain in place.

Loose leaf is a more complex material to lay and requires all the tools mentioned. However, once the process has been learned it gives superior results.

☐ Turn several gold leaves out on to your cush (A). Bring the gold forward on your knife (B) and blow it gently until it flattens out (C).

☐ Cut to required size with your knife, making sure it is slicing through cleanly (D).

☐ Rub the gilder's tip down your cheek to pick up static electricity and place the tip over the piece of gold you wish to pick up (E).

☐ Lay it in place on the oil-sized surface (F) and tap it down with the mop.

It will help enormously to get into a regular routine, and always remember to avoid touching all oiled surfaces with your hands or tools.

☐ After you have laid your surface, rub it over with the mop and then with cotton wool to remove all loose particles of gold leaf.

Carved surfaces. If you are laying carved surfaces lay the relief areas first and then the recesses. Skew the crevices.

Protective coating. Allow your gilt surface to dry for a couple of days or more. Then you can give it additional protection with fixatives such as polyurethane varnish. Do not apply the varnish too thickly, however, and brush it out carefully. Several thin coats are superior to one thick one.

Left: carved wooden squirrel is enriched by a layer of fine gold leaf.

A. *To lay loose leaf, open book and turn leaf on to cush.*

B. *Bring the gold forward with your knife.*

C. *Blow gently until leaf flattens out.*

D. *Cut leaf to proper size with gilder's knife.*

E. *Rub tip against face first then pick up leaf.*

F. *Place leaf on sized surface and tap down.*

135

woodwork

decorative wood stains

Staining is a simple technique for colouring wood. You can achieve varying results either by using the stains on their own to colour a surface or else by combining colours within a design. Any piece of furniture can be stripped down and stained but apart from

The picture on this screen is created from wood stains applied to untreated plywood. Designed by Clare Beck.

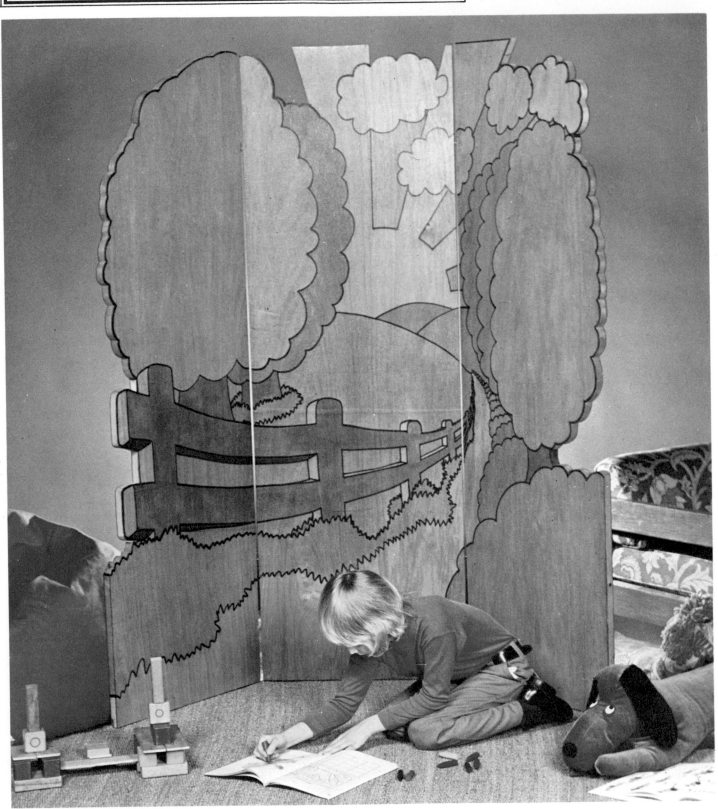

furniture there are many uses for stains. You can work with them on a small scale to decorate surfaces with a design or on a larger scale to make screens and room dividers.

Stains differ from coloured polyurethane finishes in that they soak into the wood instead of building up on top to create a coloured surface, rather in the same way as ordinary paint. Stains allow the visual characteristics of the wood such as the grain and knots, to be retained. The stain is absorbed by the wood, producing an effect of depth and translucence.

Mixing stains is similar to using water colours and has all the possibilities you would enjoy from using a paint box. It is also a more versatile technique than using a coloured polyurethane finish, because more than one colour can be applied to a surface to create patterned as well as plain effects.

Stains are made in various ways and if they are powdered or composed of water and alcohol they can be watered down. Stains such as Furniglas dyes can be used to produce a large range of tones and the colours are also intermixable. When purchasing dyes read the manufacturer's instructions and make sure that they are suitable for your particular application.

Some stains are purely decorative whereas others can be used out of doors to protect wood from fungus and insects. If your work is purely decorative you can use either but if you want to use a stain out of doors or to protect a piece of wood then be sure to get the appropriate product. Both types of stain are available in a large range of colours. If you use a stain indoors that is normally used out of doors to protect wood, make sure that it will be odourless when dry. Wood preservatives are poisonous and must not be stored near foodstuffs. Keep out of children's reach.

Finishes

To protect stained finishes, give a top coat of either matt or gloss polyurethane varnish. It is important to use the same brand of stain and polyurethane varnish, otherwise the varnish may 'lift' the stain. Wax finishes are not usually satisfactory for stains.

Suitable surfaces

The natural colour of the wood will affect the appearance and final colour of a stain. Blonde woods which include most softwoods and some hardwoods such as sycamore and birch will give the brightest colour renderings. Man-made boards with a veneered surface look particularly lustrous and beautiful when stained, especially those finished with birch veneer.

The wood must be bare and dry, ie free from paint, varnish or any other surface treatment.

Unusual surfaces. Wooden beads, dried seeds and nutshells provide opportunities to try out all sorts of ideas involving decorative colouring. They are easy to stain and can be used for necklaces and bracelets. You can stain all the beads in one colour or, more ambitiously, in a variety of shades. After staining, beads can be given a protective sheen with matt or gloss varnish. Thread the beads on to a nail or an old knitting needle to stain and varnish them.

Designs

Experiment with stains on small pieces of wood to see how they are absorbed. Try running two or three colours together, and painting small patterns freehand as illustrated.

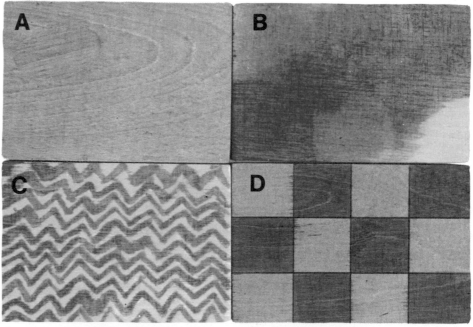

A: a single colour. B: two colours dabbed on with a piece of cloth. C: one colour is applied, then the other brushed on when the first is dry. D: squares divided with ball point pen to prevent colours running.
Below: backgammon board created with stains and birch laminated plywood.

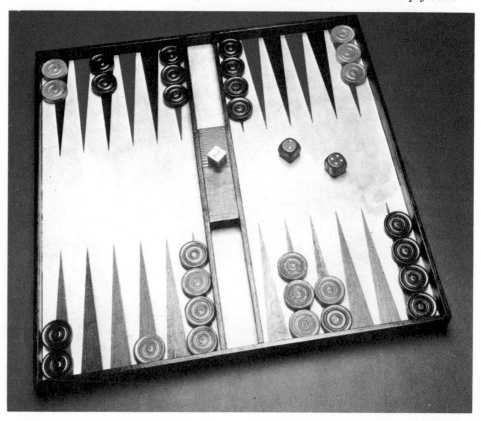

139

Outline designs using squares and stripes are easily worked out. A table top could have a central circle or a square stained in another colour. Smaller items such as chess or backgammon boards also lend themselves to this technique.

Always draw a full-size design on a piece of paper and transfer it to the surface by using tracing paper and something with a hard point, such as a

Plain wooden boxes can be purchased and decorated in a variety of ways. They can be lined with felt and used for trinkets, cigarettes and playing cards.

knitting needle or nail. For geometric designs a ruler is essential.

To stain a box
You will need:
Small wooden box with untreated surface—craft shops sell these but you can also experiment with a cigar box.
Wood stain—colour optional.
Fine grade glasspaper.
Fine steel wool.
Clear polyurethane varnish, matt or gloss.
Small, soft bristle brush.
☐ Sand the box surface with glasspaper until smooth.

☐ Wipe with slightly damp cloth to ensure a dust-free surface.

☐ Shake the stain container, or follow manufacturer's instructions, and pour a small quantity into a saucer or similar container.

☐ Stain the outside of the box by applying the stain evenly with a small brush. Let the brush strokes follow the grain.

☐ Dilute the stain with 50% water and stain the inside of the box.

☐ Allow to dry for at least two hours.

☐ Rub gently with steel wool to remove any roughness.

☐ Finish with a coat of clear polyure-

thane varnish. One coat will protect the surface and leave a matt finish. Three coats of gloss will give you a high gloss surface. Rub the dry surface down with steel wool between each application.

To create a pattern
You will need:
Oblong wooden box with untreated surface.
Wood stains—colours optional.
Small, soft bristle brushes.
Fine grade glasspaper.
Black ballpoint pen, ruler.
Clear polyurethane varnish.

☐ Sand the surface of the box with fine grade glasspaper until smooth.
☐ Wipe with damp cloth to ensure dust-free surface.
☐ Draw pattern on to box lightly with a pencil. Then use the ballpoint pen to re-draw the design. Use a bit of pressure on the ballpoint to make a slight indentation in the wood surface. This will prevent the colours from seeping into the surrounding sections.
☐ Measure out small quantities of stain and apply the chosen colours to the surface with the brush. Do not put too much stain on the brush, and only work in small areas at a time.

Stain the inside of the box. If you want to make it a lighter shade, dilute the stain with water.
☐ Finish the box as for the previous plain box.

Below: start by making a full-size pattern. Colour in the sections so that you can judge the exact effect and make any changes before actually staining the wood, bearing in mind that the colour of the wood will influence the colour of the stain you use.
Transfer the design on to the wood surface and go over it with a black ball point pen before applying colours.

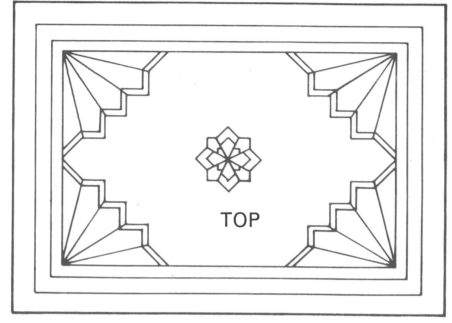

TOP

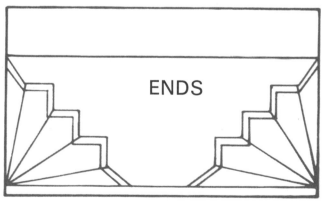

ENDS

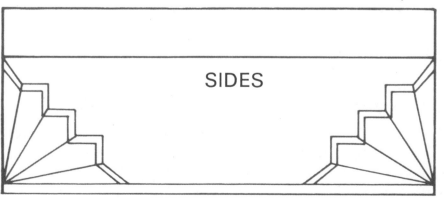

SIDES

perfect picture frames

Carpentry and cooking have a lot in common in their methods. Both have specialized tools and ingredients and require practice to make the whole process easy and enjoyable.

The most important result of learning carpentry is that it enables you to make so many of the things that are very expensive to buy.

Picture frames are particularly expensive to have specially made because there is a lot of hand work involved, but they are relatively easy and quick to make. Once you have made frames for all your own prints and pictures, you'll doubtless find friends who have something they want to frame.

There are a variety of shapes available in ready-made mouldings that can be purchased from hardware stores, do-it-yourself shops etc.

There are several ways of connecting the pieces at the corner of a frame but for picture frames the mitre joint is usually used (fig. A).

The most difficult part to do is to get the opposite pieces of the frame exactly the same length. The only way to do this is to take care and learn from your mistakes.

Practise sawing and measuring on short bits of moulding or ordinary wood to get the feel of it.

The mitre is simply the term for two pieces of wood joined at right angles after they have been sawn at 45°.

There are several ways of joining the pieces but the easiest is the nail and

Small picture framed with a mounting board. Supplied by Blackman Harvey.

Tool box

Mitre box. If you intend to make several frames a mitre box is essential. It is inexpensive and can be bought from hardware stores.

Mark the mitre box by placing the saw

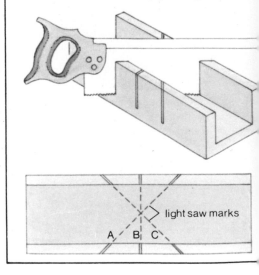

light saw marks

A B C

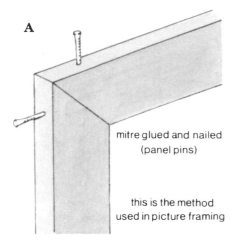

A

mitre glued and nailed
(panel pins)

this is the method
used in picture framing

*A mitre joint, glued and nailed, is the
method used for making frames.*

glue technique used by most picture
framers. The step demanding the most
care is the nailing itself for it is a
little difficult to keep the two 45° surfaces from sliding. It helps if you first
glue the pieces and let them dry in
position with a string loop all round
the edge, to hold the frame secure
before nailing the corners.

Decide how you want the frame to look.
You may have maps or prints from old
books that, because of their size, need
small, delicate frames with the wood
painted white, black or an antique
gold. Initially buy ready-made moulding which comes in a variety of shapes
and finishes to suit your purposes.

*Various shapes and sizes of mouldings.
Supplied by Blackman Harvey.*

in each of the three slots in turn and
make a slight mark in each direction
on the base of the box. These will be
used as guide lines in measuring. If
you are using a bench hook, instead
of a mitre box, carefully mark two 45°
lines and cut a groove along each one
as shown. Use a protractor to measure
the 45° angle or use a compass and
bisect a 90° angle. Saw and mark each
piece as for the mitre box.

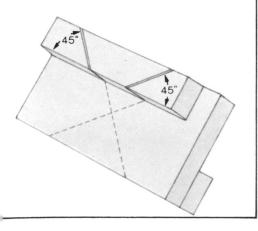

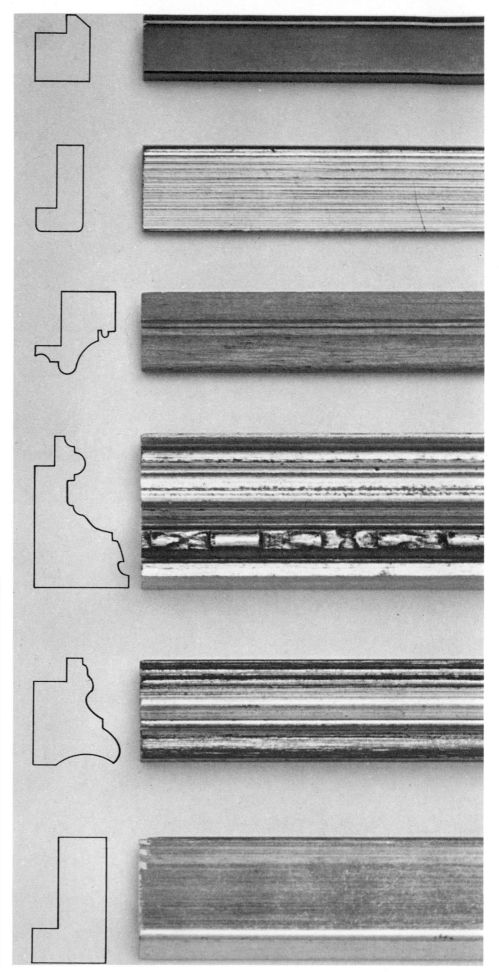

To make a picture frame

You will need:

Tools
Steel ruler
Mitre box
Panel saw—it must be a fine saw with 0.3m-0.4m (12-14points); a rough saw will have a lesser number of points. A fine tenon saw will do
Nylon cord—about 2m (2yd) for holding frame together while glue dries.
Nail punch
Hammer

Materials
Picture frame moulding: add 10cm (4″) to each dimension of the picture and add up the 4 lengths. Thus for a 30cm x 40cm (12″x16″) frame you will need 1.8m (72″) of 10mm ($\frac{3}{8}$″) half-round moulding (fig.B). The moulding can be bought from hardware stores, timber merchants and do-it-yourself shops

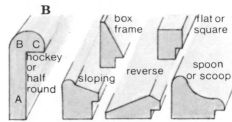

Picture frame moulding can be bought in various sizes and shapes.

Mounting board: if the picture is not going to fill the entire frame use a mounting board to surround the area between the picture and the frame
Glass: 2mm thick (18oz). Have this cut to size by a glass merchant or hardware store. Determine the size after the frame is assembled
Backing board: same size as the glass—any stiff cardboard will do
Panel pins: fine 19mm ($\frac{3}{4}$″): about 24
2 hooks or staples to hold the wire
Wire: picture hanging wire, usually brass, can be bought from large department stores
Fine grade glasspaper
Wood glue

---

1. Measure the size of the picture to get the frame size. The size of the frame is the dimensions of the inside of the rebate—ie, the size of the glass and the backing cardboard. Assume the size to be 30cm x 40cm (12″x16″).

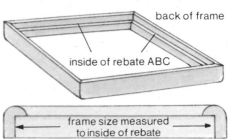

2. Cut off one end of moulding as shown, with back against side of mitre box. Start sawing towards yourself with the saw tilting forwards a little. Then level the saw and with easy, unhurried strokes saw off the end as shown.

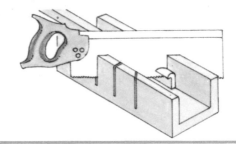

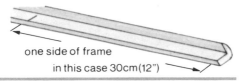

3. Measure and mark the piece of moulding as shown.

---

4. Match this mark with line C as shown and saw through the moulding. Repeat this to get an identical piece. It is essential that the lengths are exactly the same.

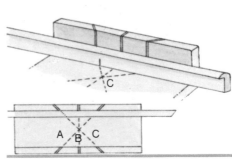

5. Carefully measure and saw two pieces 40cm (16″) long.
6. Sand the cut ends of the pieces lightly to remove rough edges. Use fine glasspaper with a sanding block.

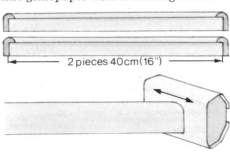

7. Prepare the nylon cord by tying a slip knot. This can then be tightened around the frame by pulling one end.

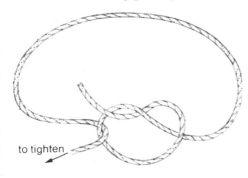

---

8. Glue the frame together. Put a dab of glue on each end and smooth it with a piece of wood. Arrange the four pieces together with cord round them.
9. Tighten cord, adjusting corners as you tighten. Leave to dry.

10. When dry, remove the cord and nail in panel pins as shown. Nail carefully, holding the side receiving the nail very firmly against a flat working surface. Use a nail punch to set nails slightly below surface of wood.

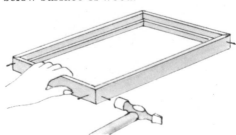

11. Take measurements of the back of the frame and order glass to fit. Cut the backing board (and mounting board if necessary) to fit inside. Wax, stain or paint the frame.

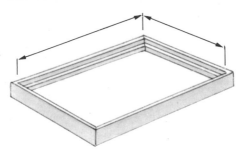

Assembling picture frame

12. Mounting board is only necessary if the picture is smaller than the frame. Clean the glass, then assemble as shown. Glue the picture with rubber-based cement to the backing board or, if it is too valuable or thin, place it between the layers and hold it in position while carefully assembling the picture. If the backing is stiff and cut to the right size it will hold the picture in position once the backing board is secured.

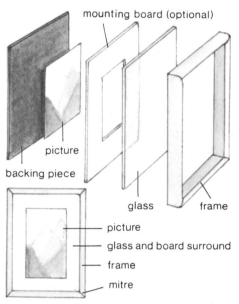

mounting board (optional)

picture

backing piece

glass

frame

picture

glass and board surround

frame

mitre

13. Nail panel pins on the inside back of the frame to hold the layers down firmly. Leave 6mm ($\frac{1}{4}''$) sticking out. To prevent dust collecting, cover the entire back with brown paper.

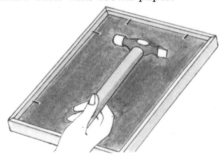

14. Put in hooks or staples. Attach the wire securely to the hooks so that the wire will not slip loose. Do not leave the wire ends too long or they will stick out from the frame.

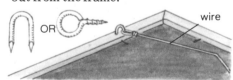

OR

wire

The completed frames can be finished in different ways. They can be left natural or you can paint them with gloss or matt paint. Designed by A. Martensson.

Introduction to marquetry

Marquetry is the art of inlaying different types of wood to create decorative patterns. The craft dates back to the days of ancient Egypt and early examples can be found in the tomb of Tutankhamun. The term marquetry is from the French word 'marqueterie' which means to variegate or to cover with patches of different colours.

Marquetry first appeared in England in the 16th century and by the end of the following century had reached a high degree of sophistication. The finest examples, however, were produced on the continent of Europe by such master craftsmen as Brulle and Riesner.

Today, the use of modern wood veneer, cut to precision-made thickness, has simplified the craft of marquetry and extended the scope of artistic expression. There are over one hundred different types of wood veneer in general use and most are available from DIY shops and timber yards. There are also a number of stores which deal exclusively in wood veneers.

It should be emphasized that marquetry requires great accuracy in measuring and cutting the veneer. For this reason it is essential to keep the cutting edge of your knife very sharp. Craft or Stanley knives with replaceable blades are ideal.

Do not attempt to cut through the veneer with one stroke but rather use several light cuts. This prevents the fragile veneer from splintering or tearing. If the veneer is warped or buckled, dampen both sides and leave to dry between blotting paper under some weights.

When fastening the veneer, use a contact adhesive, such as Evo-stik Impact, spreading the glue sparingly on both surfaces, then holding together for a few seconds.

Cutting board

This is an essential piece of equipment for marquetry work. A suitable design for a cutting board is given in fig.1. It is made from 12mm ($\frac{1}{2}$") plywood or chipboard 45cm x 61cm (18"x 24"). A strip of hardwood 12mm x 12mm ($\frac{1}{2}$"x $\frac{1}{2}$") and 61cm (24") long is glued and screwed along one long edge of the board to act as a stop.

The chessboard

Though marquetry is usually associated with furniture decoration, a useful introduction to the craft is provided by making up a simple geometric design such as a chessboard. This design utilizes the contrasting colours of certain veneers—eg the brown of teak and the straw colour of oak. The dimensions are really a matter of personal choice and those given here are for a board 35.5cm (14") square

with a playing area 30.5cm (12") square. Keep in mind that chessboards have 64 squares.

You will need:
One piece 12mm ($\frac{1}{2}$") thick plywood or chipboard 35.5cm (14") square—for the baseboard.
Two pieces 1.6mm ($\frac{1}{16}$") thick veneer 30.5cm x 20.5cm (12"x 8") in contrasting colours for the squares of the board.
One piece 1.6mm ($\frac{1}{16}$") thick veneer 37cm (14$\frac{1}{2}$") square to cover the back of the baseboard. This can be in the same colour as the darker squares of the board or in a matching dark colour.
Four strips 1.6mm ($\frac{1}{16}$") thick veneer 16mm ($\frac{5}{8}$") wide and 37cm (14$\frac{1}{2}$") long for the edges of the board. These should be the same colour as the base veneer.
Four strips 1.6mm ($\frac{1}{16}$") thick dark veneer 6mm ($\frac{1}{4}$") wide and 37cm (14$\frac{1}{2}$") long—for the border of the chessboard.
Four strips 1.6mm ($\frac{1}{16}$") thick light veneer 6mm ($\frac{1}{4}$") wide and 37cm (14$\frac{1}{2}$") long—for the border of the chessboard.
Four strips 1.6mm ($\frac{1}{16}$") thick dark veneer 12mm ($\frac{1}{2}$") wide and 37cm (14$\frac{1}{2}$") long—for the border of the chessboard.
Sellotape. Evo-stik Impact adhesive.

Garnet paper, grades 4/0, 7/0 and 9/0 and flour grade glasspaper. The abrasive surface of garnet paper is made from crushed grains of garnet stone and is ideal for fine sanding.
Trimming knife, steel rule and set square.
Cutting board.
White or clear wood polish.
Polyurethane varnish—optional.

The baseboard. The veneering of the baseboard should begin with the back. This can be simply a sheet of veneer cut slightly oversize and glued to the back. The slight overhang is trimmed flush with the flour grade glasspaper. A more professional appearance is obtained by using matching quarters of veneer (fig.2). The four pieces should be cut from similar leaves of veneer.

Edges. The edges of the baseboard are veneered next. First glue veneer to two opposite side edges. Allow to set and sand flush with the flour grade glasspaper. The remaining edges are then veneered in the same way.

The squares. The squares for the playing area are cut from the sheets of light and dark veneer.

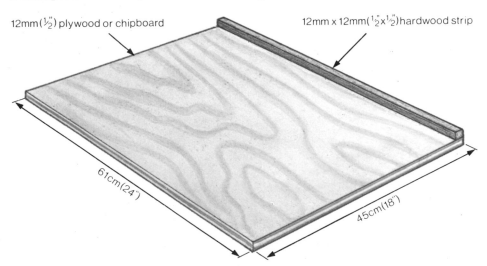

12mm($\frac{1}{2}$") plywood or chipboard   12mm x 12mm($\frac{1}{2}$"x$\frac{1}{2}$")hardwood strip

61cm(24")   45cm(18")

1. *Dimensions for cutting board which is an essential part of marquetry equipment.*

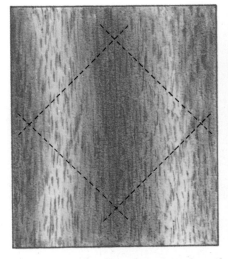
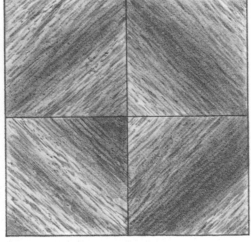

2. *A backing for the chess-board can be made from four squares of veneer.*

☐ Cut the sheets into strips 38mm (1½″) wide and 30.5cm (12″) long (fig.3). Take care to keep the veneers in the order in which they are cut.

☐ Tape the strips together in alternating colours with all the grains running in the same direction (fig.4).
☐ Place the taped strips on the cutting

board and cut another lot of strips 38mm wide (1½″) as shown in fig.5. Each strip should now contain nine 38mm (1½″) squares.

☐ Lay out these strips on the cutting board, staggering them so that they form a chequered pattern (fig.6). Again, keep the grains running in the same direction.
Make sure that the joints between adjacent strips of veneer are flush and check that the squares meet exactly at

the corners. Hold in place with tape.
☐ Eight squares of light veneer will be left projecting from the main body of the assembly and these are carefully cut off.
Border. This is composed of the three narrow strips of veneer taped together as shown in fig.7. The corners of the

border are elaborated with the insertion of contrasting dark veneer pieces 6.5cm (2½″) long (see fig.7).
☐ The borders are taped to the side of the chequered board with the corner ends overlapping. They are then cut along the diagonal to form a mitred corner joint (fig.8).

☐ The top is glued to the baseboard (fig.9). Here, the tape holding the veneers together is on the underside of the top and is left on while top is glued.

Finish

Using increasingly fine grades of garnet paper, the surface of the veneer is rubbed down. Take care not to round off any of the corners.
The chessboard can be polished with a clear or 'white' wood polish. For a very fine finish the traditional french polishing technique can be used.
Another alternative is to varnish the smoothed surfaces with a clear polyurethane varnish. The first coat can be diluted with white spirit. When the first coat is dry, sand it down lightly with the flour grade glasspaper and re-coat with undiluted varnish.
The chessboard can be incorporated

into the top of an old coffee table that needs renovating. If the table top is square and not too large the veneer can be cut to size and glued directly to the surface. Alternatively, if the top is rectangular or a fairly large square, the veneer chessboard already made can be set on to the table top.
To do this, a piece of veneer the size of the top must be cut. Into this cut a square to take the chessboard. The two are then glued to the surface of the table. The surrounding piece of veneer serves to bring the surface of the table level with the surface of the chessboard. This technique is described in greater detail in the following chapter.

pictorial marquetry

Having familiarized yourself with the basic techniques of marquetry described in the previous chapter, you can now attempt more elaborate designs. Pictorial marquetry is commonly called the 'window method' of marquetry because the background veneer acts like a stencil. The design is traced on to the background veneer and the different areas to be inlaid are cut out in the background, leaving a window. The window is then used as a stencil or guide for cutting the veneer

which is later inlaid in the window. Thus, rather than cutting into the surface of the wood and inlaying pieces of wood, a 'false' surface is cut—ie the background veneer—into which the pattern is set. The method enables you to cover large and small items, from table tops to wooden jewelry boxes. This chapter describes how to make a set of place mats using the window method.

As mentioned in the 'Introduction to Marquetry' section, there is a vast range of

wood veneers available today and the natural colours can be used effectively in most designs. However, you may wish to use bright colours and, in this case, the veneers can be dyed. If dyed or brightly coloured veneers are used, it is important to apply a sanding sealer to the lighter areas before sanding the whole picture. This will prevent any colour and dust entering the pores of the lighter wood and staining it.

Place mats

The butterfly designs used in the place mats can be adapted for many other items, such as table tops or trays. The mats shown here have diameters of 18cm (7″) and 23cm (9″) but can be altered to suit your needs. The instructions and materials are for the smaller mat, and the trace pattern and examples of inlay are given overleaf.

You will need:
Cutting board (see previous section, page 148).
Trimming knife or small light scalpel.
Carbon paper, tracing paper and pencil with a fine point.
Hack saw blade or coarse grade glasspaper.
Brown gum strip tape and masking tape.
Balsa cement and impact adhesive.
Garnet sandpaper—grades 4/0, 7/0 and 9/0—and fine grade glasspaper.
3mm ($\frac{1}{8}$″) plywood 18cm (7″) in diameter —for baseboard.
Felt for underside of mats—optional.
Furniglas Hardset or a plastic coating such as made by Rustin's.
Veneers—selection as shown and listed overleaf.

The butterfly. Draw design overleaf on to tracing paper and plan which veneers will suit the respective areas. As the butterfly is symmetrical only one side has been given.

The numbers given on the veneers illustrated overleaf are for identification. The colours of the veneers can be used as a guide in selecting your own.
☐ Select the background veneer. This should be a pale-coloured wood which is easy to cut. Here, mahogany has been used. Cut the background veneer slightly larger than the finished item.
☐ Tape the edges of the veneer to prevent splitting and hinge the tracing paper to the veneer with a strip of masking tape. Put carbon paper behind and trace with the fine pointed pencil. Transfer the main features of the design on to the veneer, omitting the small white areas on the upper

Left: early 17th century cupboard is a fine example of pictorial marquetry.

Right: marquetry place mats with a butterfly motif. Designed by Clare Beck.

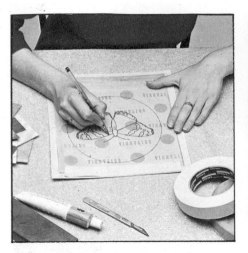

1. *Transfer design to background veneer.*

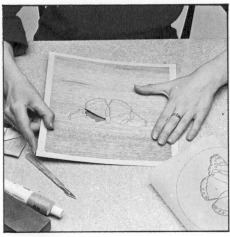

2. *Position teak veneer behind window.*

3. *Teak cut out and placed in window.*

4. *All veneers cut out and in place.*

5. *Cover front of design with gum strip.*

6. *Glue plywood back to veneer design.*

wings and the black diamond shapes on the lower wings (fig.1).

☐ Turn back the tracing paper and cut out the first piece of veneer. Start cutting at the centre of each wing and work outwards to the tip. Then cut from top to bottom of the butterfly. Leave the body until last.

Note: follow the traced line as closely as possible, using short cutting strokes.

☐ Choose the veneer for the area which has been cut out. Here, teak has been used. Position the teak behind the 'window' and fasten with masking tape (fig.2).

☐ Using the edge already cut in the background veneer as the stencil, score around the edge of the teak veneer. Remove the veneer from the back and cut out completely.

☐ Place the cut-out piece into the 'window' (fig.3). The pieces should fit closely. Hold them in position with a few strips of masking tape placed at the back.

☐ Cut out the area next to the one already cut. Place the selected veneer (Madagascar rosewood) behind the 'window' and cut as before. Continue in this way until all the main pieces for the wings and body are cut and in

place (fig.4). Do not rush the job.

☐ Very delicate areas, such as the edges of the wings, can be glued directly into position with balsa cement. To do this, spread a little cement on to the cut edge of the background veneer and press in the small piece.

☐ For the antennae, make a thin cut with several strokes. Press in a sliver of dark veneer with some balsa cement attached to fasten it.

☐ Replace the carbon paper and tracing. Transfer the small white areas on the upper wings and the black diamond shapes on the lower wings on to the main veneers already fixed. Cut out as before and glue veneers directly with balsa cement.

The butterfly is now complete and, if held up to the light, any bad joins will be noticeable. These can be corrected by cutting and fitting a small sliver of matching veneer.

Wipe the picture with a damp cloth to get a clear idea of what the finished result will be. The wet veneer looks as if it has been coated with varnish. In this way you can test whether the veneers are contrasted in the best possible way.

Keep the butterfly pressed flat under a weight in order to prevent it from buckling.

The baseboard. Cut the plywood baseboard to the required size and sand the edges smooth with the fine grade glasspaper.

☐ The surface of the baseboard which is to be veneered should be roughened with a hack saw blade or a coarse grade glasspaper to ensure that the glue will adhere properly.

The underside of the mat can be either veneered or covered with felt. Use the circular baseboard as a guide and mark the felt with tailor's chalk. Cut 6mm ($\frac{1}{4}$″) inside the marked line. The felt is only attached after the design is attached and finished.

If using veneer, cut it 6mm ($\frac{1}{4}$″) larger than the baseboard. Glue the veneer underside first following the same gluing procedure as for the design.

Fixing the design

Remove the trace pattern from the front of the finished picture and replace it on the back.

☐ Trace the exact circle size of the mat on to the back using the tracing and carbon paper. This acts as a guideline when the baseboard and butterfly design are glued.

☐ Cut the background veneer 6mm (¼") larger than the outline.

☐ Cover front of butterfly completely with gum strip (fig.5). When it is dry dampen the small strips of masking tape on the back and remove. Make sure there are no traces of balsa cement on the underside.

☐ Spread the impact adhesive evenly over both surfaces and wait until it is touch dry.

☐ Position the baseboard over the underside of the design, making sure that the grain of the veneer is running in the opposite direction to that of the baseboard. Lower the baseboard carefully on to the design using the circle marked as a guideline, and press firmly. Turn over and press gummed area firmly (fig.6).

☐ Leave under a heavy weight or in a press, if available. A number of heavy books should do. Allow to set for 24 hours.

☐ When the glue has set, dampen the surface of gum strip and peel off.

☐ Trim the veneer to the exact size of the baseboard.

☐ Check that the veneer has stuck completely. Blisters (small air pockets trapped under the veneer) can be detected by running your fingers lightly over the surface. To remedy these, slit the veneer along the grain over the blister, push in some more glue and apply pressure.

Finish

If there is a lot of variation in the thickness of the veneers, use a cabinet scraper to level the surface. This must be done carefully. Final smoothing is done with garnet paper starting with the grade 4/0 and finishing with grade 9/0. Wipe the surface with a damp cloth to remove the dust.

The wood is now ready to be sealed. For items such as table mats, which need to be heat resistant, use either Furniglas Hardset or a plastic coating such as made by Rustin's. Follow the manufacturer's instructions. If a felt underside is used on the baseboard it can now be attached with impact adhesive. Apply the glue and immediately press the felt down firmly on to the baseboard. Leave under a weight overnight.

Trace pattern for butterfly design. As the butterfly is symmetrical only half has been given. The veneers used in the design should have enough colour and grain contrast to emphasize the smaller sections of the butterfly.
1. Elm. 2. Afrormosia. 3. Madagascar rosewood. 4. Pear. 5. Sycamore. 6. Burr walnut. 7. Bombay rosewood. 8. Birds eye maple. 9. Teak. 10. Mahogany.

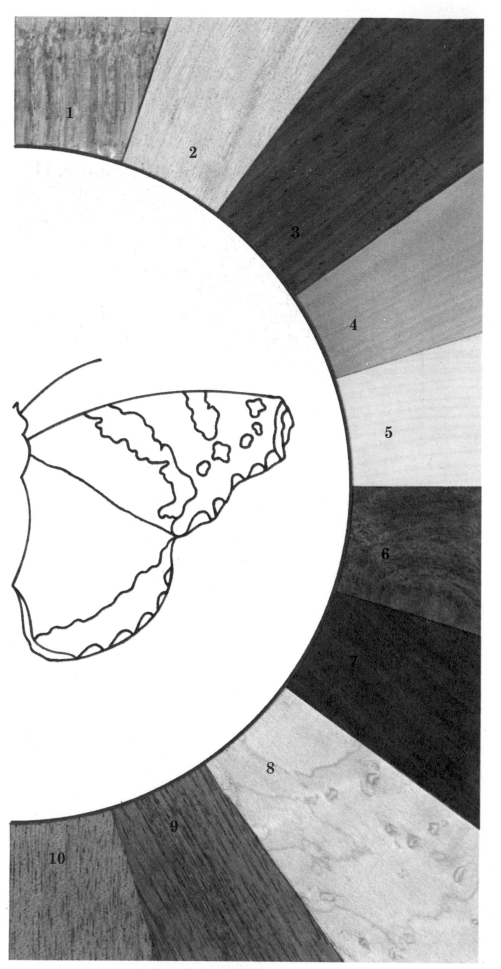

pyrography & poker work

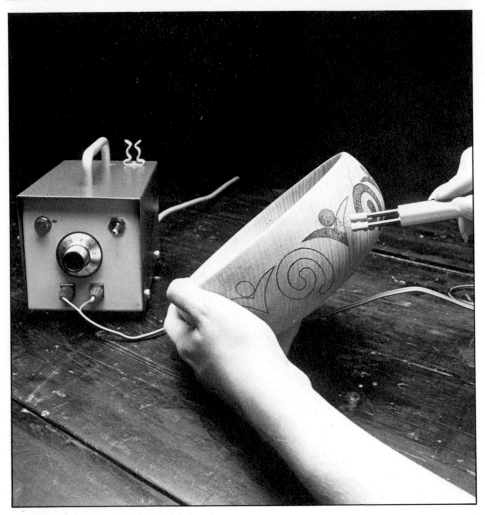

Pyrography is a rather intimidating term applied to an ancient technique of decorating wood. Pyrography—literally 'fire-writing'—entails burning designs into wood with a heated metal implement. Poker-work is a similar technique but applies to lettering and crude decorations while pyrography is more pictorial and intricate.

The art of pyrography dates back centuries but seems to have originated as a folk art in Northern Europe. In the 19th century a number of interesting examples of pyrography were produced, some of which can be seen in the Pinto collection housed in the Birmingham Museum. These 19th century artists worked with a variety of fine steel rods which they heated over a charcoal fire. The method of burning was sometimes supplemented by the use of acids and

The pyrography machine consists of a 'pencil' and a control unit which regulates the heat.

hot sand. Similarly, traditional poker-work—as the name implies—made use of hot pokers or rods of iron to burn patterns into the surface of the timber. Today, pyrography makes use of a small electric machine with an attached 'pencil'. The pencil is heated via the machine and serves the same function as the fire-heated rod in traditional work.

The pyrography machine
The skill required to master the traditional techniques of poker-work put it out of reach of the amateur but simple patterns can be made with metal rods or wire heated over a gas ring or

with a blowtorch. Iron and steel are the best metals, though strong copper or brass can be used.

The pyrography machine now makes it possible for even an amateur to carry out the most intricate detail as well as simple designs such as repeat patterns. Two main parts make up the machine; the pencil and the control unit.

The pencil is handled in exactly the same way as an ordinary lead pencil. The tip of the pencil, which is actually used to burn the design, is referred to as the point. It is made from a length of alloy wire and can be easily bent with pliers to form any shape, making possible a great variety of styles.

Spare points are available and replacing them is a simple procedure. Extra wire is also obtainable which can be worked into virtually any shape—eg to provide a 'brand' for repeat patterns.

The control unit is fitted with a dial marked from 1 to 7; this controls the heat of the pencil points.

Technique
With the aid of the pyrography machine delicate ornamentation and lettering can be burnt into such wooden objects as spice racks, house name-plates, clock faces and wooden jewelry. Wooden toys and bowls can also be decorated and detailed with the technique.

Almost any wood is suitable, depending on the desired effect. A light-coloured fine-grained timber is best to begin with if you are going to attempt delicate lines. Of the most readily available timber, birch, sycamore, holly and lime are recommended. Birch ply and various veneered boards can also be used. Leather is another suitable material for decoration.

When burning the design, different shades can be obtained by varying the pressure and speed of the pencil. In all cases try and keep a light, even pressure because if you hesitate during a stroke, the heat will cause an unsightly blob on the pattern. Too much pressure will bend the point. Begin and end each stroke with the heated point off the wood.

The more slowly you move the pencil, the deeper will be the burn and the darker the shade. Traditional poker-work relied on deep, dark burns for its effect; with the pyrography machine a greater variety of shading is more easily achieved.

For plain line work, the loop point is most suitable, but use a flat or spoon-shaped point for shading. Very fine lines are done with the edge of the spoon-shaped point. A contrasting effect of fine white lines on a scorched surface can be obtained by using a chisel with a small V-shaped blade—known as a carver's parting tool—to carve through the blackened surface and expose the white wood beneath. Completed pieces should be sealed with a clear varnish. Coloured varnish can also be used to give a different effect.

Decorative pyrography

The salad bowls and kitchen utensils in the photograph illustrate some of the designs possible.

Designs can be taken from magazines or drawn freehand. Trace or draw the pattern on to the wood in pencil to provide a guide from which to work.

You will need:

A pyrography machine with some spare alloy wire and a few extra points.

Long-nosed pliers and small screwdriver. Asbestos mat.

Pencil, tracing paper, carbon paper and masking tape.

Clear or coloured polyurethane varnish.

Medium and fine grade glasspaper.

Small V-shaped chisel (optional).

A suitable piece of wood or wooden object to decorate.

☐ Select a suitable piece of wood and smooth it down with medium then fine grade glasspaper.

☐ Draw the design either straight on to the piece of wood or trace it on lightly using carbon paper. The carbon paper and tracing paper should be held together in position with masking tape. It is not necessary to trace in every detail as this can be easily copied when you come to use the pyrography pencil.

☐ Once you have transferred your design you can remove the carbon paper and begin burning in the design. Work carefully with the pencil set at a low heat, and burn in the outline. Use the plain loop nib for this.

The detail and shading is done with a flat or spoon-shaped nib, keeping the dial at the same temperature. Darker shadows are produced with a higher temperature. Use the edge of the flat nib for fine lines. When the piece is finished, seal with a clear or coloured polyurethane varnish.

Traditional poker-work

Many objects can be decorated with the traditional poker-work method. The pyrography machine may not be necessary for very simple work and you can use pieces of wire or metal shaped into various patterns. The wire can be heated over a gas plate or with a blowtorch. The piece of wire should be a dull red when removed from the flame. Wind a cloth around the top part of the wire to prevent yourself from being burnt. You should also have an asbestos mat nearby to lay the hot pieces of iron on when you have finished using them. Alternatively drop them in a container of cold water.

For poker-work done in the traditional way you can make pokers from old wire coat hangers. Cut them up with wire cutters and bend into suitable shapes. Thicker lines can be obtained by using steel rods. The thicker the metal you use, the harder it is to bend into intricate shapes. Circular patterns can be obtained by using the ends of steel pipes similar to those used by plumbers.

You will need a pair of heavy pliers or a strong vice in which to bend the metal. Make the poker fairly long so that you can hold it far from the heated end. Either wear asbestos gloves or wrap a damp rag around the handle end of the poker. However, unless you are working on a large scale, the pyrography machine is suitable for both poker-work and pyrography.

Very intricate and detailed patterns are possible with the use of the pyrography machine. Designs on the kitchen utensils are by Diana Smith.

Ropework

A lover's knot

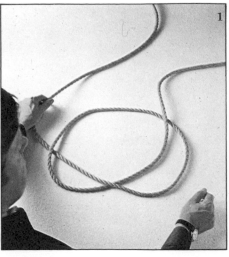

□ Using the required length of yarn, bend it in the middle of the length of yarn. Pass the left strand of the yarn through the loop and pull it to the left (fig.1).

□ Open out the knot by pulling the 2 loops that have been made.

□ Pull the loops out further still (fig.2), if you imagine them crossed, until they are about the size of the finished article.

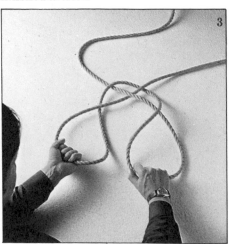

□ Grasp a loop in each hand and twist the loops once to the left (fig.3).

□ Still grasping the loops, cross the

A hard-wearing mat to use in a hall.

The lover's knot is an attractive and quick way of making a motif. The motif is versatile and may be made up in a variety of yarns, depending on the purpose it will be used for.

With medium-weight yarn, like parcel string and macramé yarns, you can make hair decorations—mounted on slides or hair combs—buckles for using on belts and bracelets, key ring tabs and, if you squash the basic shape slightly, oval buttons. The buttons look particularly handsome made in string and sewn on suede and leather or, if you use macramé yarns, sew on dresses and shirts.

Heavy-weight yarns, such as rope, make hard-wearing door mats with a rustic air. Several motifs may be sewn together to form a large and beautiful mat.

When you have made one motif you will see that the stage illustrated by fig.4 is the crucial one. It dictates the finished size and shape of the article, so even up the shape and check that the motif is the right size at this stage—later on will be too late.

Ideally the yarn should be cut to the required length for making the article. However a great length of yarn can be difficult to handle, so several lengths may be used for big projects. Providing the raw ends are left at the back of the work they can be darned in afterwards. Small articles may be made of only two strands, such as the buttons, but usually four or five strands are used.

The important thing is to fill in the gaps in the motif completely.

To make working easier the ends which you thread in and out may be either dipped in a little glue or covered with sticky tape to prevent them fraying. Always leave ends at back of work.

To make a lover's knot —buckle or mat

For a buckle motif 78mm x 42mm (3¼"x 1¾"):

You will need:
2.5m (7') length of parcel string.
For a door mat 55cm x 35cm (22"x14"):

You will need:
35m (38yd) length 12mm (½") thick manilla rep or sisal.

left hand over the right hand (fig.4).

This stage dictates the size and shape of the finished article, so make the shape even and check that it is the size you want.

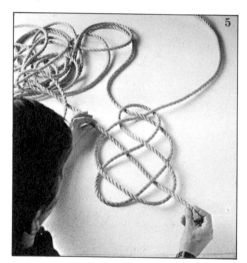

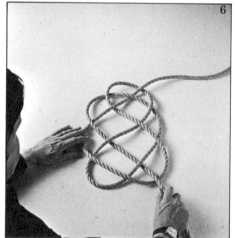

□ Release the loops and hold them in position with the left hand. With the right hand pick up the strand which lies at the top left of the shape and bend it towards the left of the shape. Weave the yarn over the outside of the middle loop, under both the central strands of the left hand loop and over the top of the right hand loop (figs.5 and 6).

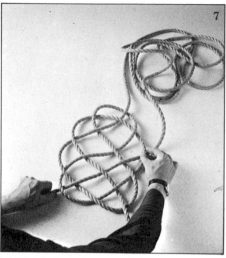

□ Hold the other strand at the top of the work, thread it under the outside of the right middle loop then over, under, over, under the other strands, working from right to left (fig.7).

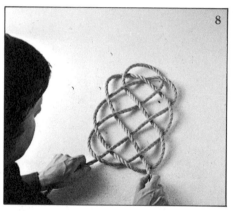

The shape should now be fairly rigid.
□ Arrange the strands in a neat shape so that the loops are about the same size and the same distance away from their neighbours (fig.8).

□ Grasp the right hand strand and bend it so that it lies parallel to the left hand strand. Thread the right hand strand under, over, under, over, under —ie following the exact path of the other woven strand but working from left to right (fig.9).

□ Continue following the path of the woven strand, placing each strand side by side. When this end is exhausted start weaving with the other one; curve it to the right and follow round the bottom loop and then weave over, under etc, following the path indicated by the yarn till all the spaces have been filled up.

To finish the ends of the strands, remove and discard the sticky tape if this was used and, using a strong needle and thread or string, tie the raw ends to the back of the article or to a neighbouring strand (fig.10).

10. *Secure the ends on the wrong side.*

Lover's knots in fine or heavy yarn.

A lover's knot makes a smart buckle.

Turk's head knots

The Turk's head is one of the most versatile decorative knots and was used originally on sailing ships to decorate nautical equipment. It is a freestanding knot made from one length of yarn and has a plaited appearance.

When it is made as a ring or loop it can be tightened around ropes or braids to make a neat finish or it can be worked to any diameter to form a bracelet, scarf or napkin ring, or a frame for a mirror or picture. Made flat it can be used for tablemats, coasters or as a soft buckle or frog fastening for clothes or bags. Pulled tight it can be used as a knob for fastening a belt or as a button.

The yarns. The easiest yarns to use for the Turk's head are those which are flexible but not too floppy. Medium-weight ropes and cords made from natural yarn, such as manilla, sisal, hemp and cotton, can all be used although they can discolour and deteriorate if they are subjected to damp conditions.

Man-made yarns, made of polypropylene, polyester (such as Terylene) and nylon, are ideal because they are easy to use, can be washed and are available in a variety of weights and colours.

The knot size. The knot can be made into any size you like. For a small knot each strand should be twisted in and out three times; these are known as tucks. For a larger knot, such as for a coaster, you should make five tucks to form a firm knot and for a tablemat you would probably need seven or even nine tucks. The tucks are always formed in odd numbers in order to achieve the correct pattern.

The width of the knot is determined by the number of times the yarn is passed round the foundation; each circuit is known as a part.

Using a jig. It is advisable to finish each knot by tightening it around a jig to ensure it is right size. A jig is a solid foundation which should be of the same size as the internal diameter of the required knot.

It could be a piece of cardboard or plastic tube or even a household jar, if the finished item is in the form of a ring. If you are making a flat knot, you can make your own jig from layers of cardboard cut to the required size and mounted one on top of the other to make the jig 6mm ($\frac{1}{4}$") thick.

A few of the many uses of the Turk's head knot, designed by Ropecraft. The small knots, napkin rings and lanyard knob are made with three tucks and three parts. The coaster has five tucks and three parts and is finished with a Flemish coil, and picture frame has seven tucks and two parts. To give firmness to the finished articles, they are glued on to a solid foundation.

Turk's head knot

You will need:
Yarn, 2.7 metres (3yds) 3mm ($\frac{1}{8}$″) diameter cord.

☐ Divide the cord into thirds. Loop the cord round the fingers of your left hand so that one-third is hanging down. Use the remaining two-thirds as the working end. Cross the working end to the left and trap under the thumb (fig.1, A).

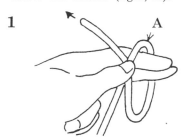

1

A

☐ Pass the working end behind the fingers again to form loop B (fig.2) and trap under the thumb. Adjust the loops so that they are slightly larger than the required diameter of the knot.

2

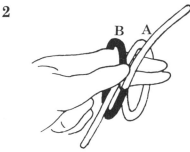

B   A

☐ Turn your fingers towards you and tuck the working end under loop A and over loop B to the left (fig.3).

B   A

3

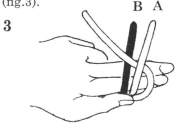

☐ Cross loop B over loop A and tuck the working end from left to right under A and over B (fig.4).

4

A   B

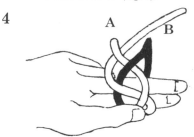

☐ Rotate the knot and cross loop B over A and pass the working end under A and over B to the left (fig.5).

5

B   A

6

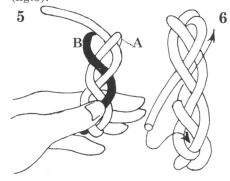

This completes three tucks. Further tucks can be added in pairs by repeating this procedure of crossing the loops alternately to the left and right and feeding the working end under and over each time. The two ends should come out of the knot over and under their respective loops.

To work the second part, take the working end and feed it back into the knot under the loop from which the tail end comes out. Keeping to the right-hand side and parallel to the tail cord, weave the working end round the knot, following the windings until you have two strands all round.

To add a third part, repeat the procedure with the tail end, weaving it round the knot in the reverse direction until there are three strands all round (fig.6).

To make the knot smaller, place the knot around the jig to hold its shape and, pulling from the end with which you started, gradually ease the yarn through the windings to the end. Repeat the process if you wish the knot to be smaller.

To make a button or knob, continue tightening the knot until it forms a tight ball. Use the two ends as a shank for sewing the button to a garment and trim the ends close to the sewing.

To make a flat knot, hold the knot in both hands with the open sides at the top and bottom. Press up the lower edge of the knot into the middle of the ring with your fingers and flatten the knot with your thumb.

To finish the knot, cut the two ends so that they are hidden behind the windings. Place a little glue on the ends to prevent them unravelling. Tuck the ends behind the windings and leave until the glue is dry.

Turk's head coasters

To make one coaster with 11.5cm ($4\frac{1}{2}$″) diameter:

You will need:
Yarn, 2.7m (3yds) 3mm ($\frac{1}{8}$″) diameter cord for the Turk's head knot border. 0.91m (1yd) 3mm ($\frac{1}{8}$″) diameter cord for the centre coil; 33cm (13″) 3mm ($\frac{1}{8}$″) diameter cord for the edge trim. (The yarn quantities are specified separately for each section as you may wish to make a multi-coloured coaster.)
Backing board, 3mm ($\frac{1}{8}$″) hardboard or plywood cut to an octagon with a diameter of 11.5cm ($4\frac{1}{2}$″) (see Design knowhow chapter 8, page 224).
Felt for the underside of backing board, cut to the same size and shape.
Jig, cut to an octagon measuring 6cm ($2\frac{3}{8}$″) in diameter.
Adhesive, such as Uhu.

☐ Apply the adhesive to the underside of the backing board and carefully stick on the felt.
☐ Place the edge trimming cord round the backing board. Check that it fits exactly and adjust if necessary. Glue the ends in a butt join. Apply glue thinly round the edge of the board and allow to become tacky. Press the trimming ring into position.
☐ Make a flat Turk's head knot with five tucks and three parts.
☐ Place the flattened knot over the jig and if necessary pull the inner end of the cord through the loops so that it touches the edge of the jig (fig.6).
☐ Holding this end down with your thumb, tighten the knot by working round the loops to take up the slack. All the strands should lie flat and parallel to each other. Do not over-tighten or the strands will bunch and cross each other. When all the strands are tightened and the inner edge of the ring fits round the jig, cut off the outer tail end.
☐ Apply the glue to the knot and allow it to become tacky. Apply glue to the section of the backing board to be covered by the knot. Remove the knot from the jig and press it glue-side down in position on to the board.

Finishing the centre. The centre can be finished with a Flemish coil. To ensure that the coil is the correct size, draw a circle of 6cm ($2\frac{3}{8}$″) diameter on cardboard and mark the centre. Double back one end of the cord about 5mm ($\frac{1}{4}$″) and place this end on to the centre of the card. Secure with a pin. Rotate the centre in an anti-clockwise direction, feeding the cord at a light even tension while keeping the coil flat on the card under the fingers of the other hand. When the coil becomes the correct size, insert a pin through the outer turns to secure it.
Spread adhesive over the coil and on to the board, allow to become tacky and place in position. Tuck the loose end under a strand of the Turk's head.

Recycling with rope

An unusual way of using rope is to wrap it round furniture which is shabby or round an item which otherwise might be thrown away. Things which can be rejuvenated or re-cycled in this way are chairs, oil cans, jars, pots of many kinds, the legs of a table, a strutted bedhead and banisters; rope can even be used on the fronts of cupboard doors or drawers if it is coiled and glued instead of wrapped.

Rope is a useful yarn for craft work and it is available in a surprisingly wide range of fibres and textures.

Types of rope and twine

Ropes and twines (string is not a term used for thin grades by the makers as they consider it too vague) may be made from natural fibres, such as manilla, hemp, sisal, jute or cotton, or from synthetics such as Terylene, nylon and polypropylene.

Those made from natural fibres are easier to handle in the heavier sizes but they do have the disadvantage of discolouring and decaying if they are kept permanently damp. However, they can be washed if they are dried quickly. Ropes made from synthetic fibres tend to be lighter in weight and cheaper than the same sizes in natural fibres, they do not decay under damp conditions, they can be washed and they are available in a variety of colours. Thinner grades are easier to handle for craft work than the thicker ones which tend to be very springy.

Manilla and hemp. These are the strongest and most expensive of the natural fibres and are normally recognizable by their coffee colour. Most rope made from these fibres is in stranded form (made from two or more separate strands of rope which are twisted together).

Sisal is one of the cheaper natural fibres and is recognizable by its off-white colour and hairy texture. Sisal dyes well and is sometimes available in different colours but these are more expensive.

Jute is another inexpensive natural fibre of a slightly darker colour than hemp. It is recognizable by its fine fibres and it is normally sold in braided form (like a tubular plait) rather than stranded.

Cotton is the cheapest natural fibre and is recognizable because it is off-white and smooth. It is more often sold by stationers as parcel string rather than by rope chandlers.

Polypropylene is the most expensive of the synthetic fibres and is recognizable by its shiny texture. It is available in white and other colours and is normally stranded although some

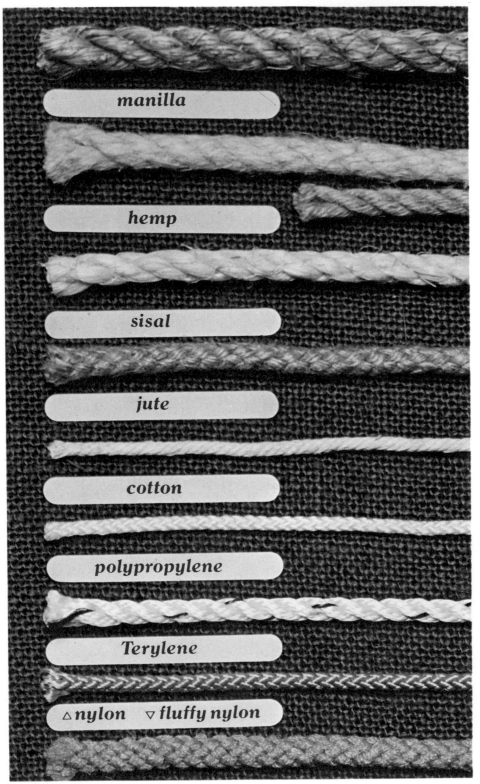

manilla

hemp

sisal

jute

cotton

polypropylene

Terylene

△nylon   ▽fluffy nylon

The different kinds of rope and twine, all available in a variety of weights.

162

thinner grades are braided.

Terylene and nylon appear very similar although nylon is more stretchy than Terylene. They are softer and smoother than most other types of rope and are available in a wide range of colours. They are normally braided rather than stranded. Nylon is also made in a fluffy version which is suitable for some forms of craft work where this texture is required.

Rope for coiling
Natural fibre ropes such as sisal, jute or hemp are normally cheapest to use for this type of project and they are available in different thicknesses from hardware shops or suppliers of camping or sailing materials. Choose a chunky rope for larger objects such as furniture or oil cans and thinner twine for small items such as a coffee jar or flower pot.

The colour. Ropes are available in a variety of natural shades ranging from off-white to brown but you can dye the lighter shades if you wish to match your colour scheme. Combining ropes of different colours is also attractive.

Attaching the rope. There is no need to glue all the rope to the surface of the item you are covering because the tightness of the coiling keeps it in position, but you do have to secure the ends of the rope to the surface. On wood this can be done simply by using a tack and burying the head inside the twist of the rope. On glass or metal you will have to glue the ends, using a general-purpose clear adhesive or a contact adhesive. You will normally achieve the best result by fraying the end of the rope for about 2.5cm-4cm (1″-1½″) and applying the adhesive to the rope and to the surface to which it is to be stuck. When the adhesive is tacky, press the rope firmly and accurately in position. Where possible the frayed ends should be covered by an adjacent coil.

It is normally easiest to work direct from the hank of rope because it is not easy to calculate exactly how much you will need. If you do run out before you have finished covering an area, glue down the end in an unnoticeable place as neatly as possible and butt the end of the new length up to it.

This lampbase, designed by Horatio Goni, was made from a motor oil can covered by coiling rope around it. The shade carrier is a bent coat-hanger.

Oil can bases
The stylish lamp base in the photograph was made from a large motor oil can. The electrical fitting was slotted into the opening and the flex passed through the can and out from a small hole which was drilled in the side at the bottom. The lampshade sits on a home-made shade carrier, fashioned from a wire coat-hanger.

To make the base

You will need:

Average-sized oil can.

Medium-weight rope, 27m (30yd) if you are using one colour only or 9m (10yd) of each colour if you are using three colours.

General-purpose clear or contact adhesive (such as Bostik 1 or Evo-Stik).

Light fitting with flex, suitable for bottles.

Drill and No.10 or 12 bit.

Wire coat-hanger.

163

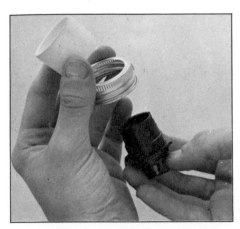

1. *Inserting the light fitting.*

2. *Gluing the frayed ends.*

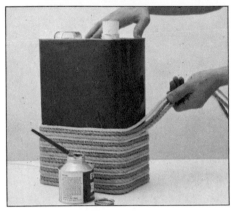

3. *Coiling the rope.*

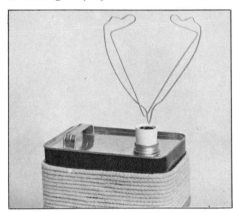

4. *Shade carrier made from coat-hanger.*

☐ Fill the can with water, rinse with a little detergent to remove all oil and dirt. Stand upside down to dry.
☐ Drill a small hole at the bottom near the corner on one side of the can. Thread the light flex through the can from the opening at the top and out through the hole. (Alternatively, if this is difficult, disconnect the flex from the light fitting and thread through the hole in the bottom and out at the top). Slot the light fitting into the hole at the top, or into the cap if possible (fig.1) and press down firmly.

Attaching the rope. Fray out the ends of the rope for about 2.5cm (1″) and smear with adhesive. Smear adhesive at the bottom. When tacky, press the rope end (or the ends held together and parallel if you are using different colours) on to the glued area. The lower edge of the rope should be level with the bottom of the can. Hold in place until adhesion is complete. Spread more adhesive in a band round the bottom of the can (fig.2).

☐ Start winding the rope round the can, covering the ends of the rope and then spiralling up the can. Keep the windings close together and as taut as possible. If you are using three strands of rope, hold them level and parallel (fig.3).

☐ At the top, cut off any excess rope, fray the ends and smear on some adhesive. Smear some adhesive on the can at a corresponding position and stick down when tacky. Tuck the ends under neatly.

The lampholder. Bend the coat-hanger as shown (fig.4) and fit the loop round the opening of the can at the base of the light fitting. Push the lampholder towards the middle of the can so that the lampshade will be balanced. Fit the lampshade, bulb and electric plug.

Coffee jar and plant pot

All kinds of dull household items can be made more attractive by coiling. For small items you will not require a large amount of twine so it is not costly to use synthetics which are available in a good range of colours and can be washed.

Coffee jars. When decorated with coiled twine empty coffee jars make attractive storage jars for the kitchen or work room. If you leave part of the jar uncovered you will be able to identify the contents easily. The lid of the jar can also be covered by coiling the twine from the centre outwards and then round the sides. The centre of the lid on the photograph was finished with a Turk's head knot (see previous section.

The plant pot. There is no need to stand a plastic plant pot in a decorative container when you cover it with coiled twine. The rim of this one is finished with a seven-tuck, two-part Turk's head knot.

A coffee jar of the type which might normally be thrown away and a plastic plant pot are given an attractive finish with coiled twine by Ropecraft.

5. *Gluing rope to chair leg.*

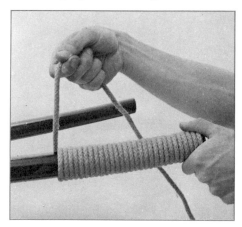

6. *Coiling rope around leg.*

7. *Securing the end with a tack.*

8. *Weaving round the middle struts.*

Covering chairs

The amount and the method with which you cover a chair will obviously depend on the style and size of the chair and how much of the wood you wish to cover. Study the chair before you begin work and plan your design. Decide where you could make a continuous length of rope cover a large area. On the chair in the photograph, for example, the back and back legs were covered with four separate lengths.

The ends of two of the lengths were glued to the bottom of the legs (fig.5), wound up the legs (fig.6), on to the side struts and part of the back cross member where they were finished neatly with a small tack (fig.7).

The other two lengths were wound round the remaining part of the cross member and then woven round the middle struts (fig.8). Two more lengths were used to wrap round the front legs in a similar way.

Utility chair given a new lease of life with coiled rope by Horatio Goni.

Diamond mesh netting

Netting is a traditional nautical craft, originally used to make fishing nets. It later became popular for shopping bags, hammocks and games nets.

Unlike macramé which is worked with several strands of yarn and a variety of knots, netting is worked with one continuous length of yarn and one knot throughout. This knot, the sheet bend—also known as the netting knot —is worked in rows and into the loops of previous row to form diamond mesh.

Materials

String. Ordinary cotton parcel string is perfectly suitable for netting and you can also use any of the fancy twines sold for macramé. Knitting yarns can be used for scarves and shawls. There is no easy way of estimating the amount of yarn you need for a specific project.

Netting needle (fig.1) holds the yarn and helps to form the knot. Needles are usually plastic and are available in various widths. The needle should always be narrower than the mesh stick so that it passes easily through the mesh.

Home-made needles. You can make a simple netting needle from a thin strip of wood of the required width by cutting a V-shaped notch at each end. Alternatively for a very narrow netting needle, as required for a shrimping net, cut off both ends of a knitting needle, heat the remaining ends and hammer flat. Use a small hacksaw to cut a notch at both ends.

Mesh sticks. These determine the size of the mesh and ensure the correct size. The sticks can be Perspex or wooden battens, about 3mm ($\frac{1}{8}$") thick, such as a ruler. You will need a variety of widths from 2.5cm-4cm (1"-1$\frac{1}{2}$"), although for some projects you may need wider or narrower sticks.

Loading the needle. Hold the needle in your left hand and pointing away from you. Place the end of the yarn anywhere on the body of the needle and hold the yarn in place with your left thumb.

☐ Lay the yarn up along the body of the needle, round the prong at the top and down the same side of the body to trap the end of the yarn (fig.1a). Pass it under the heel at the bottom of the needle and then turn the needle over. Pass the yarn up the opposite side of the body, round the prong and down the same side (fig.1b). Take it under the heel and turn over the needle again. Continue in this way until the needle is comfortably full. Cut the yarn, leaving about 45cm (18") as a working length.

Loading home-made needles. Wind twine round, passing it through notches.

Making a practice piece

Foundation loop. From the remaining yarn cut off a length about 45cm (18") long. Tie the ends together and hang the loop on any convenient hook or knob with the knot at the top. This loop is used only for practice and acts as a substitute for other methods of casting on, such as by using a series of clove hitches.

Tiny mesh shrimping nets made with a netting needle and mesh stick both made from knitting needles.

First netting knot. Pass the needle through the foundation loop from the back, leaving a tail of yarn of about 2.5cm (1") (fig.2). Hold the yarn firmly at the intersection with the loop between the thumb and index finger of your left hand.

☐ Throw an open loop from the needle to the left and across the front of the foundation loop to the right (fig.3). Pass needle round behind foundation loop and out to the front through the thrown loop (fig.4).

☐ Keeping the left thumb and index finger firmly in position and with a steady tension on the whole work, pull down the needle with the right hand to make the knot firm (fig.5). Check that the knot is seated correctly at the bottom of the foundation loop (fig.6) and that it does not slip below. Fig.7 shows the knot incorrectly seated.

First row. Having made the first netting knot, hold the mesh stick in the left hand with the thumb at the front. Lay the working yarn over the front of the stick and take it round below (fig.8) and up behind it and out through the foundation loop from the back (fig.9). Pull the needle downwards so the stick is pulled up to the bottom of the foundation loop as shown.

☐ With your left thumb at the front and forefinger at the back, hold the yarn and the loop where they intersect at the top of the mesh stick. Keep a steady tension by pulling down lightly with your left hand.

☐ Work the knot as before (fig.10), setting it at the bottom of the foundation loop and at the top of the mesh stick. If the stick is too short to complete the row, pull it out of the first loops to give required length.

☐ Continue working knots into the foundation loop in this way, always passing the yarn round the mesh stick from front to back before throwing the loop to the left (fig.11). After each knot, pull down on the working yarn with your right hand so that the knot is formed correctly at the top of the mesh stick.

Second row. Remove the mesh stick from the loops (if it feels tight it means you have worked good firm loops).

☐ With the left hand turn the loops round so that the last loop made is on the left, to be used first in the second row.

☐ Hold the mesh stick in position at the bottom of the loops and lay the working yarn over it, round and up behind it and out through the first loop from the back (fig.12). Pull down on the needle so that the mesh stick is drawn up to the bottom of the loop. Work the netting knot as before, taking care to pass the needle between the loop and the yarn descending from the left from the previous row. It often helps to use the left index finger to part these strands where the needle passes through and to use the middle finger and left thumb to hold the string and loop.

☐ Keep the mesh stick in position and work one knot into each of the first row of loops. Fig.13 shows the first two rows completed, forming the traditional diamond-shaped mesh of netting.

Third and subsequent rows. Continue working in this way, always turning the work after each row. Check that all the knots are correctly positioned before beginning the next row.

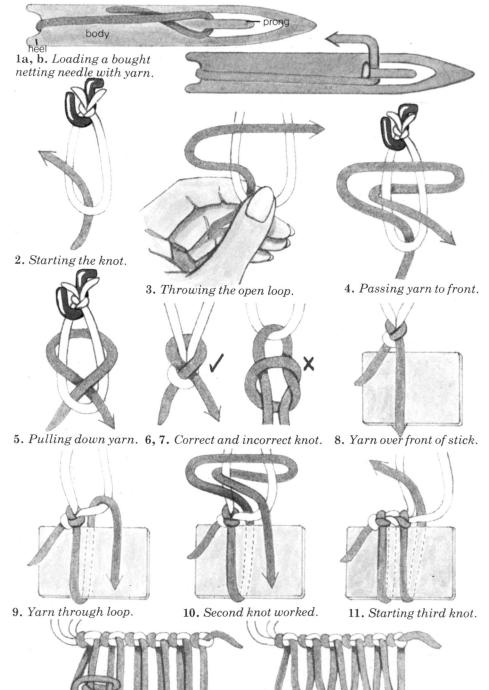

1a, b. Loading a bought netting needle with yarn.

2. Starting the knot.

3. Throwing the open loop.

4. Passing yarn to front.

5. Pulling down yarn.

6, 7. Correct and incorrect knot.

8. Yarn over front of stick.

9. Yarn through loop.

10. Second knot worked.

11. Starting third knot.

12. Loops turned to start next row.

13. Two rows completed; stick removed.

Making a hammock

The word 'hammock' derives from the Spanish *hamaca* of Caribbean origin. It was mentioned by Columbus in his diary when he found that the inhabitants of the Bahamas Islands slept in 'nets of cotton', suspended at either end and which they called 'hamacs'. Although the net hammock was novel to Columbus, Alcibiades (a 5th-century BC Athenian general and contemporary of Socrates) is accredited with

the invention of the swinging canvas bed. The navy used canvas hammocks as beds despite the fact that netting is a nautical art.

Garden hammocks and hammocks used in the tropics are traditionally made from netting.

A hammock netted in soft but strong twine makes a comfortable garden bed. Designed by Charles Holdgate.

Small hammocks are also used by campers to store luggage off the ground. With large netted items, such as hammocks, a close netting is not necessary and the process can be considerably speeded up if you use a wide mesh stick. The resulting mesh is just as firm as if worked with a narrower stick. However, some care should be taken with the finishing so that the hammock is both comfortable and strong.

The hammock

Finished length (measured between rope thimbles): 284cm (112″).

You will need:

Soft twine of about 8mm (¼″) diameter: ½-1kg (1-2lb) according to fibre.

Firm twine of about 3mm (⅛″) diameter —about 40m (45yd).

Stout rope of about 15mm (½″) diameter —about 4m (4½yd).

Pair of rope thimbles, 75mm (3″) diameter. (Thimbles are round or heart-shaped collars, made from plastic, steel or brass. They are obtainable from ship's chandlers.)

Two pieces of hardwood, 60cm x 4cm x 12mm (24″x 1½″x ½″).

Large netting needle.

Mesh sticks, 15cm (6″) and 7.5cm (3″) wide. The narrower stick could be used throughout.

Saw and wood file.

Casting on. Load the netting needle with soft twine as described earlier, on page 166.

☐ Tie a firm line between two points about 60cm (24″) apart (you could use one end of the firm twine for this because it will be removed later).

☐ Using clove hitches over the tied line, cast on 13 loops over the wide mesh stick. (If you are using the 7.5cm (3″) stick wind the twine round twice.)

The netting. Net 25 rows with the 7.5cm (3″) mesh stick. To make a strong selvedge, work the first knot of

each row round the twine hanging from the previous row (fig.1)—this should usually be avoided for edges which have to be joined but it is acceptable here. If you run out of twine, join

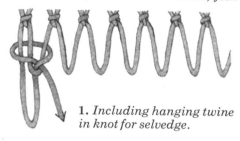

1. Including hanging twine in knot for selvedge.

a new length as described overleaf.

Casting off. Net one row over the wider mesh stick. Remove the firm line from the first row. The clove hitches will drop out so that the first row matches the last one (the slight difference in size does not matter).

The clews. These are the sections at the head and foot of the hammock which connect the netting to the thimbles. Each strand of twine is passed round the thimble to prevent chafing and wear. These strands are often known as nettles.

☐ Cut off and reserve two lengths of firm twine, each equal to twice the length of the selvedge.

☐ Cut the remaining firm twine in half and use one piece at each end of the hammock. Thread one of the pieces through the centre mesh of the first row so that the ends hanging are equal. Make a netting knot.

☐ Thread one of the ends through the thimble and draw it through so that the thimble is about 50cm (20″) from the knot. Working from the centre to one side and leaving 50cm (20″) again from the thimble, work a netting knot with the same end into each mesh.

☐ Repeat this process with the other end for the opposite side (fig.2).

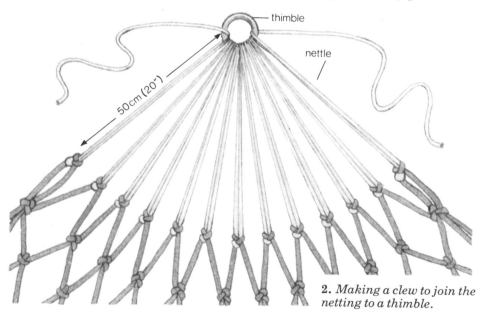

2. Making a clew to join the netting to a thimble.

Woven section. Thread both ends back to the thimble. Starting with the left-hand end, weave it under and over each strand of the hammock clew and bring it out at the right-hand side. Repeat this process with the right-hand end, passing over and under the same strands as the left-hand end but bringing it out on the left. Pull both ends tight.

☐ Work the second row in the same way but this time passing over the strands passed under on the first row and vice versa (fig.3). Draw up tightly.

☐ Continue like this for the following rows, but omitting the end strands on each row until only two remain in the centre. Tie the ends over these with a reef knot.

☐ Repeat the above with the nettles and woven clew at the foot of the hammock.

Drawing up the sides. Fold one of the reserved lengths of rope in half and pass the loop round the base of the left-hand nettle at one end of the hammock.

☐ Pull the ends of the twine through the loop and then thread the ends through the selvedges of the netting to the opposite end. Do not tie off yet.

☐ Repeat for the opposite edge and then draw up each edge to give the hammock a good shape. Tie the ends.

Rope for slinging the hammock. Cut the stout rope in half and thread one piece round the thimble at one end, passing it through the loops at the top of the strands.

☐ Secure the rope round the thimble with an eye splice (see box opposite) or tie with two half hitches and whip the ends securely with whipping twine (see fig. 4 below).

☐ Work a back splice at the other end of the rope (see box opposite) and whip. Repeat this process at the opposite end of the hammock.

Stretchers. Shape the ends of the two pieces of wood with the saw and file as shown in fig.5. Fit them between the outer strands of the clew at the ends of the hammock when it is in position as shown in the photograph on page 168–9.

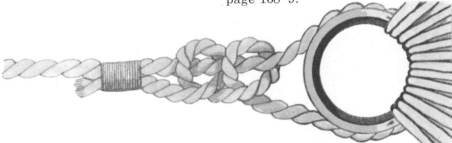

4. *Tying the rope for slinging the hammock to the thimble with half hitches.*

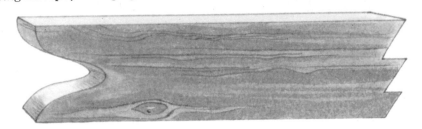

5. *V-cuts are made at each end of the stretchers with a saw and file.*

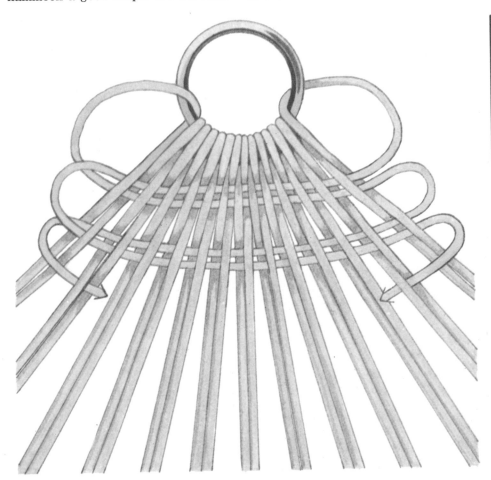

3. *Threading the twine through the nettles for the woven section of the clew.*

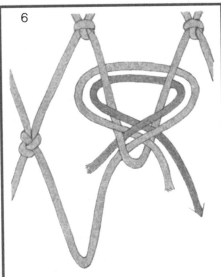

Joining lengths

The strongest method of joining on a new length is with a double netting knot.

☐ Hold the end of the old length with the beginning of the new length and make a netting knot with the double twine (fig.6).

☐ Alternatively, work a knot with the end of the old length, slacken off the knot and thread the beginning of the new length round the same path as the old length.

7. *Placing the unlaid strands across the main body of rope.*

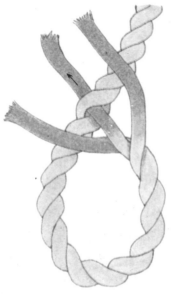

8. *Tucking the middle strand under a main-body strand.*

9. *Tucking left-hand strand where middle strand emerges.*

Eye splice

☐ Unlay (unravel) the end of the rope for about 7.5cm (3″) and loop the ends round to the right with the unlaid ends pointing across the rope (fig.7).

☐ Tuck (thread) the middle strand under any strand in the main body of the rope (fig.8). Then tuck the left-hand strand in where the middle strand comes out (fig.9).

☐ Turn the splice over. You will see that there is one strand in the main body of the rope without an end strand under it. Take the third end and tuck it from right to left under this strand (fig.10).

☐ Each end strand is now lying over a strand in the main body of the rope. Tuck each end in turn over the next strand and under the following one (fig.11).

☐ Check that all the strands are at even tension and then add further tucks in the same way to within 1.5cm ($\frac{1}{2}$″) of the end.

☐ Finish by whipping.

Back splice

☐ Unlay (unravel) the ends of the rope for about 5cm (2″). Form them into a crown knot (fig.12).

☐ You will see that each end is now pointing across a strand in the main body of the rope. Pass the end strand over this and then tuck it under the next strand in the main body. Repeat for the remaining two strands (fig.13).

☐ Go round the rope twice more in this way then whip the ends neatly.

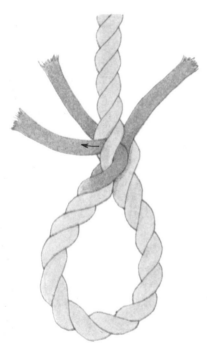

10. *The splice turned over to tuck the remaining strand.*

11. *Tucking the strands over and under following strands.*

12. *Forming a crown knot to start a back splice.*

13. *Tucking the strands under and over strands in main body.*

172

papercraft

cut-out murals

Large sheets of gaily coloured papers cut into simple shapes can make very effective murals and are an original way to decorate a room.

Invent your own designs, or copy ideas from books or magazines. But try to avoid a lot of intricate detail. Cut-outs are most effective when shapes are bold.

Suitable papers

Papers with a glossy surface look particularly cheerful, but anything from tissue paper to thin card could be used, and you will be able to choose from a wide selection at any good art shop.

Tissue paper can produce particularly subtle results when toning shades are used in double layers. Or choose jewel-like colours and stick your tissue paper mural to a glass window pane for a brilliant stained glass effect. Unfortunately the fragile quality of tissue paper makes it tricky to work on, so it is advisable to use a simpler, thicker paper for your first mural.

Glossy papers come in glowing colours and have the advantage of keeping their pristine good looks longer than most other types of paper. But all papers will lose their freshness if handled, so murals should not be fingered before you have given them a protective seal.

Preparing the wall

Any wall painted with emulsion or gloss paint is suitable for decorating with paper murals. But check first that it is clean and dry, and free from grease.

Paper cut-outs can also be stuck on to wallpaper, provided it does not have a raised or embossed finish. And, of course, the mural will only look effective if the wallpaper is in a plain colour. The surface of the wallpaper, like paint, must be clean, dry and grease-free.

Choosing an adhesive

Your choice of glue should be determined by the type of paper to be used and the wall surface. Bear in mind, too, how permanent you wish the mural to be.

A PVA adhesive is suitable for stick-ing thin card on to any wall surface. But it is almost impossible to remove the mural without damaging the paint or wallpaper too. Spread PVA adhesives very thinly over the whole surface of the paper. The occasional blob may be quicker to do but is liable to cause wrinkling and to show through the paper.

A wallpaper paste, such as Polycell, is suitable for most lightweight papers (anything up to wallpaper weight), and can be used on any surface—gloss, emulsion or wallpaper. The mural can be removed from a gloss painted surface quite easily. But if the paper cut-outs are very thin (like tissue paper) their colours may stain the wall.

Paper murals glued with wallpaper paste on to emulsion paint or wallpaper can be removed with a stripper, such as Polycell, but this is likely to spoil the paint or wallpaper as well.

A rubber-based solution such as Cow Gum is another alternative, and would probably cause less damage to the wall surface when the mural is removed.

Loosen the paper mural by soaking with petrol lighter fuel. It will then peel away quite easily. Any surplus Cow Gum remaining on the wall can be erased by using a 'rubber' made from scraps of dry Cow Gum rolled into a ball.

To make cut-out murals

☐ First plan and then sketch your mural on a sheet of rough paper, using coloured pencils to match your papers.

☐ When you have decided on the composition, lightly draw the designs on the wall with a soft pencil (or a felt-tipped pen for gloss paint). These designs can then be traced and transferred on to the chosen paper and card.

☐ Alternatively draw each design on to tracing paper, and use your sketch as a map when it comes to gluing each piece into position on the wall.

☐ It's a good idea to try your layout on the wall before finally sticking each design into position. A low-tack adhesive such as Blue-Tack will stick the paper cuts lightly on to the wall and enable you to remove them again without damaging the surface. So use this for testing, and only apply a stronger adhesive or wallpaper paste when you are sure each design is correctly positioned and the composition looks right as a whole.

☐ Take one animal or object at a time, starting with a central figure in the composition. Draw, cut and stick it on to the wall with low-tack adhesive before proceeding with the next.

☐ For the best results use a scalpel to

cut the paper. Scissors, however, are safer and quite suitable for thin papers, so use them if children are helping with the project.

Take the elephant as an example (see trace pattern overleaf); start with the basic large body shape.

Lay a sheet of grey paper on a flat surface. If one sheet is not large enough, add a second. Butt them up against each other but don't overlap the two sheets.

☐ Draw or trace the elephant shape on to the paper, trying to make the joins in the least obvious places—such as where the head joins the body. Draw the outline only. Details such as ears and eyes will be cut out of other coloured papers and stuck on top. This not only makes for easier cutting, but the superimposed details will add depth and interest to the mural.

A child's room could be transformed by this delightful menagerie mural. Elephant and parrot patterns overleaf.

☐ Now trace and cut out the tusk, eye, ears and toenails in suitably coloured papers, and stick them on to the cut-out grey body.

☐ (If details extend beyond the main body shape—like the water spout coming from the whale—they should

not be stuck down until the main shape is glued to the wall.)

☐ When the details are firmly secured and dry, turn the paper over, apply low-tack adhesive, and position the animal on the wall.

When all the animals are cut out and lightly stuck to the wall with low-tack adhesive, adjust their positions as necessary to get the best possible composition. Then take them down, one at a time, spread with a thin coat of stronger adhesive or wallpaper paste, and stick firmly into position, smoothing down with a soft rag or tissue.

Added protection can be given to your mural by sealing it once it is firmly glued to the wall and the glue has dried.

Dilute PVA adhesive with an equal quantity of water and brush a thin coat all over the paper. It will dry

Have fun designing your own motifs and themes but remember that simple shapes, like these, plus bold use of colour make the most effective murals.

clear, keep the mural rigid, and can be dusted or even sponged clean.

Alternatively seal the mural with a thin coat of poster varnish—an aerosol is easiest to use and gives the most even results.

It is a good idea to use a low-tack glue first to 'test' your composition on the wall. When everything is positioned to your liking, stick firmly with a stronger adhesive. Above: farmyard scene. Below: blue/green aquatic theme.

Decorative cut-outs

The fascination of folding and cutting paper lies in the fact that it is almost impossible to guess what the finished pattern will look like until the paper is finally unfolded and it is this that makes it such an amusing pastime for both children and adults alike.

There are several uses for these decorative cut-outs. When the patterns are completed and ironed flat they can be used for window pictures, for doilies and cake frills, bookmarks, mobiles, or, mounted on a coloured background, for gift and greeting cards. You can even make them on a large scale for use as a frieze for any room in the house.

All folded paper-cuts will produce symmetrical shapes, and the finished design depends on the type of fold used.

Suitable papers

Choose a fairly lightweight paper which creases crisply but can be ironed out quite easily once the design is complete.

Tissue paper comes in lovely colours. It folds well and irons out easily. Its fragile quality makes it particularly suited to delicate patterns and, being so thin, it is excellent for multiple repeat patterns.

Cutting very thick paper is tiring, even if you have sharp scissors and strong wrists, so use them only for one- or two-fold designs.

Avoid papers with very shiny surfaces because the finish will crack when the paper is folded, and the cracks will still be visible after ironing. It is difficult, for example, to erase fold marks from gold-finished papers so only use them for simple double folds.

Cutting techniques

Always fold your paper cleanly and firmly, and be sure your scissors or knife is very sharp or frayed edges may result.

The thinner the paper, the more folds you can make and the more layers you can cut simultaneously. But don't be tempted to cut too much at once or the resulting patterns are likely to be uneven because the scissors or knife may not reach the innermost layers of paper.

Stapling them together helps prevent folded layers of paper from slipping. Be careful though to place the staples in areas where they won't leave telltale marks to spoil the finished work.

Lightly sketch or trace the intended design on the top fold, making sure the design is firmly joined at the folds themselves—or you will end up with several separate motifs instead of one continuous connecting design.

Following the pattern sketched on the top sheet, cut through all the layers simultaneously with your knife or scissors.

Simple folds and cuts

Here are three easy folds to try out:
☐ Fold a sheet of paper in half to produce two symmetrical patterns, one on each side of the central fold. You could draw an abstract pattern, or half a heart—which would be whole after cutting and unfolding.
☐ Fold a sheet of paper in half, and then in half again, to produce a four times repeated pattern (fig.1).

1. Paper folded twice as shown above left, cut with sharp pointed scissors along lines, as indicated, will produce four times repeated pattern as shown below and used for window decoration, right (panel 3, row 2).

Right: each panel in this pretty window decoration was made by the twice fold technique described in fig.1.

Bowl of fruit, above, with trace
pattern right, is made using single fold
technique. Below: other patterns with
dotted lines indicating single fold.

Smiling angel made from pattern left.

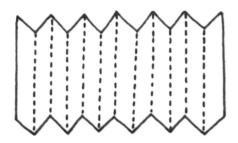

Fold a sheet of paper concertina-fashion to form a continuous line of patterns (fig. 2) with as many repeats as there are folded sections to the paper. This is the way to make the traditional row of gingerbread men holding hands, or any simple figure.

Above: trace pattern for balancing clown uses concertina fold technique.

Right: the clown and other concertina fold designs unfold to produce delightful chains of freize-like figures.

Decorating with découpage

The word découpage means 'cut out' and the craft is concerned with decorating objects with cut-out paper prints or illustrations, and then varnishing them. Originally the idea was to 'sink' the print under many coats of varnish so that the print would look as though it had been inlaid in the surface of the object. This is very effective for wooden objects, such as boxes or even chairs. However, you can also decorate glass and metal objects with découpage or cover a large area such as a floor or wall entirely with prints, and in these cases the prints need not be sunk. In any case modern varnishes have lessened the number of coats necessary making découpage inexpensive and fun. All you need to be able to create unusual and attractive pieces is time and patience.

Below: these découpage objects were all designed by Alan Wheeler.

Découpage was a popular pastime in 18th-century France, when ladies of the court used to amuse themselves by copying the lacquered Chinese and Japanese furniture that was all the rage at the time. Découpage was known as 'poor man's lacquer' and, in Britain, 'Japanning'.

Early in this century the craft of découpage came into vogue again, this time in America where it is still very popular. Découpage studios sell a variety of prints, varnishes and finishes many of which are exported to specialist shops and art shops in other parts of the world. Even if you don't have access to these découpage materials you can buy suitable alternatives at DIY and craft shops.

In this chapter you will see the basic method of applying découpage to a

Right: objects, which might otherwise not be worth a second glance, can be transformed with découpage.

wooden box, and in the next you will see how to plan and decorate a large screen, and how to decorate glass and metal.

Choosing decorative prints

There are innumerable sources for attractive prints and illustrations—art shops, junk shops, sales, stationers and museums are all possibilities. Almost any prints are suitable, from catalogues or old books, to posters, wallpapers and wrapping papers, but do remember that if they are thick card or paper they will be much more difficult to sink. Try to choose prints on thin paper, and to use prints of similar thickness on one object.

Christmas cards and postcards can be used if you soak them in water and peel off the thick backing paper. If it will not easily peel off, you may be able to rub the backing off in tiny pellets. Don't risk soaking your favourite card as you may destroy it!

If you have a plain black and white print you can colour it with water colours, felt-tipped pen or coloured pencils. Do this before cutting it out.

Materials

The main materials used in découpage are the prints, sealer, adhesive and varnish. There is a lot of scope for using a variety of products and you should make sure that they are compatible—that, for example, the varnish you have chosen will not dissolve the sealer you have used. If in doubt, test a small area.

Sealer. Prints and illustrations must be sealed to prevent glue or varnish from seeping into them. You should do this before cutting them out. You can use a commercial sealer such as Treasure Sealer, Dufix, or a white PVA sealer. If these are not available you can make your own sealer by mixing equal parts of white spirit and varnish. Magazine illustrations have to be sealed on the reverse side as well as the upper surface, so that the print does not show through. Some magazines are printed on such thin paper that even sealing may not entirely prevent heavy print from showing. You can test for this by sealing a trial piece first.

Adhesive. The type of adhesive you choose depends on the surface of the object you are decorating. For wood, a PVA adhesive such as Evo-Stik can be used. If the surface is metal or glass you should use a general-purpose glue such as UHU. Wallpaper paste is an alternative which has the advantage of making the print easy to slide into position on the object.

Varnish. Almost any varnish is suitable for découpage, although traditional varnishes take longer to dry than polyurethane varnishes and this can

be very important when you have to apply several layers and allow each one to dry thoroughly. Both types give prints a yellowish tinge, which makes it difficult to retain a clear blue or green base colour.

There are also a number of specialized découpage varnishes such as Oriental Lacquer, Fun Finish and Instant Finish. These are designed for specific projects so their suitability should be carefully checked with the mail order catalogue or the shopkeeper. They have a quicker drying time than traditional varnishes, some drying in one hour rather than twenty-four hours. They also need fewer coats to achieve a good finish.

Rustin's Plastic Coating is a useful alternative to varnish as it gives a very clear finish which leaves the original colours virtually unchanged. It is sold in two parts, lacquer and hardening solution, which are mixed equally in a glass or ceramic container. Unlike varnish it works best when applied quite thickly, and it dries in about two hours at room temperature.

Decorating a wooden box

A small wooden box is a good object to

start on and can be decorated in many different ways.

You will need:
Plain wooden box.
Assorted prints.
Primer and emulsion paint (optional).
Wood filler (optional).
Sealer.
Water colours, felt-tipped pens or crayons (optional).
Adhesive or wallpaper paste.
Fine sandpaper, sanding block.
Wet and dry paper.
Fine steel wool.
Wax polish and duster.
Varnish.
Pair of large scissors, pair of small scissors with curved blades; scalpel.

Preparation

Fill any holes or cracks carefully with a proprietary wood filler, then sandpaper the whole box thoroughly. Wooden surfaces can be left with their original finish or primed and painted with emulsion paint. Make sure that the base paint goes on smoothly; any

Cut out small details in the print with a scalpel since any flaws in the cutting will show through the varnish.

The care and patience taken to decorate the box have been worthwhile, as this finished box by Alan Wheeler shows.

flaws in the basic foundation will show through the layers of varnish. You will need two coats to make a really good job of it. When choosing the basic colour remember that the type of varnish you use will affect it.

Sealing
Remember all prints should be sealed before being cut out (magazine illustrations on both sides): this stiffens them and makes them easier to cut. Paint on the sealer thinly and evenly, covering the whole print.

Cutting out
The cutting out is very important as every tiny detail will show through the varnish on the finished box. It is therefore worth taking a lot of trouble at this stage.

Cut away any white surround with the large scissors first, then cut the details with the small curved scissors. If you use the small scissors with the curve turning away from the direction you are cutting, you make a slightly

bevelled edge which gives a smoother surface for the varnish. Leave any fine detail until last so that it doesn't get damaged while the rest of the design is being cut. Then cut it out carefully with a scalpel.

Sticking down
Cover the back of the print evenly with adhesive and press it down on the box with your fingers. Working from the centre outwards, smooth the print so that no air bubbles remain and no print surfaces overlap. Make sure that all the edges are properly stuck down so that varnish does not seep underneath. Wipe off excess adhesive and allow to dry.

Varnishing and sandpapering
The drying times and number of coats of varnish vary, and the point at which you decide the object is finished—or even whether you wish to sink the design—is obviously a matter of personal taste. Broadly, a traditional or polyurethane varnish will need up to 20 coats to make an embedded finish, while a specialized product will only need up to eight coats and a plastic

coating about six. If you are using a traditional or polyurethane varnish you should sandpaper between all coats following the tenth coat since sanding at an earlier stage could damage the prints. The special découpage products and the plastic coatings can be sandpapered between every coat.

Clean the surface of the box first to get rid of dust and fluff. Brush on the varnish evenly, taking care to catch all runs before leaving it to dry. Work in a good light so that you can see any runs. If they do occur, allow the varnish to dry and then sandpaper the uneven spots before putting on the next coat.

When sanding the surface between coats, use fine sandpaper wrapped round a sanding block. For a very fine finish, wet and dry paper is the best to use. Wash all surfaces with soap, rinse and dry thoroughly before the next coat of varnish.

Finally, for a really glowing finish, and to get rid of sanding and brush marks, rub down the surface with wet and dry paper and then with fine steel wool. Wash, rinse and dry, then wax polish the box until it shines.

More surfaces for découpage

There is no limit to the area you can decorate with découpage. With immense patience and innumerable prints you could, in theory, decorate an entire room; découpage floors, like the one shown here for instance, can look superb. In fact, the découpage base may be made of almost anything with a hard and durable surface: glass, metal, ceramics and even plastics are suitable.

A découpage screen

A screen composed of three or more panels is also a suitable subject for découpage, and planning and decorating one so that it is totally covered with pictures can be a very rewarding project. The finished screen can be displayed on a wall, as in the photograph, or used as a traditional room divider. The Victorians and Edwardians were particularly fond of découpage screens and used to cover them with decorative prints, pictures from newspapers and magazines, and greeting cards. The numerous coats of varnish or shellac over the pictures gave them a yellowish glaze.

If you look in antique shops and sale rooms there are still many fascinating old prints to be found. These need not be in good condition as you will probably be cutting them up anyway. Alternatively, you may prefer to use modern designs and pictures, from posters, wrapping paper, greetings cards, wallpaper, newspaper clippings, and from many other sources. You could start with plain paper of simple design as a base and add borders or friezes of cut-outs. If you are using wallpaper, make sure it is not too thick, since it will create an uneven surface. Remember that prints used should be of a similar thickness in each project. When you are planning your screen, it often helps to decide on a theme or a group of colours. Make sure that you have enough prints to cover the area—you may need more than you think—and that you have a good variety. Light and darkness, interest and drama are important elements for a large area such as this, which can easily look monotonous if there are not enough contrasts.

If you are using an old, fabric-covered screen as a base for découpage, remove any tacks, strip off the fabric covering, rub down the frame and attach pieces of hardboard to it; otherwise construct your own frame.

Above: (left) découpage makes an unusual patchwork floor; (centre) a mirror embellished with découpage; (right) jars with their original prints. Below: (left) a pretty attaché case covered with prints; (right) a découpage screen used as a wall panel.

To make panels you will need:
Hardboard cut to the size of each panel.
Wooden battens 50mm x 25mm (2" x 1")
for each panel, three times the length
and three times the width. (These
strengthen the back of the hardboard
and prevent warping.)
A woodworking adhesive.
Panel pins 20mm (¾").
Hammer and screwdriver.
Decorator's size, such as Polycell.
A hand saw.
Screen hinges which allow the panels
to fold both ways. 2 hinges per join, and
screws.
Chisel.
Gloss paint, primer and paintbrush
(optional).
☐ Saw the battens into the correct
lengths and glue and nail them together
and then to the rough side of the
hardboard (fig.1). Allow the panels to
dry flat, away from direct heat. Keep
them flat during all stages of your
work.
☐ Coat the hardboard and frame with
decorator's size to seal it.
☐ Chisel out an area the size of each
hinge on the battens. Screw on one
side of each hinge only (fig.2).

To decorate screen you will need:
A selection of cuttings, prints etc.
About 0.5 litre (1 pint) clear
polyurethane varnish for each panel, or
Podgy. (Podgy is a product specially
designed for découpage and can be
used, not only instead of varnish, but
also instead of sealer and glue, since it
combines these three functions. It is
much quicker to use than conventional
products: one coat of Podgy over your
prints is the equivalent of several
coats of varnish.)
A wood-to-paper adhesive such as
Bostik 3, or Podgy.
Chalk or pencil, wallpaper roller.
Scissors.
A soft cloth to dust the surfaces
between each coat of varnish.
A 50mm (2") soft household paintbrush.
☐ Cut out the prints carefully as
discussed in the previous chapter.
☐ With each panel flat on the floor or
a table, move the prints around on
them until you are satisfied with their
layout. Cut away the parts of the
design which overlap: the double
thickness would be more difficult to
cover with varnish.
☐ Mark the position of each piece in
chalk or pencil on the board (fig.3).
You could number the back of each
piece and mark the same number on
the area where it will be. Then its place
on the board can be easily found when
gluing.
☐ Starting from the centre and dealing

*You can make a screen like this original
Victorian one if you use old prints from
junk shops or Victorian magazines.*

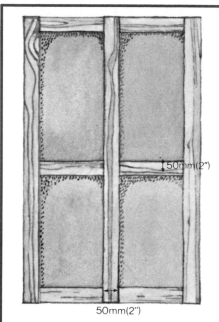

1. *Position of battens on the panel.*

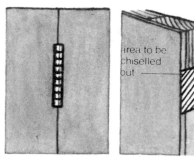

2. *Affixing the hinges.*

3. *Mark positions of the prints.*

4. *Work over the edge of the screen.*

with one print at a time, glue the
prints evenly and stick them down
with glue or Podgy. Make sure that
all the edges are firmly stuck down,
particularly if you are using glue,
since the varnish could seep underneath. Roll out any air bubbles with
the wallpaper roller and wipe away
any excess glue. It is best to work right
up to and over the edges of the screen
(fig.4).
☐ Dry the panels thoroughly in an
airy room, keeping them flat. The
adhesive must be absolutely dry and
the prints perfectly stuck down at the
edges before you start to varnish.

Varnishing. Using long, even strokes,
brush on a thin coat of varnish. Work
as quickly as possible and try not to
let the varnish strokes overlap each
other. After each coat, go round the
corners and edges with a brush to
prevent runs. If they do occur, sand
them smooth as described in the
previous chapter. Rub the surface with
a soft cloth to remove dust and hairs
before applying each coat. Three or
four coats of varnish are usually
enough for this type of découpage, and
will give a tough glaze which can be
wiped clean with a damp cloth.

Assembling. If you like, you can prime
and paint the back of the screen with
gloss paint. Attach the second side of
each hinge to the corresponding panels.

Other surfaces

Découpage on glass, metal, plastic or
ceramic objects, as with découpage on
a screen, requires no sinking of the
design beneath layers of varnish.
Therefore fewer coats of varnish are
needed and there is no sanding down
between coats.
You must decide for yourself how many
coats of varnish will be necessary and
whether to coat the whole object or
just the print itself. When applying
découpage to a mirror or a glass jar, it
is better to coat the print only, extending the varnish fractionally over the
edges, as varnish will dull the glass.
Of course you can also apply découpage
under glass. Seal the back of the print
or prints with acrylic sealer or Podgy,
to prevent absorption. Spread glue
over the inside surface of the glass and
place the right side of the print on the
glued area. Press out excess glue from
the centre of each print to the edges.
When it is dry use a vinegar and water
solution or compatible solvent to wipe
away excess glue, since it will leave a
haze on the glass if not removed. Then
cover the back of the design with a coat
of clear polyurethane varnish. If you
wish, you can paint a background
colour over and around the design.
This method could be applied to a vase,
plate or ashtray, or to a glass-topped
table.

Flowercraft

pressed flowers

One of the joys of working with pressed flowers is that it enables you to produce the most delicate designs without being able to draw. Instead of draughtsmanship the qualities required are neat fingers, patience and a love of plants. The natural beauty of the flowers makes them a perfect material for creating a work of art.

Suitable flowers

The best flowers for pressing are simple ones. Those with too many large petals, a prominent seed area or a thick bulky stem are too clumsy to press well.

Common but insignificant wild flowers can look beautiful when pressed and are invaluable for decoration. Buttercups and daisies are easy to press. Daisy stems are useful for adding to flowers which have stems unsuitable for pressing, either because they are damaged or they do not suit the design. The stems of plants such as the primrose, clover and clematis are other useful substitutes.

When choosing specimens bear in mind the line and curve of the whole flower, as this is important in an arrangement. Dog violet, for example, has a gracefully curved stem. Larger varieties such as delphinium, hydrangea or azalea can only be used successfully if the individual florets are picked off and pressed separately. You will find there is ample scope for experimentation both in the type of flowers you press and the time it takes to press them.

Leaves, grasses, sedges and ferns are as important to collect as the flowers themselves. Apart from often being very delicate they give texture to an arrangement. They are usually picked when young and before the seeds have formed.

If, as with cowslip, the leaves look too large for the flower, try to find a smaller leaf from a seedling. Ivy leaves are very decorative as is the brilliantly hued autumn foliage of prunus or Virginia creeper.

You can obtain an attractive contrast by turning a pressed leaf to display its underside.

Picking for pressing

Flowers should be picked with scissors or secateurs so as to avoid pulling up roots accidentally. Pick your material under the best possible conditions, preferably just before the flowers come to full bloom, Given a few days of fine, dry weather, you can continue to collect your plant material as long as such conditions last.

Pressed flowers superimposed on one another were used to create the embossed effect on this attractive free-standing flower picture.

Flowers and leaves to press

Acer (maple)	Ivy (variegated)
Ageratum	Larkspur
Anemone	Lobelia
Aquilegia	Lily
Artemesia absinthium (silver leaf)	Narcissus
Buttercup	Nemesia
Callistephus (single)	Pansy
Campanula	Pelargonium
Celandine	Polyanthus
Chrysanthemum (carinatum)	Poppy
Cineraria	Primula
Clematis	Prunus
Coreopsis	Raspberry (leaf)
Cosmos	Rhododendron
Crocosmia	Rose
Crocus	Rudbeckia
Dahlia (single)	Salvia
Daisy	Scabiosa
Delphinium	Senecio greyii
Fuchsia	Snowdrop
Gaillardia	Tulip
Geum	Viola
Honeysuckle	Virginia creeper
Iris	Wallflower

It is most important that floral material should be obtained as dry as possible in order to give satisfactory results. If flowers are the slightest bit damp when pressed they will lose their colour or go mouldy. Only pick perfect specimens.

Flowers should be pressed as soon as possible after picking. Wild flowers wilt especially quickly. Collect the flowers and put them in a polythene bag and close it securely with a rubber band. Do not gather too many flowers or they will crush each other. Never put flowers in water once they have been picked or leave them in the bag longer than a couple of hours as the condensation created in the bag will ruin the material.

Temporary press. If you are away from home, take a simple home-made press with you. Make this from two rectangles of cardboard, about 35cm x 43cm (14″x 17″), held together with two rubber bands. Lay out the flowers between sheets of newspaper or blotting paper cut the same size as the press and place the sheets between the two rectangles of cardboard. Secure with the rubber bands. This will give temporary and satisfactory results until you return home.

Pressing methods

Flowers can be pressed in various ways for an interesting variety of results.

Pressing in books. Place the flowers carefully between the pages of a thick book made of absorbent, not shiny, paper. Do not use your best coffee table volumes, instead obtain some old wallpaper pattern books or telephone directories.

You will need:
Books for pressing.
Cardboard name tags and felt-tipped pens for labelling.
Weights such as bricks.

Sort your flowers and leaves into similar groups for easy access when designing your pictures, cards, lampshades etc. Press flowers of the same thickness next to each other so that they receive the same amount of pressure.

Common wild flowers can be pressed complete with stems and leaves. Buttercups and daisies could even have their heads turned to one side.

Individual florets such as those of a primula or delphinium should be snipped off.

Petals of flowers with hard centres should be gently pulled off for pressing. They can be reassembled for your designs with a centre from a different flower if necessary.

Press as many flowers as will comfortably fit on one page without touching each other.

Insert a name tag with details of

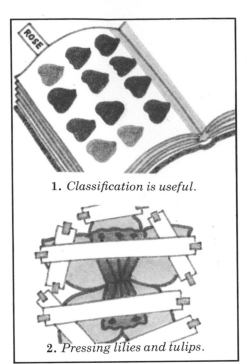

1. *Classification is useful.*

2. *Pressing lilies and tulips.*

To make a press
You will need:
2 pieces of wood, 35.5cm x 43cm x 20mm (14″x 17″x ¾″) thick.
4 x 1cm (⅜″) diameter bolts, about 10cm (4″) long with washers and butterfly screws.
Hand drill with 1cm (⅜″) bit.
Drill holes in corners of each piece of wood, matching top and bottom pieces exactly.

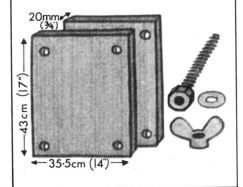

20mm (¾″)

43cm (17″)

35·5cm (14″)

pressing date and colour of flower (fig.1). Leave several pages of your pressing book between every layer of flowers.

Place heavy weights such as bricks on the book and leave undisturbed in a dry, well-aired room for four weeks.

Pressing using a flower press. A flower press can be bought from a craft shop or you can make your own. You can experiment with substitute presses such as two pieces of wood or hardboard or sheets of corrugated cardboard held together with elastic.

You will need:
A press.
Blotting paper, newspaper or tea towel.
Layer of corrugated paper (optional).

Sandwich your plant material between blotting paper, newspaper or tea towel cut to fit between the four bolts. To press several layers use corrugated paper between each layer. Insert the bolts and tighten the butterfly screws to apply pressure. Check the pressing at least every other day. Some flowers contain more moisture and if blotting paper or cloth is damp it must be changed for a fresh layer.

Lilies, tulips and similarly-formed flowers need to be pressed between wood or hardboard. Cut several strips of card, each about 2cm x 7.5cm (¾″x 3″). Gently open out the first petal of the flower, working from left to right. Place a card strip over the petal and secure each end to the wood or hardboard with sticky tape. Repeat this until the entire flower is covered (see fig.2). Daffodils can be pressed like this if the trumpets are slit in half vertically. Place the second piece of wood or hardboard on top and secure with rubber bands.

Drying time for all the methods described depends on the condition of the flowers, the outdoor weather conditions and the temperature in the room in which the material is drying. This can vary from four weeks to a few days.

Store your pressed material in used kitchen containers such as margarine tubs, transparent-topped cheese boxes or clear plastic sandwich containers so that the contents, which should be sorted into colours, shapes and species can easily be seen. Material can also be kept in polythene bags or cardboard folders.

If you see a flower which you know is not very common or if there is only one of its kind in the vicinity, do not pick it but give it a chance to become more established. Before importing or collecting from abroad, the relevant Ministry of Agriculture regulations should be carefully checked.

A few pressed flowers and leaves can be arranged to make delicate flower pictures. This chapter explains how to prepare and press plant material and the next Flowers and plants chapter illustrates further their creative applications.

fabric flowers

These giant fabric flowers make an unusual display that will never wilt.

Fabric flowers can change a simple outfit into something special—and when you make them yourself they add a further touch of originality at surprisingly little cost.

Wear them on a hat, in the buttonhole of a jacket, on a velvet choker or at the neck of a dress. Quick and easy to make, these decorative accessories will add a flourish to old and new garments alike.

There is an enormous variety of flowers that can be made—from large extravagant cabbage roses to sprays of tiny discreet flowers. You can even make giant specimens of these everlasting fabric flowers and brighten up a room with a flamboyant display of them.

Fabrics

Almost any fabric can be used providing the desired petal shape will hold with starching.

It is advisable to select fabrics that lend themselves to the texture of the flowers. The shiny finish of silk and organza, for example, is particularly suited to roses. Crisp, brightly coloured cottons, on the other hand, are suitable for carnations. The use of gingham, as illustrated overleaf, gives a gay and variegated effect.

The sprays of small blossoms can be made from almost any fabric. An unusual idea is to use millium, an insulating lining fabric which has a gold and silver finish on either side; as both sides are visible, this has a striking shimmering effect.

Some flowers—a blossom spray, for example—may benefit from the addition of a leaf for a more professional finish. Again, almost any fabric can be used, but the soft texture of velvet is particularly appropriate.

A touch of realism may be added by shading petals and leaves with fabric paint such as Dylon Fabric Paint.

These suggestions are guidelines rather than hard and fast rules and are intended to inspire, rather than limit you. Adapt the patterns given here, or design your own, to make different flowers. Use real flowers as guides, and be adventurous with fabric textures and colours. If you are a home dressmaker, you can experiment with scraps and even make flowers to match your clothes.

Basic principles

The main technique involved in making fabric flowers is that of 'moulding' the cut-out shapes from flat and lifeless pieces of fabric into realistic petals. The professional artificial flower-maker uses a flower iron to do this—a specially shaped ball on the end of a stick—and a cushion filled with sawdust on which to work.

Beginners who are reluctant to make

this initial investment may, however, find substitutes in the shape of teaspoons or, better still, melon ball scoops, both of which will provide sufficient curve. Do not use your best spoons as they need to be heated. Use a small firm cushion or ironing pad on which to press the fabric.

To heat the spoon, use a camping gas burner, gas stove, or small blowtorch. It is advisable to use an oven glove when heating the spoon in order to protect your hand. Hold the spoon in the flame for a short while, and test the heat by pressing the spoon on to a scrap of the fabric to be used. The length of time required to heat the spoon will depend on the fabric, just as one needs to regulate an iron according to the material.

Place the cut-out petal shape on the cushion and press the back of the spoon on to the fabric to produce the required curve. This may result in a crinkled edge but this can be eliminated later.

Patterns

Patterns are given overleaf for two kinds of rose, a blossom for a spray, a carnation and a leaf. It is advisable to make templates in thin card from these trace patterns. You can then draw round the template in pencil on the fabric. Templates ensure accuracy in cutting out, and, once made, they can be used repeatedly.

For all fabric flowers
You will need:
Relevant card template and pencil.
Sharp scissors.
Small, firm cushion or ironing pad.
Old teaspoon or melon ball scoop.
Adhesive such as Copydex.
Florist's stem wire.
Florist's green binding tape for the stems (gutta-percha).
Spray starch.

A rose
You will also need:
30cm (12″) by 20cm (8″) of fabric.
Sharp kitchen knife or metal knitting needle.
☐ Using the rose pattern with three petals given overleaf, trace and cut out six shapes in fabric.
☐ Make a small hole in the centre of each shape with the point of the scissors.
☐ Place one cut-out shape on the cushion or ironing pad.
☐ Heat the teaspoon or melon ball scoop and press the back of it on to the centre of each of the three petals so that their edges curve upwards.
☐ Apply a little adhesive to the top left-hand side of each petal and stick them together so that the side edges overlap (fig.1).
☐ Make a loop in the top of a stem

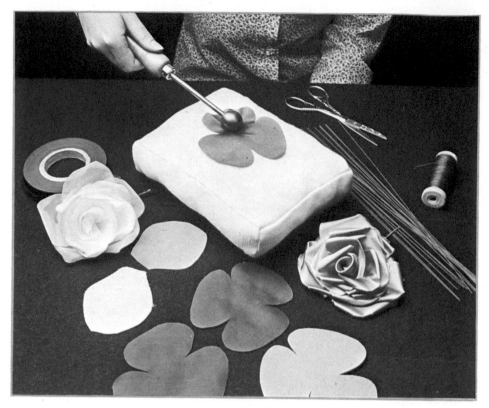

Moulded rose (right) and single petal rose (left), designed by Pamela Woods.

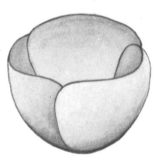

1. Overlap first set of petals.

a   b

2. Thread petals on wire and pleat.

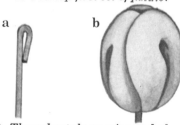

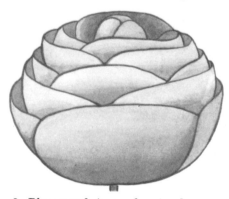

3. Place petals in overlapping layers.

wire (fig.2a). This is to prevent the first set of petals from slipping off when threaded on.
☐ Thread the first set of petals on to the wire.
☐ Make a pleat in the centre of each petal and secure with adhesive so that the petals close up further into a bud shape (fig.2b).
☐ Repeat the moulding process with the other five sets of petals.
☐ Apply a little adhesive to the inside centre, around the hole, of each of the five sets of petals.
☐ Thread them one by one on to the stem wire, pushing each one firmly under the previous one. Arrange them so that the petals lie in alternate layers (fig.3).
☐ Leave the adhesive to dry.
☐ Coat the whole flower with spray starch and place to dry on a colour-fast surface, so that the wet flower does not absorb the colour of the surface. Surplus starch will disappear on drying.
☐ The petals should now be shaped. If you are using fabric that does not fray, use a sharp knife. Holding the blade of the knife between forefinger and thumb, ease the edges of the open petals one by one over the blade with the thumb so that they curve outwards. If you are using fabric that frays, use a heated metal knitting needle. This will also flatten any crinkled edges.
☐ Cover the stem wire with florist's green binding tape, winding it several times round the wire just below the petals to prevent them from slipping down the stem.

Above: blossom spray and carnation, designed by Pamela Woods. Below: detail.

A single petal rose

An equally successful method of making roses, which does not involve the moulding technique, is that of attaching individual petals with florist's binding wire. This method can also be used for many other fabric flowers.

□ Spray the fabric to be used with spray starch and leave to dry.
□ Cut one piece of fabric 7.5cm (3″) square.
□ Cut out 14 petals from fabric, using the trace pattern given on this page for a single petal.
□ Fold the square of fabric in half diagonally.
□ Bind the binding wire round the stem wire and then bind in the folded square of fabric, by coiling it into a bud shape and gathering all the raw edges into the binding wire.
□ Curl the top edges of each petal using a knife or metal knitting needle as for the previous method.
□ Make a pleat in the base of each petal to form a cup shape.
□ Join on each petal in turn by binding it on at the base with binding wire. Each petal should overlap half of the previous one.
□ Cover the base of the final petals where they join the stem with green binding tape and bind the stem.

A tiny blossom

You will also need:
12cm (5″) by 6cm (2½″) of suitable fabric.
Pearl stamens.
Florist's binding wire.

□ Using the blossom pattern given on this page, trace and cut out two shapes in fabric.
□ Make a hole in the centre of each set of petals with the point of the scissors.

□ Fold four pairs of pearl stamens in half together so that eight pearls are grouped in a bunch (fig.4a).
□ Bind them tightly at the point at which they fold to the top of the stem wire with binding wire (fig.4b).

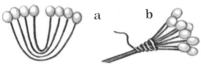

4. Bind pearl stamens to stem wire.

□ Mould the petals as for the rose. If you are using millium, treat the gold side as the upper side for one set of petals, and the silver side for the other set. In this way, both the gold and silver finishes will be visible in one blossom.
□ Thread the first set of petals on to the stem wire and push it up firmly under the stamens.
□ Apply a dab of adhesive around the central hole of the second set of petals, and thread it on to the stem wire, pushing it up firmly under the first set.
□ Bind the stem with florist's binding tape, ensuring that there is enough tape just below the flower head to hold it in place.
□ Spray the finished flower with spray starch and leave to dry.
□ You can make up a blossom spray with any number of these tiny flowers, depending on how large a spray you require. Arrange the flowers into a group, add a leaf if desired, and bind the stems together with binding tape.

A carnation

You will also need:
30cm (12″) by 20cm (8″) of fabric.
Pinking shears.
One small artificial fruit.
Florist's binding wire.

□ Using the carnation pattern given opposite, cut out six shapes.
□ Trim the edges of three of the circles with pinking shears.
□ Trim away 1.5cm (¼″) from the edges of the other three circles so that they are smaller than the first three.
□ Make a hole in the centre of each circle of fabric with the point of the scissors.
□ Join the stem of the artificial fruit to the top of a stem wire by binding the two together with florist's binding wire (fig.5).

5. Bind artificial fruit to stem wire.

☐ Cut three slits in each circular shape at equal intervals as shown in fig.6a.

☐ Working on each circle in turn, apply a little adhesive to both inner edges of each slit and stick them together so that the flat circles of fabric become cup-shaped (fig.6b).

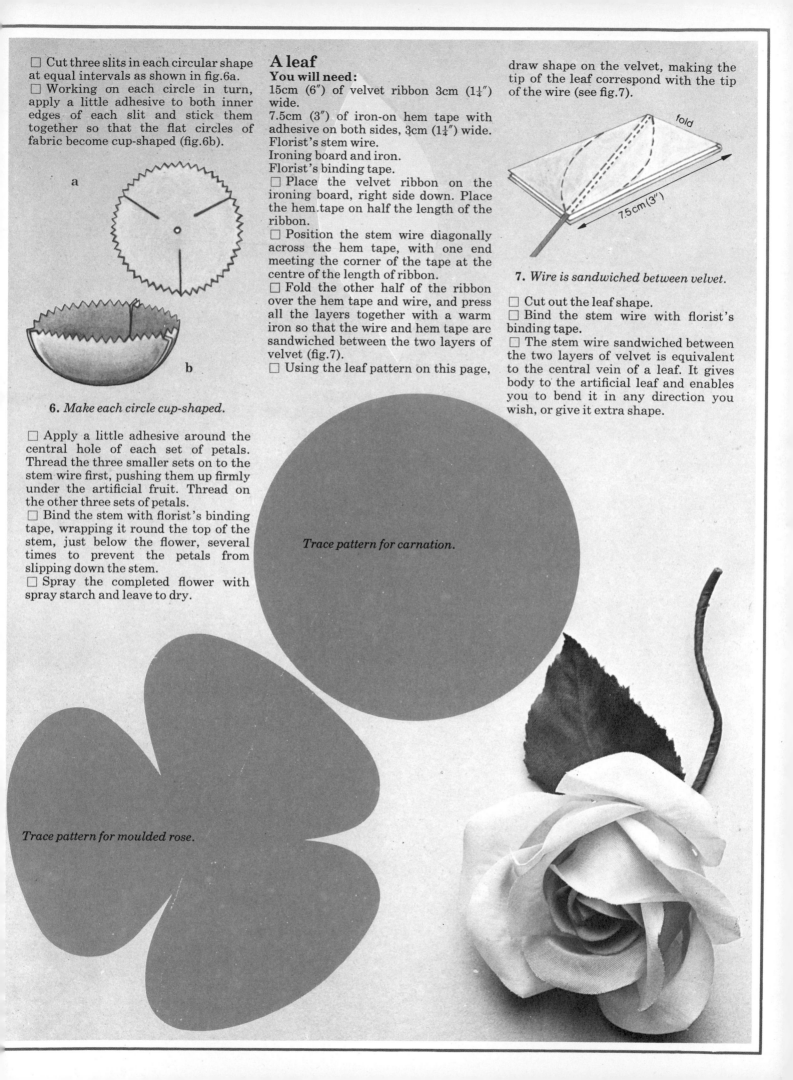

6. *Make each circle cup-shaped.*

☐ Apply a little adhesive around the central hole of each set of petals. Thread the three smaller sets on to the stem wire first, pushing them up firmly under the artificial fruit. Thread on the other three sets of petals.

☐ Bind the stem with florist's binding tape, wrapping it round the top of the stem, just below the flower, several times to prevent the petals from slipping down the stem.

☐ Spray the completed flower with spray starch and leave to dry.

Trace pattern for moulded rose.

A leaf
You will need:
15cm (6″) of velvet ribbon 3cm (1¼″) wide.
7.5cm (3″) of iron-on hem tape with adhesive on both sides, 3cm (1¼″) wide.
Florist's stem wire.
Ironing board and iron.
Florist's binding tape.

☐ Place the velvet ribbon on the ironing board, right side down. Place the hem tape on half the length of the ribbon.

☐ Position the stem wire diagonally across the hem tape, with one end meeting the corner of the tape at the centre of the length of ribbon.

☐ Fold the other half of the ribbon over the hem tape and wire, and press all the layers together with a warm iron so that the wire and hem tape are sandwiched between the two layers of velvet (fig.7).

☐ Using the leaf pattern on this page,

draw shape on the velvet, making the tip of the leaf correspond with the tip of the wire (see fig.7).

fold

7.5cm (3″)

7. *Wire is sandwiched between velvet.*

☐ Cut out the leaf shape.
☐ Bind the stem wire with florist's binding tape.
☐ The stem wire sandwiched between the two layers of velvet is equivalent to the central vein of a leaf. It gives body to the artificial leaf and enables you to bend it in any direction you wish, or give it extra shape.

Trace pattern for carnation.

flowers from feathers

On close inspection feathers bear a considerable resemblance to the leaves and petals of flowers. The curves of body feathers, for instance, are very like the curve of the petals in many flowers, while the pointed, oval shape of many wing and tail feathers are amazingly leaf-like. What is different is colour and texture and by using the glossy, often speckled colours characteristic of feathers to mimic blossoms and leaves, many beautiful and exotic looking 'flowers' can be created which, unlike their master images, will last indefinitely.

General rules

To construct a flower, first consider the basic structure that you wish to recreate—that is a seed on a stem with one or more petals round it and, sometimes, with leaves as well.

The seed centres of feather flowers can be made from several things—dried cones, grasses, small dried flowers, beads or bunches of small feathers, such as barbs from ostrich or peacock feathers, or whole small feathers.

Stems. All feather flowers, however made, are mounted on wire stems. Stem wires are obtainable from florists and floral suppliers and are properly called stub wires. Thin binding wire is normally required as well to secure several components together and to attach them to the false stem (or stub wire) as shown in fig.1a. Stems are then covered with special floral tape called gutta percha. Gutta percha sticks to itself and comes in several shades and, like floral wire, it is available from florists and floral suppliers. It is also possible to use strips of crepe paper for covering stems instead of gutta percha.

To cover stems always begin as high up under the 'petals' as possible (fig.1b). Rotate the stem with your thumb and forefinger until there is enough tape round the base to cover all underpinnings. Then twist the tape in an overlapping spiral down the wire stem and cut it off at the bottom. If crepe paper is used then a dab of glue at the ends will be necessary.

Design

Shape, colour and textures are the three variables, apart from size, which you must consider when creating feather flowers and arranging them.

Shape. Since many flowers are quite naturally round in shape there is always the danger, as with real flowers, of making an arrangement which is too repetitive. One way to overcome this limitation is to assemble a few flowers together in a spray or to create a leafy branch to produce a more linear structure.

Do not expect all your flowers to face forwards, they can also bend down or simply turn sideways, in which case their profiles are important and prominent 'stamens' can produce a delicate feature in the arrangement.

Fantasy feather flowers mixed with dried plant material make a fascinating 'floral' arrangement. Flowers were made and arranged by Pamela Woods.

1a  1b

1. *Feathers are mounted on wire stems with binding wire, then covered with tape.*

Choice of colour is personal but colours should blend with the environment in which your arrangement will be placed. Remember also that feathers can be dyed using a hot water dye. Make sure the feathers are completely submerged and moved constantly for a minute.

The textures of feathers play an important part in the design of flowers. Contrast is obtained by using fluffy with smooth or straight with curly. Each quality should appear in moderation, however, particularly the fluff, which in profusion can completely smother a flower design.

Arrangements. Unless you particularly choose to make a bowl of matching flowers there are many different kinds you can assemble in one vase. Feather flowers can also be mixed with dried flowers to make arrangements which vary the colours and textures to an even greater degree.

Styles. A selection of feather flowers is given here and each technique can be varied by choice of feathers and seed centres to make other 'species'. By looking at real flowers you can find inspiration for feather ones.

Sunflower

This velvety flower is built on a hemisphere of floral foam or oasis, into which the feathers, bead centre and stem wire are pressed.

You will need:
Floral foam ball about 6cm (2½″) in diameter.
1 medium-sized coloured bead for centre.
About 36 striped partridge body feathers.
40 chicken hackle feathers.
3 stub wires.
Binding wire.
Gutta percha.
All-purpose glue.
Knife.

Selecting feathers. Choose only the stripy partridge feathers. If there is any variation in size use the larger ones first. Choose the chicken hackles for similarity of their tips as that is the part that is visible, and cut the base if any are too long.

Floral foam comes in two densities and with the less fine type you will have to use glue to get the feathers to stay put.

Making the flower: this flower is worked flat, with no stem until later.

☐ Cut the foam ball (fig.2) in two and place one hemisphere on your working surface.

☐ Start with chicken hackles first and push them into the foam all round the edge to form a circle (fig.3). If you are using the more porous type of foam you will have to secure the feathers by poking a hole for each one with the end of a stub wire and giving the feather a

dab of glue before pushing it into the foam.

Note that the flower is worked backwards, that is, starting with the outer petals and working inwards to the centre.

☐ Then make overlapping circles with the partridge feathers (fig.4) until the entire dome is filled.

☐ Thread the bead with binding wire and twist the ends together (fig.5) and push the bead into the centre.

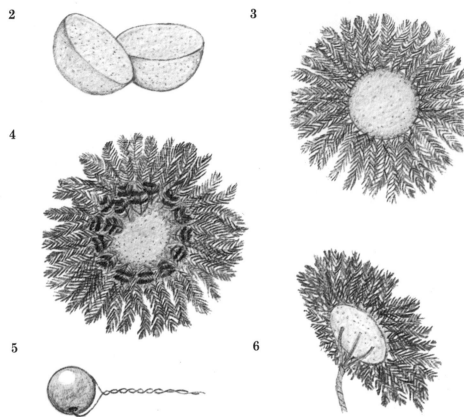

☐ Bind three stub wires together with gutta percha but leave the top 5cm (2″) separate.

☐ Put some glue on the tip of each wire and push them into the back of the flower (fig.6).

If necessary you can always cover the back by sticking a few little feathers in to mask the foam.

Leaves

Many varieties of wing and tail feathers

2-6. The sunflower is made on a foam base. Feathers are pushed into it until the surface is covered, a wired bead is used as a centre. Finally, stem wires are twisted together and inserted into the back of the 'flower'.

can be used to make leaves. The main criterion is that they should be flat. The leaves shown are made from turkey wing feathers.

Leaves normally require cutting, stripping and, to a lesser extent, curling. Feathers can be stripped by pulling away the tufts you don't need. To cut feathers use large, sharp scissors.

☐ Hold the feather in the centre, as close as possible to the cutting place, and cut the top of the feather into a

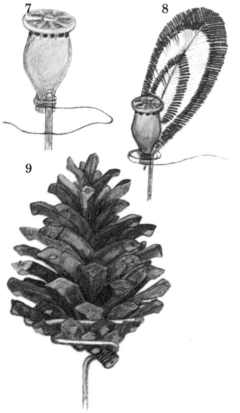

7, 8. *Poppy seed head is mounted on a wire stem and feathers are bound round it.* 9. *shows how to wire a fircone.*

Sunflower, leaves, lily, pheasant spray and fircone feather flower. All are made and designed by Pamela Woods.

pointed shape with a pair of scissors.
☐ Strip off the lower part of the barbs until only enough remains to make a leaf. The stripped shaft becomes the natural stem.

To make a spray of leaves, attach each leaf to a stub wire and cover with gutta percha, then bind leaves along another stub wire with gutta percha.

If you want to make an undulating shape to leaves, curve the lower half of the feather one way and then the tip another.

Lily
This is a good flower to make if you want a large, exotic, tropical type of lily.

Choose some special little firm feathers to make a bunch for the centre; seagull, pigeon wing feathers or those little red feathers from the side of pheasant tails. Then choose some chicken hackles to contrast with the centre feathers, or dye them accordingly.

The red curly feathers which form the petals are the soft flat ones from the underside of goose wings, and you will need about 18 of these.

☐ Strip the fluff from the little centre feathers and most of the barbs from the side of each one. Then curl each feather over to one side to form a slight hook shape. Bind them together tightly at the top of a stub wire. If you pull the binding wire very tightly the feathers will then kink and fan out.

☐ The hackles are used as they are, but the flat ones require curling. Attach the hackles with continuous binding and arrange them so that they all fan outwards.

☐ Divide the goose feathers into three groups with six feathers in each, then curl the first group just at the top, the second ones half the way down and the last group completely curled.

☐ Use the group of goose feathers curled only at the top first and add each one separately around the centre. Bind very tightly with care and arrange them so that they radiate evenly.

☐ Then add the half-curled feathers in the spaces between the first petals.

☐ Finally add the completely curled feathers, binding with the same wire throughout.

☐ This is a heavy flower which will almost certainly require more than one wire stem to support it; so twist a few together then bind the base of the petals and stem as one. Cover with gutta percha and bend the flower head over so that the explosive centre is clearly visible.

Pheasant flower spray
You will need:
Tiny poppy seedcase.
7 pheasant feathers.
Stub wire.

Binding wire.
Gutta percha.
☐ Bind a stub wire to the poppy seed so that the head stands just above the top of the wire (fig.7) but do not cut off the binding wire from the reel.
☐ Bind each petal separately (fig.8) to the base of the seed head by successive encirclements with the binding wire. The top of each feather should curve outwards.

The success of your flower depends on binding the petals evenly and tightly and not allowing them to twist round in the process.

☐ Cover the base of the petals and stem with gutta percha.

☐ Make three or four flowers this way, then take a stub wire, bind one flower to it with gutta percha, then add the next flower a little further down and then another further on to make a spray. Bind with tape to the end.

Fircone flower
This imaginative combination of natural materials would blend into a dried arrangement or a predominantly feathered one.
You will need:
1 fircone.
7 turkey body feathers.
Stub wire.
Binding wire.
All-purpose glue.
Gutta percha.
Select your feathers for size and similarity of shape. Some turkey feathers have wide fan-shaped tips and these are the ones to use, so keep the little ones for another flower. The curve also varies enormously and as this must be uniform, do not use the flat specimens.

☐ Trim the base of each feather if there is any variation of length, but do not remove any of the fluff.

☐ To put the fircone on a stem make a hook in the top of a stub wire and push it into the fircone between the scales at a point where they start to open. Weave the wire between the scales for some way and then make a spiral to support the fircone (fig.9).

☐ Straighten the wire so that it holds the cone upright.

☐ Push some glue between the scales at the same level as you put the stub wire in.

Be liberal but not excessive with the amount of glue. The feather must be fixed by the central shaft and not just the fluff.

☐ Now push a row of feathers well into the glue, between the scales so that they encircle the cone. They should all touch each other to form a cup-shaped flower. You may have to hold them in position for a moment until the glue sets.

☐ Finally cover the wire stem with gutta percha.

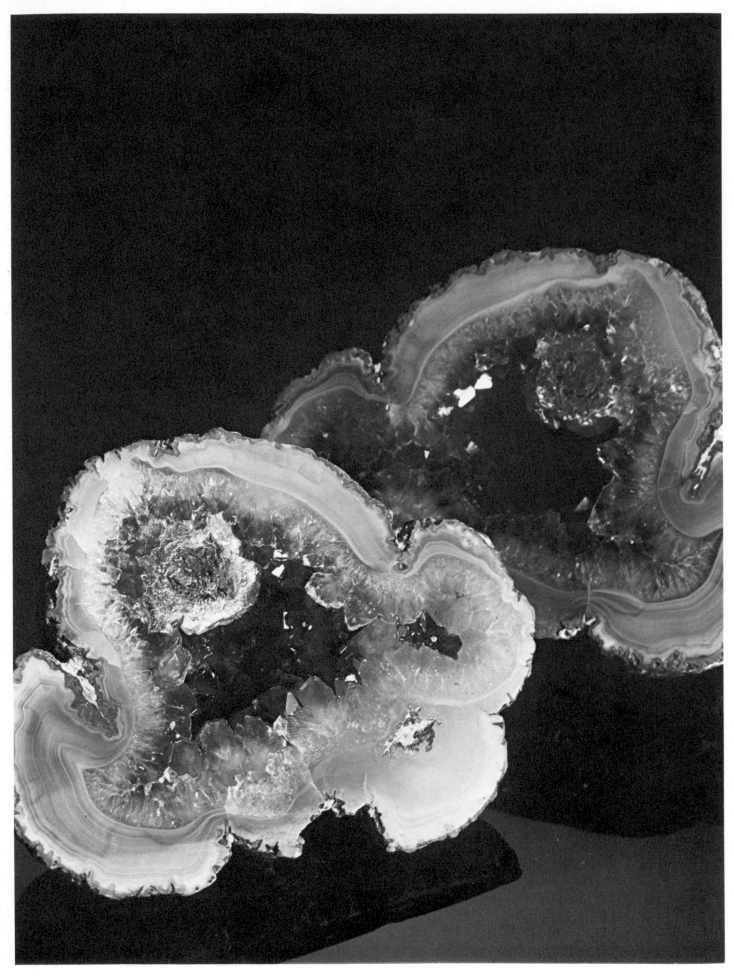

204

shells, stones & seeds

Displaying shells

Shellcraft—decorating and making objects with shells—was very popular with leisured ladies of the 19th century and has recently undergone a revival. More and more people are now discovering the rewards of using these natural materials, which need cost nothing, for decorations.

Designing with shells

Every shell is intrinsically beautiful, however common the species. Shells which you have found while beachcombing will probably form the bulk of your collection, while those from other countries, which you may have bought from a shop, will add even more variety of colour and shape.

When collecting shells for decoration the most important considerations must be colour, structure (including texture) and especially the outline shape of the shell. Classify them accordingly, and also for size, and store them in glass jars for easy identification.

Shapes. You will find that most shells fall into the following categories of shape: spiral (snails such as whelks, nerites, winkles); cone- or tent-shaped (limpets, top shells); dome-shaped (cockles, which have interesting 'ribs' along them which are often an asset to a design); flattish (the smooth donax shells which have the quality of very thin porcelain, shiny abalones, and the ridged scallops); spiky (murex shells); smooth and rounded (cowries); and long and pointed (turritellas). These shapes are shown in fig.1. More information on types of shell is given in the previous chapter.

Take care when sorting bivalves (scallops, cockles) because, since their shape is mirrored in their opposite shell, confusion of the two sides can spoil a pattern. These and other flattish shells are effective when contrasted with rounded or pointed shapes in a design.

Limpets can be used either way up; their interior surface is often totally different in colour from the outside and is usually shiny.

The spiral cones of the snail are many and varied, from the tiny shells of the nerite family, which can be less than 1cm ($\frac{1}{2}''$) long, to the giant helmet shells.

Abalone shells look very effective when broken up into chips and used for a mosaic effect. To break up abalone shells, put them into a polythene bag and crush them with a hammer. You can buy pieces of abalone for this purpose: these are cheaper than buying the whole shell.

When planning a design, choose shapes and colours which go well together. Shells can be used so that their individual beauty is emphasized,

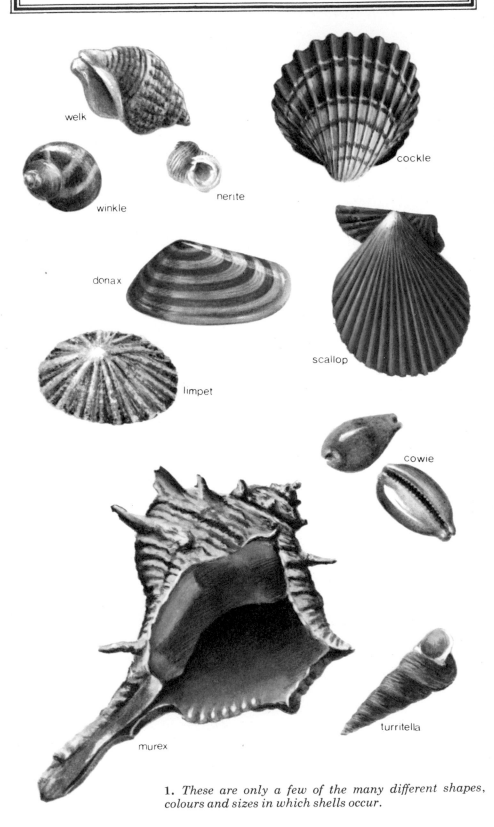

welk

winkle

nerite

cockle

donax

scallop

limpet

cowie

murex

turritella

1. *These are only a few of the many different shapes, colours and sizes in which shells occur.*

or as a part of a larger design to which each shell is subordinate.

When creating a pattern covering a small area, the emphasis should be on small rather than large shells. Whatever pattern you choose you are bound to need many small shells. They are especially useful for covering curved surfaces such as around bottles and circular boxes, since large shells will not stick to curves so easily.

You will also need a great number of one type of shell. These must be as similar to one another as possible, both in size and shape.

Larger shells are more difficult to incorporate in a design but may be used when a three-dimensional collage effect or a large, central shell is required in a pattern. You will also need large shells when making a figurine or for embedding in clear plastic. This last method is often used for preserving valued objects and has an effective magnifying quality which emphasizes small details. Clear acrylic plastic is also suitable for use as a stand to exhibit a turritella or similarly tapering shell, since it does not detract from the delicacy of the shell's shape.

Gluing and varnishing

There are various ways of fixing shells to a surface or, in the case of figurines, to one another. Clear general-purpose glue such as UHU or Bostik 1 is often successful but the type of·adhesive to use usually depends on the material to which the shells are to be attached. Glass surfaces require epoxy resin adhesive such as Araldite, but since this type of glue forms a very strong bond it is very important to be accurate in your work since it is virtually impossible to correct any errors.

Where a pliable bond is required, use Oasis Fix or Blu-Tack. When making models or figurines, plasticine mixed with clear general-purpose glue is an ideal adhesive. For curved glass surfaces such as bottles or jars which are to be completely covered with shells, use a cement filler such as Polyfilla. If any gaps remain between the shells you can fill them with sand which will stick to the cement.

Most shells look better with a shiny surface. Two coats of clear polyurethane varnish applied to a shell will enhance its colours and make it look as if it were still sea-washed. Aerosol cans of varnish spray are suitable and are readily available. The varnish forms a protective coating which is also waterproof.

Household items

There are many household items which seem to be quite ordinary objects but which, when covered with shells, take on a quite different identity and make

unusual and interesting ornaments. Old biscuit tins, bottles, coffee jars, tobacco tins, jam jars and even matchboxes are suitable objects for covering with shells.

The decoration of such objects usually requires a number of shells which are uniform in size and shape for a particular strand of the pattern. Bands of small shells in contrasting patterns and colours look best for this kind of work, with perhaps a larger shell placed in the centre or at each corner of the design.

When completely covering the flat surface of an object (such as a box) with shells in a symmetrical pattern, it is usually best to start at the centre by marking the spot and sticking the first shell there. Work from the centre towards the edge of the surface to be covered, working row by row until you reach the edge. Work in rows round the sides of the box.

The round box

133 nerite shells, 84 olive shells, 46 marginella shells and broken abalone chips were used to decorate the round

Two boxes and a wine bottle are decorated with shells. By Pamela Woods.

box shown, which measures 12.5cm (5″) in diameter and 5cm (2″) high. You will also need clear general-purpose glue, a re-usable, pliable adhesive such as Bostik Blu-Tack, and a box to be decorated.

☐ Since the centre of the design of the lid of this box is filled with abalone chips which are not symmetrical, start by gluing a row of shells round the edge of the box and add as many more rows as you need until you have a space in the centre measuring about 7.5cm (3″) in diameter for the abalone chips.

☐ Cover this central space with a thin layer of Blu-Tack and embed the abalone chips in it, completely hiding the Blu-Tack.

☐ With the lid on the box so that you know where not to stick the shells, cover the sides by gluing on more rows of shells until the surface is entirely covered.

Straight-sided boxes

The straight-sided boxes illustrated

have a more three-dimensional pattern than the round box, although one has rows of tiny shells along its edges, bordering the larger shells displayed on the top and sides. The other is simply a pile of special shells on the lid, and is a good way to make use of individual shells you may have collected.

Match-boxes
An ordinary match-box can become more interesting if the lid is decorated with shells stuck to flock-paper.

☐ Cut flock-paper to fit all sides of the box except the side on which the matches are struck.

☐ Select the shells you want. Use only two or three types of shell for such a small area.

☐ Since this will be a simple design which does not cover the whole surface, mark with chalk or pen the position of the shells to ensure accuracy, then glue them in place.

Bottles
You can decorate a bottle with shells to use as a vase, lamp base or candle holder. Cover the surface of a bottle with Polyfilla and embed the shells in horizontal rows. Start by covering the base with shells, with one type of shell in each row.

Other circular objects such as ornamental glass dishes and bowls (which do not require washing) can be made more unusual with bands of small shells stuck to them, perhaps in just one row round the rim. Follow the simplicity of line of a functional object, by adding the simplest of decoration. Make sure that identical shells in a row all face the same direction.

208

Decorating frames

Pictures and mirrors look very attractive with their frames covered with a pattern of shells. The existing frame must be fairly simple in shape with a flat surface to which the shells can be easily stuck.

If possible, remove the picture and glass or the mirror from the frame before you start. Otherwise cover the picture or mirror with a cloth to avoid either scratching the glass or chipping the shells. Always work with the frame lying flat on a work surface covered with newspaper.

Use a cement filler such as Polyfilla, or clear general-purpose glue such as UHU, for attaching the shells to the frame. If the entire surface of the frame is to be covered with shells, apply a thin layer of adhesive at a time to a small area of the frame and embed the shells in it. If you want some gaps between the shells, mark with felt-tipped pen the position of each shell on the frame and dip one shell at a time in the Polyfilla mixture or glue so that just enough adheres to the base of the shell to allow it to stick to the frame without the adhesive showing. When your design is complete, leave the frame lying flat overnight to allow the adhesive to set.

A simple border of shells, such as several rows of pearly univalves which are all the same size, can be extremely effective. It is best to use shells of one colour when framing a picture from whose impact you do not want to detract too much. Flat shells or pieces of large shells such as abalone chips can be overlapped by sticking on the largest pieces first and smaller pieces on top of them. Use small whole shells for embellishing the basic pattern. Apply very small shells with tweezers.

A favourite photograph becomes even more striking when framed by rows of shells.

Above: this box has been used for a magnificent display of various large and small shells.

Figurines

If you have collected a great number of shells, intending to create patterns needing many matching shells, you are bound to find that you have some left over which do not match any others. Use this assortment to make small animals, birds, insects and made-up characters, fixing the shells together with epoxy resin or plasticine mixed with glue. A bivalve makes a good base for a figurine; limpets make excellent skirts or hats; and tiny shells used for eyes will immediately bring a shell figurine to life.

Left: use odd, left-over shells to make amusing figurines which will delight your children. By Pamela Woods.

Three-dimensional shell designs

Victorian ladies of leisure used to spend hours patiently making shell flowers from a great number of tiny shells. These arrangements, many of which still survive under glass domes, can be copied, but it is possible to produce attractive results more simply. Shells which are translucent lend themselves particularly well to use in three-dimensional objects such as flowers or lampshades, because light can pass through them easily.

The different shapes of shells can be used for different parts of a flower arrangement. Flat shells make ideal petals which can be wired or glued to one another at their hinges. They can also be used to form a base for a flower —a container to hold a small amount of cement filler such as Polyfilla in which small shell 'petals' are embedded. Coiled shells and cowries can be used for buds when mounted individually on wire stems. Pointed shells and razor shells can be wired and used as bulrushes. Different types of coral can be used to represent foliage. When you have selected a number of shells for use in a particular arrangement, you may wish to colour them. Lacquer paints of the type used for modelling are suitable, either to colour the whole shell or part of it. Another way of colouring shells is to dip them into a pan of boiling fabric dye and water until the colour has been absorbed. More detailed information about painting and dyeing shells is given in a later chapter.

Floral lampshade

A functional as well as unusual way of using large shells such as scallops is to make a lampshade like the one shown opposite. Resembling a flowering water-lily the wrong way up, it is surprisingly easy to make and is much more robust than it looks.

You will need:

Three scallop shells, each about 12.5cm (5") in diameter.

Twelve quin or 'queen' shells, six of about 7.5cm (3") in diameter, and six of about 6.5cm (2½") in diameter.

One light fitting of miniature 'bayonet' type.

One 40 watt spherical miniature 'bayonet' bulb.

Epoxy resin adhesive such as Araldite.

Adhesive tape such as masking tape.

Hack saw.

File, coarse wet and dry paper.

A piece of thin card, at least 20.5cm sq (8in sq) from which to make a template. Pencil, ruler, pair of compasses, scissors.

In order to shape the three large scallop shells (which form the top part of the shade, the 'leaves' of the lily) so that they fit well together, first make a template from the thin card.

This intricate Victorian display incorporates a variety of shells.

210

☐ Using the compasses, draw a circle with a radius of about 2.5cm (1″) on the card. Draw a second circle of the same radius with the point of the compasses on the circumference of the first circle (fig.1). With a pencil, draw two lines,

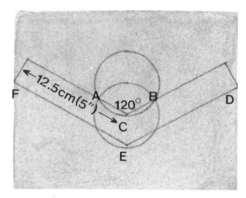

1. Draw a template with a 120° angle.

joining the points at which the two circumferences intersect each other (A and B) with the centre of the first circle (C). The angle formed is 120°. Extend the two lines forming the angle to about 12.5cm (5″) each, and cut along them and lines parallel to them (lines DE and EF in fig.1), to form a template.
☐ Place the template over the back (convex side) of each shell in turn (fig.2), with the 120° angle placed

Large scallops and quin shells are used effectively to make a pretty lampshade. Designed by Jerry Tubby.

☐ Place the three scallop shells, convex surface uppermost, in a circle with their hinges towards the centre and their edges aligning. Then draw

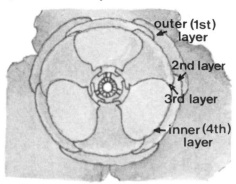

4. Position of the quin shells.

☐ First take three of the 7.5cm (3″) quin shells and, with the concave surfaces of all the shells uppermost, glue them to the 'leaves' in a circle round the threaded ring. Secure with masking tape and leave to dry.
☐ When these shells are firmly attached to the scallops, the second layer of 'petals' can be added. Glue three more quin shells of 7.5cm (3″) diameter centrally over the gaps between the shells in the previous row and with their hinges about 5mm ($\frac{1}{4}$″) away from the threaded ring. Secure as already described and leave to dry.
☐ The third and fourth rows of 'petals' are added in the same way. Each row consists of three quin shells of 6.5cm (2½″) in diameter. The shells in each row are placed centrally over the gaps between the shells in the previous row, and progressively farther away from the threaded ring. The petals will hang about 7.5cm (3″) below the leaves formed by the scallop shells, as in the photograph and fig.5. The diameter of

3. Position of the scallop shells.

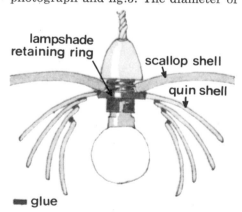

5. Assembled lampshade and fitting.

a circle at their centre large enough for the lamp fitting to pass through it, but not so large that the threaded ring, which normally retains a lampshade, passes through as well. File away the area within the circle on each shell (fig.3).
☐ Apply epoxy resin adhesive to the straight edges of each of these shells and glue them together in a circle (see fig.3). Secure them in place with adhesive tape until the glue is dry.
☐ Glue the retaining ring to the centre of the three shells on their concave surfaces, so that it frames the central hole. Leave to dry.

the space at the bottom of the shade, through which the light bulb will shine, should also be about 7.5cm (3″).
☐ When the glue is completely dry on all parts of the lamp, wire up the fitting, fit the 40 watt bulb and switch on. The lamp will throw a soft light and the colours of the shells will glow with a delicate translucency.

centrally on the edge of the hinge. Draw on the shell along the lines AC and BC.
☐ Using a hack saw, saw each shell to shape along these lines, resting the shell on the edge of a table and holding it firmly. (Do not attempt to place the shell in a vice when sawing or it will crack.) File the edges smooth.
☐ Finish the sawn edges with coarse wet and dry paper. Place the paper, abrasive side up, on a work surface, wet it thoroughly with water and move the edges of the shell backwards and forwards across it, using medium pressure. This will ensure a smooth edge and a good fit with the other two shells when they are assembled.

2. Place the template over each shell.

Fig.4 shows how to assemble the 'petals' of the lily.

Three flowers

The three flowers in the photograph resemble a dahlia, a poppy and a bulrush. You could make several of each of these and arrange them all together in a vase, or separately.

You will need:
One double razor shell.
Seven banded tops or similarly shaped univalves.
One large limpet.
One small limpet.
Seven small scallops.
A cement filler such as Polyfilla, mixed with water to a pliable paste.
Six floral stem (stub) wires.
Thin floral binding wire, at least 1.5m (5') long.
Gutta-percha, scissors, a pointed instrument such as a pair of compasses.
Lacquer paint such as Humbrol's modelling paint and brushes (optional).

To make the 'bulrush', cover a stem wire with gutta-percha (this is floral tape which sticks to itself) and then bend the top of the wire to form a hook about 5cm (2") long.

☐ Open the two valves of the razor shell carefully and put a teaspoonful of Polyfilla paste inside one end of one valve.

☐ Embed the hooked end of the wire in the Polyfilla paste and close the shell. If necessary, twist a piece of binding wire round the shell to hold the two valves together until the Polyfilla paste has dried.

To make the dahlia, cover a stem wire with gutta-percha. Take the large limpet and coat its outside with a liberal amount of Polyfilla paste. Bend one end of the wire round to make a loop which is slightly smaller than the diameter of the limpet. Embed the loop in the Polyfilla paste on the limpet (fig.6).

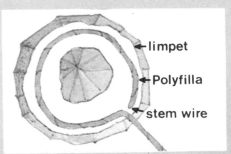

6. Embed wire in Polyfilla on limpet.

☐ Arrange seven banded tops round the limpet, pressing them into the Polyfilla paste so that they are evenly spaced and with their pointed ends facing outwards.

☐ Place a small limpet over the centre of the flower, on top of the large limpet. Leave to dry.

☐ Take one more stem wire and bind it to the first looped wire with gutta-percha. You will find that the weight of the flower head requires this extra support.

To make the 'poppy', take the seven scallop shells and, if you wish, paint the edge of each shell. The flower has seven shell petals.

☐ Using a pointed instrument such as the sharp end of a pair of compasses, make two holes one above the other in the base of each shell.

☐ Cut 14 lengths of binding wire, each about 10cm (4") long, two for each shell. Thread one length of wire through the top hole of one of the shells and another length through both holes. Pull the ends through until they are level and twist them together (fig.7). Repeat the process with the

7. Thread binding wires through shell.

other scallops so that they all have short twisted wire stems.

☐ Twist the thin wires on one shell round one end of a stem wire (fig.8).

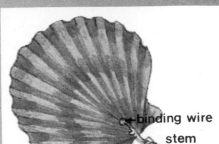

8. Attach binding wires to stem wire.

Add the other six shells to the stem wire in the same way, arranging the seven shells so that they are evenly spaced with three shells in the centre and four outside. Place two more stem wires beside the first stem wire and bind them all together with gutta-percha.

A dahlia, a poppy, and a bulrush are all made from shells. Designed by Pamela Woods.

To make the cowrie sprays, use 11 cowries. Cut 11 15cm (6") lengths of binding wire and wrap one round each shell (fig.10), twisting the ends together

10. Wrap wire round each cowrie.

to form the stems. Dip each one into the paint and leave to dry. Assemble into three sprays of three shells and one of two by simply twisting the ends of the binding wire together.

To make the container which holds the flowers, take the larger cockle and put a large blob of Polyfilla paste on its apex. Place the remaining cowries in a circle round the edge of the paste and set the other cockle in their centre, concave side up on top of the first cockle. Fix a piece of Oasis with Oasis fix to the centre of the second cockle and push the stems of the flowers into it, to form a pleasing arrangement.

Nacreous shells of various kinds make a beautiful flower decoration.

Cockle shell design

This incorporates two cockle shells which are used as a base.

You will need:

15 small wedge shells, and tiny abalone chips, seven keyhole limpets (which have a hole in the centre), five pieces of scallops, 19 cowries and two cockles. Seven olive shells.

Three compressed cotton wool balls, which are known as 'puffballs'.

Green and red lacquer paint, brushes. Glue, Polyfilla paste, Oasis, Oasis fix. Stem wires and binding wire about 3m (9') long, gutta-percha. Hack saw.

To make a five-petalled flower, cover a stem wire with gutta-percha and glue it to a puffball. Coat the ball with glue. Press the backs of the wedge shells round it to form petals; press abalone chips in the centre to cover the puffball. Make three of these flowers.

To make the limpet flowers, cut a 15cm (6") length of binding wire and fold it in half. Put some Polyfilla paste into the cleft of an olive shell and press the fold of the wire into the shell. When the Polyfilla paste is dry, thread the ends of the wire through the limpet from the inside and make a twist at the back of the limpet to secure it in position (fig.9), before straightening the

Two cockle shells form the base for this arrangement. Designer Pamela Woods.

rest to use as a stem. Make seven of these flowers.

To make the 'leaves', use a hack saw to trim the scallop pieces to leaf shapes. Cover five stem wires with gutta-percha and glue one to the back of each leaf shape. Paint each leaf green with lacquer paint.

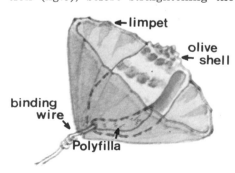

9. Thread the wire through the limpet.

Hand polished stone slabs

Instead of the usual tumbling process, which is anyway only suitable for small stones or pebbles, large stones can be polished by hand. In fact only flat stones are suitable for hand polishing, and the method, known as lapping, involves both grinding the flat face of the stone against more resistant materials on a surface called a lap, and then giving it a final polish by means of a leather or felt buff and powdered materials, in order to produce a shine. This is a more time-consuming process than tumbling, but the advantage of finishing a stone in this way is that the end result can be controlled more easily; you decide what part of the pattern will show in the finished stone, which can also be much larger than the pieces suitable for tumbling. Most slabs are improved by lapping; even slabs bought from a lapidary shop often require further polishing to make them really glossy.

Polishing flat stones and slabs is

214

accomplished commercially on machines incorporating rotating and vibrating discs, known as laps or lapping plates, which are made of cast iron. You can buy a lapping unit from a lapidary shop but it will be rather expensive unless you intend to make this a full-time hobby. Start by hand polishing, which will produce excellent results, with a little hard work and patience, before deciding whether to invest in specialist equipment.

Most lapidaries who work at home prefer to buy their slabs from dealers. It is possible to buy flat stones and slabs of many types of rock and of interesting shapes, colours and patterns.

The advantages of these over smaller stones is that it is possible to see the whole pattern in the stone rather than just a part of it. If the slab is quite thin the light will show through it and enhance the pattern even more.

Buying ready-cut slabs saves time and enables you to select a design which appeals to you rather than gamble on finding a good pattern hidden inside a chunk of uncut rock. However, if you have bought or collected uncut pieces of rock (roughs), you can have them custom-slabbed commercially: softer materials, such as amber, coral, malachite and turquoise can sometimes be cut by marble masons, but harder

rocks such as agates will need to be slabbed by lapidaries. It is a good idea to join a local lapidary club since you may be able to use their equipment; otherwise your dealer will probably be willing to saw up your roughs for a small charge. Alternatively it is possible to slice roughs into slabs yourself, using a slabbing saw.

A simple, well-lit display of polished slabs and uncut rocks shows off their intrinsic beauty. From left to right, back row: petrified wood, moss agate. Front row: hematite, azurite (the blue encrustation), banded agate, rhodonite, red agate.

The guidelines given for polishing stones according to their hardness do not necessarily have to be followed: the list below gives some tried and tested combinations for giving the final polish to a stone:

Stone	Polish	Lap
Amazonite	Tin oxide	Felt
Aventurine	Cerium oxide	Felt
Bloodstone	Cerium oxide	Leather
Coral	Tin oxide	Leather
Garnet	Cerium oxide	Felt
Hematite	Cerium oxide	Leather
Iolite	Tin oxide	Felt
Jasper	Cerium oxide	Felt
Jet	Cerium oxide	Felt
Labradorite	Tin or aluminium oxide	Leather
Malachite	Tin oxide	Cork
Obsidian	Cerium oxide	Felt
Rhodonite	Tin oxide	Cork
Sunstone	Tin oxide	Leather

For a fuller list of stones and their relative hardness on the Mohs' scale, see Lapidary chapter 2, page 276.

Grinding

The first objective, when aiming for high polish on a slab, is to remove any cutting marks or blemishes by grinding. The technique can also be applied to marble, slate, or even a flattish pebble.

If the slab is thick and too heavy to hold by hand, it is best to rest it on newspaper on a flat surface and 'sand' the top surface with wet and dry silicon carbide paper stretched over a wooden block. Use a coarse grade at first, for example 80 grit, progressing to 320 and finally 400 grit. Use the paper with water and a small amount of detergent.

Power sanders may be used, but in this case do not use water if the equipment is connected to mains electricity. Be careful not to breathe the dust produced and take care not to make more scratches than you remove, by washing the stone between every stage, to ensure that no piece of grit remains on its surface.

If the slab is small enough to be hand held, then polish it by moving it over loose grit. Use a sheet of plate glass as a lap, resting it on several sheets of newspaper. Use loose silicon carbide grits and water, and progress from coarse to fine grit as already

The first stage in polishing a small slab is to grind it against loose grits and water on a glass lapping plate.

described.

□ Use a plastic squeeze bottle to hold the water, and squirt it over the glass. Sprinkle a little of the coarse grit (80 or 100) on it, then rub the slab all over the glass, in a figure-of-eight pattern, continually for a few minutes.

□ Move the slab around in your hand from time to time, to avoid wearing it down unevenly. Add more grit when necessary (that is when you no longer hear the noise of the friction), and occasionally wash and dry the slab and inspect it under a good light for any scratches.

□ When the surface of the slab is completely smooth and free from blemishes, ·wash and dry it again, along with the lap (glass) and your hands.

□ Destroy the top sheet of newspaper to ensure that no grit remains and repeat the process using 320 grit and finally 400 or 600 loose grit, until the dried slab shows almost a semi-polish. Remember to wash everything thoroughly between stages, as one particle of grit in the final polishing area can ruin the smooth surface of your slab.

You can straighten the edges of a slab if necessary, by the same process.

Finishing

The slab should now have a smooth satin surface. The easiest method of finishing the slab is to apply two coats of hard varnish such as polyurethane, but a serious lapidary would not approve of such a method.

For relatively soft stones (up to 5 on the Mohs' scale), a polish may be obtained by rubbing the surface with a

To give a final polish to a slab, rub it with a damp pad and an oxide powder.

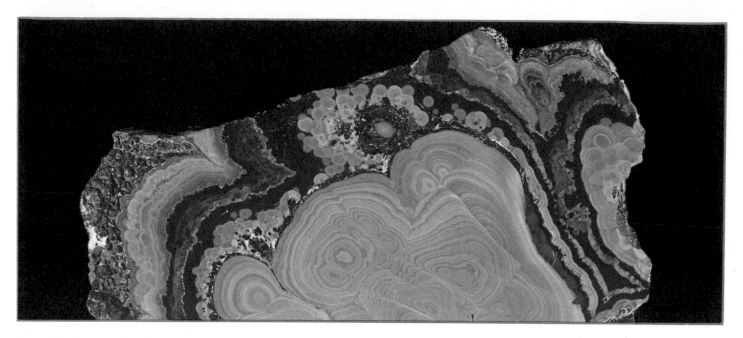

damp leather pad and putty powder (tin oxide). The leather polishes best when it is almost dry, but still takes a long time. For harder materials such as jade, opal, sodalite and amethyst; and others up to 7 on the Mohs' scale, leather and ruby powder are generally considered to be the best polishing agents. (Ruby powder, or aluminium oxide, is crushed corundum, either natural or synthetic.) For quartz and agate, and other materials of 7 or over on the Mohs' scale, felt and cerium oxide produce a beautiful gloss.

However, these are by no means the only combinations which can be used and it is worth experimenting with different polishing powders and laps (felt, leather, and even cork) for yourself.

Some uses for slabs

Slabs with interesting shapes, colours or patterns can be beautiful objects just as they are. They may be displayed on stands manufactured specially for the purpose, available from rock shops. They may also be used as wall plaques by using a ring clip of the type used to display plates.

Your polished slab would also make a fine clock face. Battery-driven clock movements are available from many electrical suppliers and are not very expensive. Numbers or markers may be attached to the face with an adhesive such as Araldite or Permabond. The problem with such a project is drilling the holes for the spindle to which the hands are fixed. Drilling is dealt with in a later chapter, but at this stage the drilling is best carried out by a lapidary or glassworker. Softer materials with a hardness of 6 or below might be drilled with masonry drills but, if you are not an expert, hours of work could

be ruined if the drill were allowed to wander over the polished surface of the slab.

One of the simplest ways of using a thick slab is as a paperweight. If the shape is interesting there is no need to trim or smooth the edges. Such a block may also be used as a plinth for a model, a bronze figure, a seashell or a pen holder. Stick a piece of felt on the base with an epoxy adhesive such as Araldite or Bostik 7.

This beautiful slab is malachite with bands of azurite (blue copper carbonate crystals) encrusted in it.

However, there is no need to incorporate your slab into anything functional. A simple display of polished stones makes a beautiful addition to any décor. More ways of using slabs which are both decorative and functional are discussed in the next section.

The high polish on this banded agate slab was made by the hand polishing method described.

Advanced slab projects

A few projects for using slabs were given in the previous section on Lapidary, on page 214. However, if you have access to a slabbing saw or a slab-trim saw with which you can further shape slabs, there are many more uses to which such stones can be put.

If making an object from more than one slab, it is important to ensure that the slabs you use have patterns which match and blend well together. For example, any banding in the material looks best when it runs in the same direction on all pieces. Matched pairs of slabs can only be obtained from the opposite sides of a single saw cut.

Book ends

There are several ways of making book ends by slabbing roughs. A block of rough such as an agate nodule (a nodule is a stone ball more or less spherical in shape and solid right through) may be sawn in half to form matching book ends.

Colourful banded agate makes a beautiful decoration when sliced at different angles, and book ends are an excellent way to exploit the banded pattern, as the photograph shows. If the base of the rough stone is fairly flat it will just need lapping (see Lapidary chapter 6), but if it has an uneven surface it will be necessary to saw off one side of the stone first, to make a flat base (fig.1). Next, slice off a small piece of rough at right angles to the base (fig.2), before sawing it into two halves. The two sides to be displayed can then be polished to show the matching patterns in the stone.

A book end may also be produced by gluing two slabs (which each have one end trimmed) together at right angles, with epoxy resin such as Araldite (fig.3).

Yet another way is to use two matched slabs for each book end, sawing them into rectangles and lapping their faces and edges. Polish the faces which will be visible in the way described on page 216, and then glue them together with epoxy resin at right angles to each other (fig.4). Stick felt to the base of all types of book ends, to avoid scratching or marking the surface on which they are to be placed.

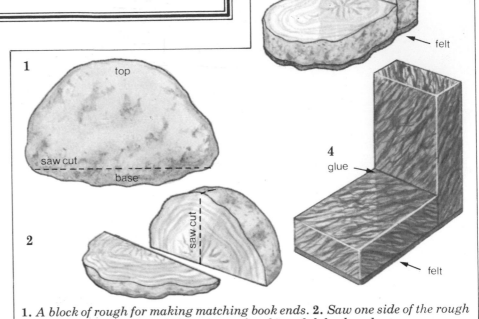

1. A block of rough for making matching book ends. 2. Saw one side of the rough before slicing in half. 3, 4. Two ways of making slab book ends.

Matching banded agate book ends made by sawing a block of rough in half.

A paper knife

If you own or have the use of a slab-trim saw, a slab made of a hard material such as jade, agate or petrified wood may be trimmed to form a paper-knife. Fig.5 shows a design for such a knife with an outline resembling a rounded spatula or palette knife: the handle is rounded to an oval cross-section and the blade portion is ground to an edge. Fig.6 shows a design with a pointed blade forming a diamond shape. You can use either of these designs or vary them if you wish, but keep the shape fairly simple and draw its outline on the flat surface of the slab with a felt-tipped pen before you start.

Choose a slab from which you can make a knife about 15cm (6″) long, 3cm (1¼″) wide and 4mm (³⁄₁₆″) thick and make sure that the lines of the pattern in the stone will travel lengthways in the knife. It is less likely to break than if the lines travelled across it.

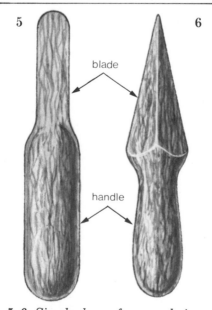

5   6

blade

handle

5, 6. *Simple shapes for paper knives.*

This paper knife from Aspreys was designed by Colin Griggs.

When the slab has been trimmed to the required shape, remove scratches by holding the knife in a clamp (the clamp on your machine if it has one) and sanding it with silicon carbide paper glued to a wooden stick with epoxy resin. Start with coarse paper and progress to a finer one (see under Grinding on page 216). Give the knife a final polish with another wooden stick round which you have wrapped a piece of felt dampened with water and sprinkled with aluminium or cerium oxide, depending on the stone. Hand polish the knife vigorously all over until it shines. Remember that all the polishing processes will take several hours of hard work.

Slabs may also be trimmed to form knife handles, either for a paper knife or cutlery. The handle must be drilled to take the shank of the blade.

A box

A very handsome box suitable for holding cigarettes or jewelry can be made from slabs. Choose a fairly soft material such as marble, calcite onyx or alabaster for your first box. You can use slabs of different materials if you wish.

Brass hinges and other fittings such as that on the box shown are readily available from cabinet makers. Hinges may be recessed in the stone, but if they are not, the box lid may be levelled by sticking small felt pads on the opposite side of the lid from the hinges. For a simple, rectangular box with outside measurements of 10cm x 7.5cm x 5cm (4″ x 3″ x 2″) follow fig. 7 for measurements, using slabs which are all 5mm ($\frac{3}{16}$″) thick. The dotted lines indicate the areas to which epoxy resin is

applied, on the inside surface of the slabs.

Whatever size and shape of box you choose, the method of construction and number of slabs needed are the same.

You will need:

Five slabs 5mm ($\frac{3}{16}$″) thick for a box without a lid (see fig. 7).

Two more thinner slabs if you wish to make a lid, either removable or hinged, one which will be cut to 10cm x 7.5cm (4″ x 3″) and about 3mm ($\frac{1}{8}$″) thick and one which will be cut to 9cm x 6.5cm (3$\frac{5}{8}$″ x 2$\frac{5}{8}$″) and about 1.5mm ($\frac{1}{16}$″) thick after lapping.

Stiff card, transparent sticky tape, epoxy resin, set square.

80, 300 and 600 loose grits and lapping plate.

Leather or felt lap and tin oxide.

Water.

Clamp, rubber bands.

Felt-tipped pen, pencil.

☐ Before cutting and grinding the slabs to their final shape, construct a box from stiff card and sticky tape, numbering all the pieces so that they can be used as templates for drawing the shapes on the slabs. Select the best areas of the slabs for pattern and freedom from flaws, and outline and number shapes with felt-tipped pen.

☐ Begin by trimming the slabs round the templates to the correct size.

☐ Lap each side of each slab with a glass lapping plate (or on an electrically driven lapping unit if you have the use of one) and coarse (80) grit until all the saw marks have been completely removed.

☐ Lap the faces to be on the outside of the box with 300 and 600 grits.

□ Using coarse grit, lap the edges of the base so that all corners are right angles. Check that angles are right angles with the set square; the base decides the final shape of the box, so it is most important to work accurately.
□ Repeat this lapping process with the edges of the sides of the box, using coarse grit and checking the angles with the set square. Do not proceed to finer grit as a slightly rough surface enables the glue to adhere to the surfaces more efficiently.
□ Take the base and set side A (see fig.7) against it. Draw a pencil line across the end of this side at the level of the upper face of the base (along the dotted line indicated in fig.7). Do the same with side B, and stick a strip of sticky tape across the bottom of each side, up to the pencil lines.

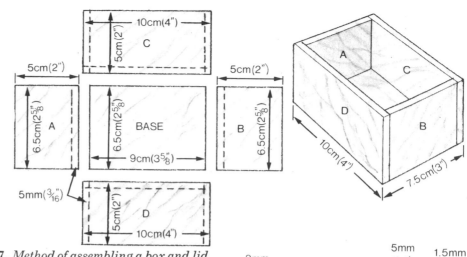

7. *Method of assembling a box and lid.*

□ Hand polish the top of the base and the inner surfaces of the two insides with felt or leather and tin oxide and water. (See page 216-217 of the previous section of this technique). After you have completed the polishing, remove the sticky tape carefully and clean the slabs thoroughly.
□ Apply epoxy resin to the unpolished strips on sides A and B and place them in position against the corresponding edges of the base (see fig.7). Place in a clamp (the clamp on your saw can be used for this), in order to hold the slabs in position while the glue is drying.
□ When the glue is dry (after about an hour), remove the assembled slabs from the clamp and check that they are correctly aligned. If there is any irregularity, lap each side with coarse grit until base and sides are in line with each other.
□ Taking sides C and D (see fig.7), place them in position against the assembled slabs. Pencil a line across their ends at a level with the upper face of the base and down their sides where they adjoin the first two sides A and B (along the dotted lines indicated in fig.7).
□ Fasten a strip of sticky tape across their ends and down their sides to align with the pencil marks, and hand polish the inner faces of these sides as before.
□ Remove the sticky tape and apply epoxy resin to the unpolished areas. Position them against the other sides and base, and place in the clamp or secure with rubber bands until the glue is dry.
□ Check the box for any irregularities in alignment; if there are, lap the ends with coarse grit until they are all flush with each other. Make sure that the top edges of the sides are level, especially if you are going to make a lid.

An onyx box like this can be made with or without a hinged lid.

□ Lap the outside faces of the sides with 300 and 600 grit and then polish with leather or felt and tin oxide (see Lapidary chapter 6 for the method).
□ If you wish to make a lid, take the two thin slabs and lap their faces with coarse grit. Then lap the smaller slab, measuring 9cm x 6.5cm ($3\frac{5}{8}$" x $2\frac{5}{8}$") and 1.5mm ($\frac{1}{16}$") thick, along each edge so that it fits the opening of the box exactly. Check corners of both slabs with a set square to ensure that all are 90° angles.
□ Lap both faces of each slab with 300 and 600 grit. Polish the edges of the smaller slab and apply epoxy resin to one of its faces and to the same area in the centre of the larger slab. Glue the small slab centrally to the under surface of the larger slab, so that there is a 5mm ($\frac{3}{16}$") distance between the edges of the smaller slab and those of the larger slab (see fig.7).
□ Place a weight on the two slabs until the glue is dry. Then place the lid in the opening of the box to check that the edges of the upper (larger) slab align with the outer edges of the box. Lap any projections with coarse grit until they are flush with the sides of the box.
□ Lap the top, bottom and sides of the box lid with 300 and 600 grit and finally polish with leather or felt and tin oxide.
□ If you wish to hinge the lid, simply glue two hinges of suitable size in position, using epoxy resin. To keep the lid level, stick two small felt pads on the lid opposite the hinges, or glue a flat piece of brass in the middle of the opening edge of the lid. This also enables you to open the box more easily.

seed collages & mosaics

Seed collage is not just a means of making pictures. Almost any surface can be used as a base for seed design provided the glue is suitable for the base and the surface being used is one which will not be given too much harsh treatment.

If the surface is one which should be level, such as a table, then it may be necessary to split some of the seeds so that the height of all will be approximately the same. However, in cases such as this it is better to choose seeds that are already more or less the same height.

To split seeds: use a sharp knife and, if possible, hold the seed to be split with tweezers. Cut on a cutting board or similar surface and slice through the seed with the part of the blade nearest the handle.

Improvised containers

Containers like those shown in the photograph are good subjects to begin with since they can be made from throw-away objects. The vase was a humble washing-up liquid bottle and the two tins contained toffees and a cake. The candle holder was a goblet-shaped, plastic yoghurt carton which has been lined with metal foil and sprayed with a non-flammable spray for safety. Other disposable containers such as glass bottles, coffee jars and tins can all be used to make ornamental but useful objects as diverse as ciga-

Old cartons and containers become colourful ornaments when covered with seed mosaics. These are by Roger and Glenda Marsh.

222

rette boxes, cake tins and lampshades. If the container is already patterned give it a coat of emulsion paint before you begin so that any speck of background that shows through the seed collage will be neutral.

Mirror frames

This is an unusual and very decorative use of seed mosaic and frames can be cut from plywood like the one shown or you can apply seeds to an old mirror or from a junkshop.

To make the mirror shown you will need:

1cm (⅜″) thick plywood cut in a circle with a diameter of 80cm (32″) and a hole in the centre with a diameter of 40cm (16″) for the glass. This means the width of the frame will be 20.5cm (8″).
Sheet mirror glass 46cm x 46cm (18″x 18″) and 3mm (⅛″) thick.
Tweezers.
Plastic strip for spreading glue.
All-purpose glue such as Copydex.
Sandpaper, carbon paper.
Clear gloss polyurethane varnish.
White or neutral emulsion paint.
4 mirror clips and screws, available from DIY shops.
2 screw eyes and picture wire.
Blue colouring for pearl barley.
227 gms (½lb) each of pearl barley, tic beans, yellow split peas, haricot beans, red or kidney beans, Cyprus tares.
4 walnut halves.
40 beech masts including casing.
160 rose hips.
450gms (1lb) soya beans.
Seeds given may be substituted by others of your own choosing.

☐ Sand the edges of the frame lightly and apply two coats of emulsion paint on both sides and on the edges.

☐ If you are using the seeds listed, dye the pearl barley blue with ink or food colouring diluted in a little water. Dry them individually on tissues.

☐ Next, enlarge the section pattern (fig.1) to a width 20.5cm (8″) and, using carbon paper, trace it on to the front of the frame.

☐ To lay the seeds, follow the key guide (fig.1). Work one section at a time, laying the design first and then the background. Lay the seeds as closely together as possible. The beech mast is laid by gluing the entire flower-like shape on to the plywood base.

☐ Finish with two coats of polyurethane varnish.

☐ To attach the mirror glass to the back, screw the mirror clips to the frame and clip in the glass.

☐ Then screw in the two eyes. Wire and hang the mirror.

Top right: seedwork mirror frame made from plywood by Roger Marsh.
1. Section pattern for mirror design and guide to seed placement.

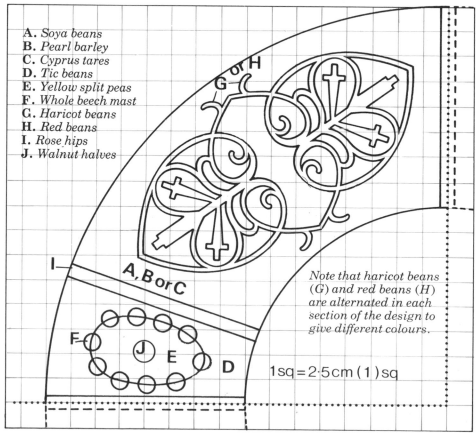

A. *Soya beans*
B. *Pearl barley*
C. *Cyprus tares*
D. *Tic beans*
E. *Yellow split peas*
F. *Whole beech mast*
G. *Haricot beans*
H. *Red beans*
I. *Rose hips*
J. *Walnut halves*

Note that haricot beans (G) and red beans (H) are alternated in each section of the design to give different colours.

1sq = 2·5cm (1″) sq

223

Mosaic tables

Tables with tops covered in seedwork are best put under glass like the one shown, but designs can also be worked on old table tops and then covered with at least three coats of polyurethane varnish. However, for uncovered designs of this type you should try to choose seeds which are roughly the same height when laid so that the surface will be as smooth as possible.

Finally, select a table that will not receive too much wear and tear.

The dimensions of the mosaic in the table shown are 62cm (24½″) x 45cm (18″) and the pattern given (fig.2) could be used in full or part to make a similar table.

The key (fig.3) shows where the seeds are laid. Those used here are as follows: dried peas, butter beans, red beans, haricot beans, mung beans, Cyprus tares, lentils, yellow split peas, Sudanese dari, paddy rice, rhubarb seeds, marrow seeds, gold of pleasure, rose hips, coffee beans. It is unlikely that any household would have all of these in stock but something similar can easily be substituted.

Work the design described previously. If you intend to cover the table with glass you will need to split the rose hips to make an even surface.

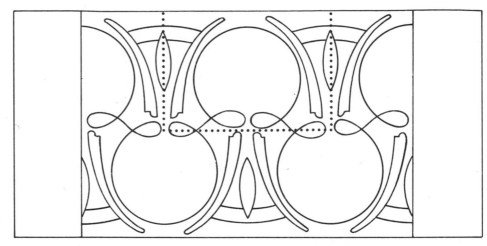

2. Top: diagram of the table mosaic shown opposite. The pattern can be used in its entirety as in the photograph or a section could be used to cover a smaller table or other type of surface.

3. A graph pattern below is a section of the table mosaic design and a guide to seed placement. Since several types of seeds are used in the design shown however it is possible to substitute those given with seeds of your own choice or ones which you may find it easier to obtain. The table shown here was designed and made by Roger Marsh.

A. *Dried peas*
B. *Butter beans*
C. *Red beans*
D. *Haricot beans*
E. *Mung or moong beans*
F. *Cyprus tares*
G. *Lentils*
H. *Yellow split peas*
I. *Sudanese dari*
J. *Paddy rice*
K. *Rhubarb seeds*
L. *Marrow seeds*
M. *Gold of pleasure*
N. *Rose hips*
O. *Coffee beans*

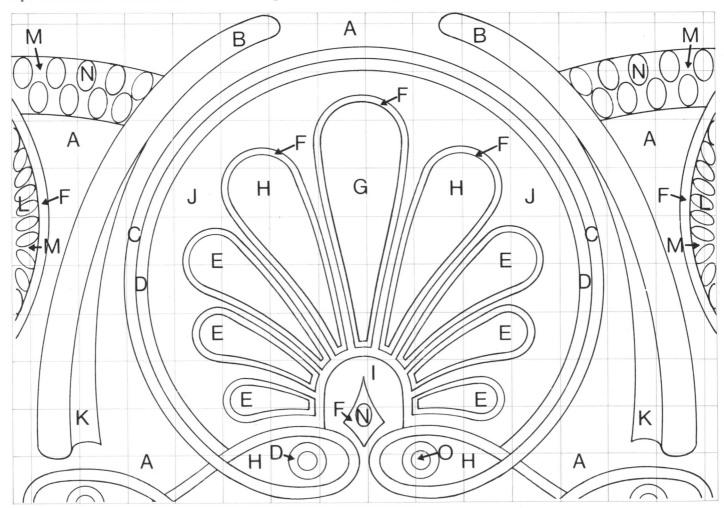

Glass & acrylics

cutting & gluing glass

Glass can be cut quite simply and with a little practice you will be able to cut lines and curves in plain or stained glass to make shapes to your own design which can be stuck together to form windows, panels or screens. In this section a stained glass window is made by cutting and gluing. A technique of mock leading is used as well. Plain glass can be used and then painted with transparent glass paints which are specially made to adhere to glass. Alternatively use traditional stained glass. This may be very expensive, so try the glass paints first. In both cases a backing sheet of clear glass provides support.

The sun window

Tools

Glass cutter. Use a steel wheel glass cutter.

Radius glass cutter. A cutting wheel mounted on an adjustable arm which revolves on a central pivot fastened to a suction cap. The radius cutter is not absolutely necessary though it is useful for cutting circles.

Pliers.

Wallpaper roller or rolling pin.

Goggles.

Materials

Two sheets of glass about 3mm ($\frac{1}{10}$") thick, bought from a glass merchant, one sheet to be cut up and painted, the other sheet to be used for backing. If you are using real stained glass buy several smaller sheets in amber, blue, yellow and green.

Transparent glass paint, if you are starting with plain glass and then painting it. There are several kinds of suitable paints available which can be bought either in the form of a kit or on their own.

Epoxy glue, such as Araldite Rapid, to stick one piece of glass to another.

'Leading', the resin kind which comes in two parts and is mixed together to form a long roll. This leading is not essential but it does make the design stand out and gives it a more 'finished' look. Leading sometimes comes as part of a glass staining kit.

Silicon carbide paper, the fine wet and dry variety, for smoothing rough edges.

Methylated spirits for cleaning glass.

Light machine oil, such as sewing machine oil, for lubricating the cutting wheel.

Turpentine for cleaning brushes.

Sheet of cardboard the same size or bigger than the glass.

Lampblack.

This decorative plant holder can easily be made using cutting and sticking techniques. A plain piece of glass is cut to shape, colour painted and leaded as described in this chapter, and glued on to an ordinary metal shelf bracket. Using bottle cutting equipment which is quite simple to use, a green bottle is cut to make a plant holder. Supplied by Craft Materials Supplies.

Right: the finished window, simple but effective. It can either be made with traditional stained glass or using transparent glass paints.

Designed by Anthony Wilson.

Plain white paper the same size as the glass.
Masking tape, ruler, felt-tipped pen or wax crayon.

Method

Draw the design on to a piece of paper the same size as the sheet of glass. Keep the design simple with not too many intricate curves or sharp corners. Not only are they difficult to cut but stress points at corners could shatter the glass. Keep the sections of the design on the large side because larger pieces of glass are easier to cut than smaller pieces.

Cutting. Lay the design on a flat surface which is covered with a piece of protective cardboard. Place the glass over the design and tape the top corners to keep it firm (fig.1).

I. *Tape the glass over the design, clean with methylated spirits, and mark the lines of the design on the glass. Cut the bottom section first.*

If real stained glass is being used, each segment of colour is cut one at a time. It may help to draw the design on to stiff card, then cut it up into sections to make a set of templates or patterns with a separate template for each section of the design. Draw each section separately. If using templates be sure to cut just inside the line.

Before starting work on the glass clean off any dirt and grease with methylated spirits. Then mark the lines of the design on the glass with crayon.

Start cutting bottom sections first.

Lubricate the glass cutter beforehand by wiping it with a piece of felt which has been soaked in light machine oil. Hold the cutter so that the handle rests between the first and second fingers and thumb, and the bottom of the hand remains clear of the glass.

Score the surface of the glass along the line with the cutter. Draw the cutter towards you, keeping the action smooth. Don't press too hard, or backtrack because the glass may break at a point where you do not intend it to.

The scoring should be completed in one operation, the object being to score the surface of the glass evenly so that the piece can be easily tapped apart. Once the score mark is made, turn the glass over and lightly tap it with the end of the glass cutter along the silvery score line. Keep the glass flat on the table. It will start splitting but keep on tapping until the two pieces separate. Patience and a light hand are essential at this stage.

If you are making a design with small strips or pieces of glass score the line as before and then, wearing goggles and using the jaws of a pair of pliers, break off the glass in small pieces.

Cutting circles. A radius cutter is the special tool needed for cutting circles or semi-circles, but you can make a perfectly satisfactory circle by using an ordinary glass cutter fastened to a length of string. The other end of the string is held down in the centre of the circle.

If you are cutting glass for the first time it is a good idea to practise on some waste pieces of glass first—just to get the feel of the cutter.

Smoothing rough edges. When all the sections are cut, rub the edges with wet silicon carbide paper. Don't overdo the smoothing because the pieces may then not fit back together. On the other hand, allowance should be made for the glue you use to take up a small amount of space between the edges.

Painting. If you have been using a sheet of plain glass the different parts of the design will need to be colour-varnished. Load a fairly coarse brush with paint and drop on to the glass, working from edge to edge. Do not brush the paint too much because it tends to spread out on its own and find its own density. Paint on the reverse side of the design and leave the paint to dry overnight in a dust-free room—if the atmosphere is dirty bits and pieces will adhere to the glass.

Gluing. When all the sections are varnished and dried they can be stuck to the backing sheet of glass. Starting at the bottom, put a little glue along the cut edges of the first piece and place it in position (fig.2). There is no need to glue the whole flat surface of the glass. The glue from the edges will spread out underneath the cut sections to hold them in place.

Hold the glass cutter firmly but lightly and score the surface of the glass by drawing the cutter towards you.

A radius cutter is the right tool for cutting circles. Hold the centre steady and swing round the cutting arm.

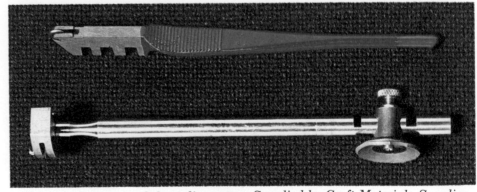

Glass wheel cutter and the radius cutter. Supplied by Craft Materials Supplies.

2. *Glue cut pieces of glass on to backing sheet with a little glue squeezed along the edges of each piece.*

Make sure when sticking the glass that the varnished side is placed down in contact with the backing sheet. This will have the effect of protecting the varnish and of adding extra translucency to the colour. Stained glass is often smooth only on one side and this side should be stuck to the plain glass.

Position the other sections in place, coating the edges with just the right amount of glue so that a little squeezes out on the backing glass.

Don't worry if the glue oozes out on to the top of the glass—leave it to dry and then gently scrape off any excess with a sharp knife or blade.

Mock leading. When all the sections are in place and the glue is completely hardened, the 'leading' can be added along the joins. Roll out the leading on a dry wood board and position it along the joins, then roll over with a hard wallpaper roller or rolling pin dipped in water (fig.3). Finally smooth the leading with a moistened finger.

The leading putty takes about three hours to dry; when it is hard rub a damp cloth over it. Fine wire wool can remove any stubborn smears and raise a lustre on the glass.

Finish off the leading with a soft cloth dipped in lampblack and finally buff it with a duster.

How to use the window

The window is now ready and can be put into a window frame in the usual way or left free-standing.

Alternatively, glue wire around the edges of the glass (using epoxy glue) or attach to the glass with the 'leading'. Leave a loop at the top of the glass and hang in front of your window or other source of light.

This lampshade can be made from a large bottle, and decorated. Supplied by Craft Materials Supplies.

3. *Roll out leading into a long, thin strip and apply along the glued edges of design for a complete finish.*

Cutting the lampshade

An attractive lampshade can be made quite simply from a glass carboy or demijohn bottle.

Draw a line with a felt-tipped pen around the bottle, making sure that it is the same distance from the top all the way round. Then score the line with the glass cutter in the usual way.

Tap the cutting line from the inside of the bottle. You may have to improvise a tapper; a small stone tied to the end of a ruler or metal rod would be sufficient. If you have a bottle-cutting kit use the tapper provided (the actual bottle cutter is not suitable for large bottles).

After edges have been rubbed smooth, as described above, paint with glass paints. Apply leading as described in the method given above.

painting on glass

Painting on glass is one way to turn ordinary utensils, bottles and jars into more individual and attractive objects. It is also a means of re-cycling wine bottles, jam-jars and similar throw-away containers which can be converted with very little effort into canisters, vases for flowers, decorative cosmetic jars and ornaments.

Household items like glass ashtrays look very original with a design on the bottom or even covered entirely with paint. Drinking glasses can be personalized and inexpensive glass mixing bowls can be decorated to bring puddings and salads to the most elegant dinner table.

Many simple shapes can be painted freehand on to glass and there are numbers of others which require no ability to draw whatever.

Paint and preparation
When buying paint specify that it is to be used on glass. Craft shops and art supply shops stock transparent and opaque enamel which is designed especially for this purpose. Normally, this is oil based so you will need to buy white spirit for cleaning up.

Inexpensive water colour brushes are perfectly suitable for this type of work but for especially intricate designs you should use a sable brush.

Before painting, always wash bottles and jars thoroughly with white spirit or washing soda to remove all trace of grease, otherwise the paint will not adhere properly to the surface.

Although glass paint is hardwearing,

Old bottles and jars can be re-cycled and drinking glasses and bowls gaily decorated by simple painting methods. These involve rolling containers in paint, using masking tape and stick-on labels and tracing patterns from paper cut-out designs.

232

surfaces which receive constant washing are unlikely to retain their colour for any length of time so objects such as vases, decorative bottles or undersides of table tops are really the best surfaces for glass painting. However, cheap drinking glasses and mixing

bowls can be quickly decorated on the outside for the fun of it.

Marbled effect

A multi-coloured or 'marbled' effect is easy to get and can be made on the outside or, provided the top is broad enough, the inside of a container.

To marble the outside of a glass container, pour two or three colours on to a piece of card and roll the bottle or

Above: leafy lamp is created from painted glass jar shown below.

jar in the paint. A wooden dowel or rod inserted in the container will help to roll it.

Allow the container to dry suspended over newspapers by a cord so that the excess paint drips off. This will add to the 'marbled' effect.

Marbling the inside of a container is even easier but remember that you need a fairly wide-mouthed container for the best results. Simply pour the

1. *Marbling the inside of a container.*

paint into it as shown in fig.1 and revolve the container slowly. Pour out any excess paint and allow to dry.

Images may then be painted freehand

on the outside, thus combining two techniques.

Tracing

Glass lends itself to this technique quite naturally. You simply tape an image to the inside of the glass and paint it on to the outside by following the lines. This way, colourful scenes can be painted on drinking glasses or handsome silhouettes applied to glass vases.

If the container is too narrow to insert a paper pattern then the outline can be traced on the exterior with a greasy pencil such as a chinagraph and filled in. The pencil marks can be rubbed off when the paint is dry.

Lettering is excellent for tracing from inside or out and kitchen canisters can be labelled in this manner.

Stick-on shapes

This is another versatile means of glass decoration.

Self-adhesive labels are available from most office supply shops in the shape of circles, stars and rectangles and larger labels can be cut into any shape you wish.

Arrange the labels on the glass and then paint the glass surface. When the paint is dry, peel the labels off carefully. Stubborn or uneven edges can be evened up with a craft knife.

Examples on previous spread
The tall yellow jar with blue circles was done in this way. The circles represent labels that have been removed. The inside has been painted with transparent blue paint.

Masking tape is useful for a number of designs and is indispensible for making clear, straight lines—a low-tack variety is recommended, especially for taping over a previously painted area.

2. *Using masking tape to make lines.*

The drinking glasses shown were decorated by masking off the area on either side of the desired stripes (fig. 2) before painting them in. The graduation of the lines shown is another good decorative idea.

The multi-coloured 'hard edge' jar was also painted using masking tape.

Table tops

Plate glass table tops are fascinating surfaces for decoration. Making a backgammon board adds a useful dimension, but all sorts of designs using the techniques described above could be employed.

A backgammon or chessboard can cover the entire surface of a small table or only the centre portion of a larger one such as a coffee table. Many shops sell glass-topped tables but if you are having glass cut for a table frame or to cover a table you should have the edges rounded off to take off the sharpness and give a more 'finished' appearance.

The surface which you paint will be the underside of the glass and this will automatically protect it from abrasive cleaners, fluids and scratches. (Remember however that your finished design will be a mirror image of the original drawing.)

To make the backgammon board
66cm (26″) x 33cm (13″).

You will need:
Graph paper and pencil.
Yellow, blue and red paint (or your own choice).
Brushes.
White spirit.
Low-tack masking tape.
Glass table top and frame or glass topped table.
Razor blade or craft knife.
Old newspapers or sheet.

Use graph paper to enlarge the design in fig. 3a. Trace it onto the graph paper and then draw it up in proportion to the size you require.

☐ Protect working area with newspapers or old sheet.

☐ Place the pattern on to a smooth flat working surface and put the glass on top of the pattern. If the edges are rounded put it bottom side up.

☐ Mask off the border with masking tape (fig.3b) and paint inside the tape strips. Allow to dry thoroughly before proceeding further.

☐ Remove the tape carefully and clean up any unevenness in the painted lines with a razor blade or craft knife.

☐ Mask off the blue triangles (3c) and paint them. When dry, remove the tape with extra care since part of it has been placed over previously painted areas and there is always the danger of it pulling up some of the paint.

☐ Mask off the red triangles (fig.3d), paint them and allow to dry before removing the tape.

☐ Check the surface to make sure all is in order: you can remove odd flecks with a blade and touch up any gaps with a fine brush.

☐ Place the glass in position and your table top is complete.

3a. *Pattern for backgammon board.* **3b.** *shows how to mask off borders on glass.* **3c. and 3d.** *indicate use of masking tape to outline each area for painting.*

Backgammon board in alternative colour way by Neil Lorimer decorates table.

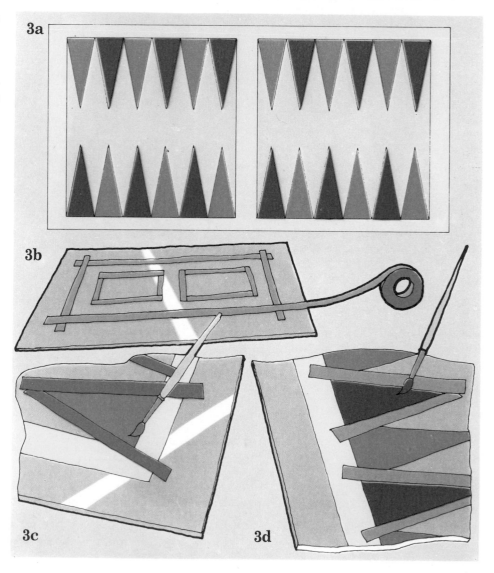

3a

3b

3c

3d

vitreous glass mosaics

It seems to be the ambition of everyone interested in mosaic to make a mosaic table and, surprisingly enough, this is not difficult for a beginner. In a big, bold table design the tesserae—as all stones used in mosaic are called—do not necessarily need cutting and shaping but can be used full-sized. You simply lay them down in a pattern.

Another advantage of starting mosaic with a large item such as a table is that suppliers will not sell less than 30cm sq (12″sq) of tesserae in any given colour, so to begin you must automatically become the owner of a considerable quantity.

Beginners in mosaic should be warned about one thing—mosaic work is at some stages a pretty messy business because it involves mixing cement. It is therefore a great asset to have a work area such as a junk room, garden shed or attic where you do not have to be too careful of your surroundings and where you can leave the work undisturbed to dry for several days.

Tesserae

There are many kinds of stones, or tesserae, that can be used in mosaic—marble, glazed and unglazed ceramic

Vitreous glass is the classic mosaic material and can be bought in a range of brilliant or soft colours.

tiles and smooth pebbles, to name just a few—but the classic mosaic material is glass.

Vitreous glass squares can be bought in a standard size of 2cm (¾″) each from any mosaic dealer. The front of each square is perfectly flat and the back is bevelled, as illustrated in fig.1.

1. *Each glass mosaic square is bevelled and has incised lines on the back to give better grip.*

The bevelled side also has a pattern or grid of lightly incised lines. Both features are designed for better grip and adhesion when the squares are applied to a surface.

The price of glass mosaic varies greatly according to the colour range, gold—as you might imagine—being the most expensive. To some extent the cost may determine your choice of colours but do be sure to select colours which will give a strong contrast of light and dark.

Mosaic designs

You can work the design illustrated or you can plot your own design on graph paper as long as you stick to designs that involve the use of squares (fig.2).

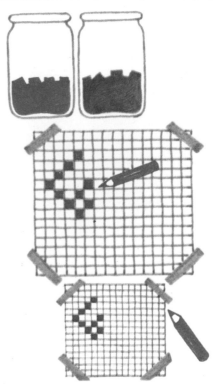

2. *Designs are worked out in graph paper first. Jars keep colours separated.*

Cross stitch embroidery and canvaswork patterns are a good source of ideas since each little square can represent one tessera. Another source of inspiration could be a modern geometric painting such as one by Mondrian. Remember that the designs must be confined to those with straight lines and right angles which do not involve cutting or shaping the square tesserae.

Mosaic table top

The materials below are given for a table top 48cm x 96cm (18″x36″).
You will need:
Sheet of paper 48cm x 96cm (18″x36″).
Sheet of 1.25cm (½″) blockboard or marine plywood 48cm x 96cm (18″x36″).
0.28lit (½pt) of a polyvinyl acetate glue which can be diluted with water, yet sets waterproof, such as Unibond or Polybond.
0.5sq m (5sq ft) of vitreous glass mosaic in the colours you require.

2 x 3kg (7lb) bags of grey portland cement.
Large container for mixing cement in, such as old plastic washing-up bowl.
Trowel.
Cement comb (optional).
Old rags, and for sensitive hands, rubber gloves.
Jam jars for storing tesserae.
Thick, blunt pencil. Ruler.
Adhesive tape. Paper adhesive such as gloy.
Silicone wax or furniture polish.

Most of these materials such as glue, trowel, cement and cement comb and PVA glue are obtainable in hardware and DIY shops. The DIY shop or your local timber merchant will supply you with blockboard or marine plywood for supporting your mosaic. No matter what shopkeepers may tell you, do not buy chipboard or external quality plywood as it will almost certainly warp. Laminated board is suitable but it is very expensive.

Preparation

Put different colours of tesserae into separate jars so that you can easily find the colour you want when you are ready to begin.

Decide on a proper working area, preferably one in which you can leave the mosaic for a time (the messy stages come later). Place the blockboard on a work table and tape the sheet of paper securely to it.

Begin to draw the design. First work out your design in miniature on graph paper. Then divide the working sheet into graph-like squares, each square representing one piece of mosaic (fig.2). Since the size of your table (and paper) is 48cm x 96cm (18"x 36") and each tessera is 2cm (¾"), it looks at first glance as though there should be 48 squares in the length and 24 in the width, but this is not so. You have to allow for cement joins between each square.

So divide your paper into 46 squares in length and into 23 squares across. In this way each square will be only a fraction larger than 2cm (¾") and the difference is made by using a blunt pencil which gives a thicker line round each square. This may sound imprecise, but you will see how it works out as you progress.

When the grid is completed, fill in the actual shape of the pattern lightly with pencil. Use the colours in the mosaic if you wish. Now you are ready to begin laying the tesserae.

Laying tesserae

Tesserae are not laid directly into cement. Instead, each square is glued with paper adhesive face down on to paper and the whole design is embedded into the cement later on. Although this

Simple, yet subtle mosaic pattern is based on the traditional Greek key design.

237

is a much easier way of working it means that for the time being you will be working in reverse. The mosaic will be stuck face down, leaving the bevelled side facing you. (As the design in this chapter does not have an 'up and down' or 'right and left' side, you will not have to worry about actually thinking in reverse.)

Start at the top left hand corner of the paper. Pick up the mosaic stones one at a time and give each a dab of glue on the flat, ie right, side. Then put each stone firmly into place, face down, leaving the thickness of black line between each tessera (fig.3).

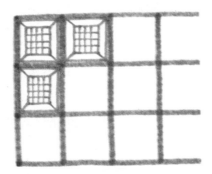

3. *Glue mosaic face down on paper. The pencil lines leave spaces for cement.*

Do not use too much glue or the paper may buckle. Worse still, the tesserae may slide around and fail to keep their place in the design.

Work about 30cm sq (1sq ft) in this way and then weight the mosaic down with heavy books to dry. Place a sheet of newspaper or lining paper between the books and the tesserae to keep it flat. Before you lay each piece of mosaic, examine it closely. Being mass-produced, some tesserae are imperfect and whereas a certain irregularity is part of the charm of glass mosaic, pieces that are badly misshapen or have broken corners should be rejected. (They can come in useful later when you start to cut mosaic.)

When the entire mosaic has been laid, leave it under weights for a day or two until you are absolutely sure it is dry.

Cementing

Preparing to cement. If until now you have been working in a room with a carpet or household furniture near or under you, the moment has come to move—to the garden shed if necessary. Failing any such place, spread a sheet of polythene to protect the floor where you are working and put several layers of newspaper on the table. No matter where you work you will need a flat surface to hold the board and you will need to leave it there for several days after it is cemented.

Remove or cut the tape binding the

paper to the board and carefully slip the board from underneath the tesserae-covered paper.

Prepare the board by priming each side with a mixture of one part water-soluble glue (remember it must be the kind that sets waterproof) and three parts water, mixed in a large jam jar. You will eventually need as much as 1.2lit (2pt), but this can be mixed in several batches if you prefer. Allow one side to dry for two hours before priming the other. When you have finished be sure to wash your brush out well. Once it has dried the glue is no longer water-soluble. For priming do not use a brush which has a trace of oil or turpentine on it for this may wreck the cement adhesion.

If the priming brings up the grain of the board, and makes it rough to touch, so much the better, because it will help to provide better adherence for your cement mixture.

To mix the cement. Up to 0.9kg (2lb) of cement is needed for every 30cm sq (1sq ft). For the table put about 2.7kg (6lb) into a mixing container and make a hole in the middle as if you were making pastry.

Gradually pour in some of the same glue mixture used for priming the board. Stir well until you get a fluffy paste, rather like whipped cream, which just about keeps its shape. It is impossible to say how much liquid you will need because so much depends on the way you mix it but, broadly speaking, 0.5lit (1pt) should be enough. Take great care not to add too much glue, however. To soften the mixture, work it well rather than adding more diluted glue.

Applying cement. When you have the right consistency—and this will take a bit of hard work—spread the mixture evenly with a trowel over the backs of the tesserae. The joins between the stones will fill up as you spread the first layer. Continue until the whole mosaic is covered with an even layer of cement about 3mm ($\frac{1}{8}$") thick. The outlines of the tesserae will be barely discernible.

Then, immediately as you have no time to lose, mix another batch of cement with glue mixture but this time only 1.4kg (3lb)—half as much as before—and spread it on the board in a thin, even coat. If you use a cement comb for spreading the cement you will find it easier to get an even distribution.

Applying cemented tesserae. You must now unite the two cemented surfaces by putting the board down over the sheet of mosaic. If possible, get someone to help you lower the board on to the tesserae as it is difficult to manage alone and once put down there is little possibility for adjustment.

When it is in place, cover the top of

the board with weights and leave it for a week (fig.4). If you are using an old

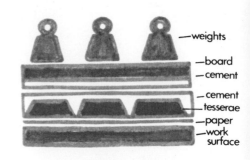

4. *After cementing, mosaic is weighted down to dry for a week.*

work table you might drive a couple of nails half-way in on each side of the board (not through it) to keep the mosaic from being jostled.

Be sure to check the outside edge of the mosaic and push back in place any overflowing cement.

If the work is to be left in a shed or other outbuilding, make sure there is no chance of frost.

Cleaning up. Throw left-over cement into the dustbin, not down the drain, and wash out the mixing bowl and trowel thoroughly. Keep any diluted glue because it will be needed at the end of the week. Unmixed cement can also be kept if the bag is carefully closed. Otherwise it may deteriorate.

Cleaning the surface

The final stage consists of taking off the weights and turning the board right side up so that the surface can be cleaned and grouted.

Facing you will be a rather stained piece of paper with the dim outline of the underlying tesserae.

Resist the temptation to pull the paper off. Get a rag and a bowl of hot water and soak the paper well, going over and over it until the hot water penetrates to the gum beneath and you feel it ready to move. At this stage your paper should come away in two or three big sections—if not, then go on wetting it patiently.

When it is finally revealed, the design will still be in need of a good deal of cleaning to get rid of the gum on the surface and any remaining bits of paper which have stuck in the joins. Possibly some cement will have moved forward to the front of the design.

Scrub vigorously with a nylon scouring pad and hot water. Do not use a metallic cleansing pad as tiny particles will get into the cement, and rust.

Final grouting. There will be many small gaps between the squares and these must now be filled. Use the same diluted glue and cement mixture as before, only this time rub it into the

Mosaic tables can be used indoors or out and in modern or traditional decors. This design is by Trata Maria Drescha.

front of the mosaic so that it fills in any remaining gaps in the joins.

This is a rather discouraging moment. No sooner is the surface clean than you must make it dirty again. You can use your fingers to rub the cement into the joins or you can use a large screwdriver or other similarly shaped tool. When all the joins appear to be filled take a handful of absolutely dry cement and sprinkle it over the surface. Make a firm pad out of an old rag and rub it vigorously all over the mosaic. The dry cement will be pushed partly into the joins and partly over the edge of the board. The harder and faster you rub, the tighter and better grouted the joins will be.

Now sweep up all loose particles of cement and leave the mosaic overnight to set. It will look rather grey and dusty but no actual lumps of cement should be stuck to the surface.

Wash the surface the next day with detergent liquid and hot water, drying it as you go.

If it still looks grey (the grain of some mosaic has a stronger tendency than others to pick up cement dust) dip some cotton wool in pickling strength vinegar (acetic acid), avail-

able from pharmacies, and rub it all over the surface. The acid will neutralize the alkali of the cement and the grey will disappear.

When thoroughly dry, wax with a good, colourless silicone wax or furniture polish. This will bring out the colour and also help to make the joins more resistant to spilt liquids and general dirt.

Finally, paint the underside of the board with a coat of oil paint. This will prevent the wood from warping and counteract any slight warp that may have developed during the drying process because of inadequate weighting.

Making a table

There are two simple ways to turn your splendid slab of mosaic into a coffee table. The simplest is to buy a metal table frame, constructed for the purpose, and screw the board into the angle irons (they have holes already drilled in the iron for this) (fig.5). You must grout in the little gaps which will inevitably exist between your mosaic and the metal frame. This can be done during the final grouting, described above, to save additional cleaning of the surface.

Alternatively, you can frame the mosaic with strips of hardwood beading 2.5cm x 6mm (1″x¼″) glued to the sides of the board. The wood should have two coats of polyurethane before you attach it so that it will not change colour or be affected by any spot grouting which may be necessary round the edges. The frame should be masked with tape before you try to grout any gaps.

To complete the table buy a set of wooden legs and attach these by screwing into the board underneath.

5. *Attach finished mosaic to table frame.*

239

cutting & gluing acrylic

Acrylic sheeting is probably better known by various trade names such as Perspex or Plexiglass. It is a thermo-plastic which means that it becomes pliable when heated and can therefore be used for moulding and bending. It also has excellent clarity and can transmit 92% of light.

Acrylic is an extremely versatile material to work with—it can be dissolved with solvents such as chloro-form, stuck together, cut, drilled and moulded to produce a wide range of useful and attractive objects. Ordinary wood-working or metal-working tools can be used for cutting acrylic although acrylic does tend to blunt saws and files rather quickly. Special glues are needed for sticking acrylic as many types of glue attack the plastic or will not adhere.

Acrylic comes in a variety of different forms: it can be bought in sheets, tubes, rods and blocks, and it is also possible to buy bags of offcuts which are cheaper and ideal for craft work.

Acrylic also comes in a wide range of colours: all colours of the rainbow in both clear and opaque, as well as black and white, luminous colours, and some special types such as mother-of-pearl. It is also possible to buy acrylic with special types of patterned surfaces.

Acrylic is a rather brittle substance and can become scratched or broken if not worked with sufficient care. When you buy acrylic sheeting it will be covered with protective adhesive paper. This paper should be kept on the acrylic during sawing and drilling, in fact until the last possible moment to prevent the surface of the acrylic becoming damaged.

In this section and the next one, ways of cutting, gluing and bending acrylic are described—a new and exciting craft for you to try. You can make a variety of different objects, starting with a letter rack and pencil holder described here.

Letter rack

This letter rack is very simply con-structed from a series of different coloured acrylic rectangles. It is 14cm x 10cm (5″x 4″) and 14.3cm (5⅝″) high.

You will need:
Acrylic sheet 3mm (⅛″) thick in the following colours and sizes:
Yellow 14cm x 10cm (5½″x 4″).
Orange 11.5cm x 10cm (4½″x 4″).
Red 9cm x 10cm (3½″x 4″).
Dark red 6.5cm x 10cm (2½″x 4″).
Red 13.2cm x 10cm (5″x 4″) for base.
(You could ask your supplier to cut the pieces to size for you or you could follow the instructions given here and cut the acrylic yourself.)

Hack saw or mechanical saw such as a Black and Decker (one with a fine-toothed blade).
Medium-sized wood file.
G-clamp.
Sharp knife such as a Swann-Morton scalpel.
Silicon carbide paper, medium and fine.
Soft cloth for polishing.
Thin stick such as an orange stick.
Metal polish such as Brasso.
Acrylic glue such as Tensol No.6.
Masking tape.
Pencil and ruler.
Set square.

Cutting. Leave protective paper on the acrylic and mark out rectangles using pencil, ruler and set square to get right-angled corners.

☐ Secure the acrylic sheet on to work-ing surface with a G-clamp, using a piece of wood to protect the acrylic from pressure (fig.1).

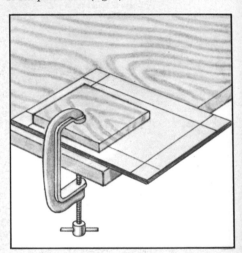

1. *Wood protects acrylic in G-clamp.*

Acrylic offcuts are ideal for craft work.

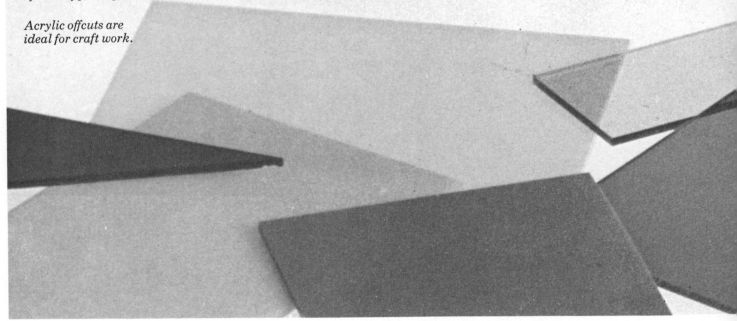

Brighten up your desk with this attractive acrylic letter rack. Designed by Doreen Cavanagh.

the position of the four uprights on to the base (fig.3).

3. *Position of uprights on the base.*

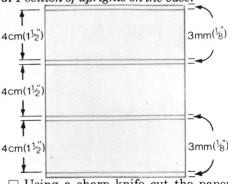

4cm(1½")   3mm(⅛")

4cm(1½")

4cm(1½")   3mm(⅛")

☐ Using a sharp knife cut the paper along the pencil lines but do not damage the acrylic underneath. Peel off the strips of paper (fig.4).

4. *Peel off strips to expose acrylic.*

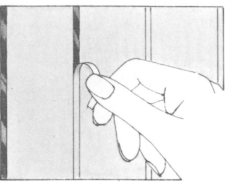

☐ Using a thin stick, paint some glue along strip A and along edge B (fig.5).

5. *Glue two edges.*

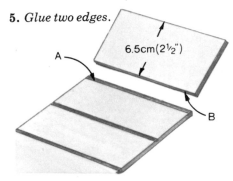

6.5cm(2½")

A

B

☐ Using a set square to make sure you are holding the upright at right angles to the base, put the two glued surfaces together and hold for a minute (fig.6).

6. *Check angle of 90°.*

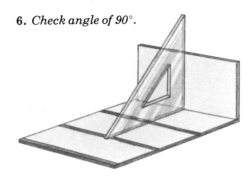

The finished letter rack in yellow, orange, and red acrylic sheeting.

☐ Using a hack saw or mechanical saw start to saw acrylic. Cut slightly outside the line to allow for sanding down afterwards.

Be very careful not to chip or crack the acrylic during sawing. This can be avoided by securing the acrylic firmly and sawing slowly and smoothly. Any great strain put on the acrylic by jerking or forcing the saw through it may cause chipping or crazing. If you are using a mechanical saw, beware of sawing too quickly. Heat generated by friction will melt the acrylic which will then join up again after the saw has passed through it.

☐ Once you have cut one side of the rectangle move the acrylic into position for sawing the next edge.

Finishing. When all the pieces of the letter holder have been cut out, the edges must be 'finished'.

☐ Using a wood file, file down edges to pencil line until they are as smooth as possible.

One 10cm (4") edge of each of the uprights (ie the edge to be glued on to the base) can be left unfinished. All other edges and the four edges of the base need further work.

☐ Place the medium silicon carbide

paper on a flat surface and put a few drops of water in the centre of the paper.

☐ Rub the edges of the acrylic rectangles on the silicon carbide paper in a circular motion, making sure that the cut edge is placed flat on the surface of the paper (fig.2).

2. *Smoothing the edges.*

☐ Continue rubbing until the edges are as smooth as possible, then repeat the action using fine silicon carbide paper. The edges can be left with a smooth matt finish or they can be polished.

☐ Using a soft cloth, metal polish and lots of elbow grease, rub the edges until they are as smooth and shiny as possible.

Sticking. The acrylic pieces can now be stuck together to make a letter rack.

☐ Using a pencil and ruler mark out

□ Repeat the process for the other three uprights making sure that they are in the right order (fig.7).

7. *Order of uprights.*

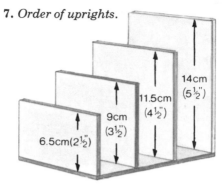

Although it takes some time to reach full strength, acrylic glue sets very quickly so you have to work fast. Beware of putting on too much glue.
□ When you have finished gluing, peel off the rest of the protective paper and your letter rack is complete.

Pencil holder
It is about 15cm ($6\frac{1}{4}''$) square and 13cm ($5''$) high.
You will need:
Tools, glue as for letter rack, and masking tape.
Acrylic sheet 3mm ($\frac{1}{8}''$) thick, 15cm x 15cm ($6\frac{1}{4}''$x $6\frac{1}{4}''$) for base.
Acrylic tubing in the following sizes:
Two 6cm ($2\frac{1}{2}''$) outside diameter, 8cm ($3''$) long.
One 5cm ($2''$) outside diameter, 13cm ($5''$) long.
One 3.8cm ($1\frac{1}{2}''$) outside diameter, 4cm ($1\frac{3}{4}''$) long.
Bench hook or other L-shape to wedge tube against during sawing.
As acrylic tubing does not come with protective paper, you must first of all wrap outer surfaces with masking tape. If you have not bought the tubing cut to the required lengths, follow these instructions for cutting the tubes.
□ Using a pencil and ruler, mark off the required lengths on tubes.
□ Wedge tube against bench hook and saw through tube (fig.8). Saw just outside the line to allow for finishing. Once you have cut through the thickness of the tube wall, start to turn the tube towards you as you saw, so that

8. *Wedge tube in L-shape for cutting.*

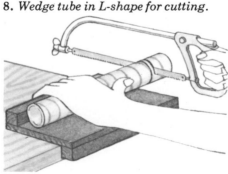

you are cutting one rather than two thicknesses at the same time.
□ Cut base as for letter holder.
□ Finish off cut ends as for letter holder. Only one end of each tube and the four sides of the base need polishing.
□ Using a set square check to see that the sides of the tube make a right angle with the base.
□ If the tube does not stand up straight, sand down where necessary.
Sticking. Mark out location of tubes on base as shown in fig.9. Put the two similar tubes diagonally opposite each other.
□ Draw the outlines of the tubes by placing tube in position and drawing

9. *Mark positions for tubes on base.*

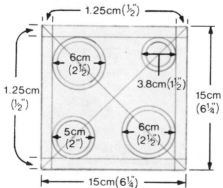

This pencil holder will help keep your desk tidy. Designer Doreen Cavanagh.

round the inside and outside edges on to the base.
□ Cut along pencil lines and peel off paper (fig.10) as for the letter rack.

10. *Peel off paper to reveal acrylic.*

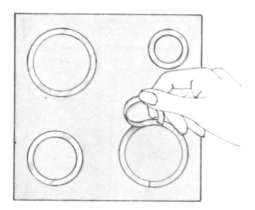

□ Apply glue to unpolished end of tube and to the corresponding location on base. Peel off paper inside circle.
□ Put the two surfaces together and hold firmly for a minute.
Stick the other three tubes in the same way.
□ Peel off protective paper and masking tape when glue is completely dry.

243

Bending acrylic sheet

Acrylic is a thermoplastic. This means that it becomes pliable when heated and can be bent and moulded to create a variety of different objects. Two kinds of bend can be made using sheet acrylic: an angular bend along a straight line, and a curve. The straight or angular bend, which is the simpler of the two types, is discussed in this chapter.

Angular bend. The basic technique for the angular bend is to heat an acrylic sheet along the line where the bend will be. When the acrylic becomes pliable, the sheet is bent along the heated line, then cooled and hardened in a dish of water or under a running tap. The tool used for heating is called a strip heater.

Strip heater

Basically a strip heater is a bar mounted on a support, with pieces of wood on either side on which to rest the acrylic during heating—the bar does not actually touch the acrylic (fig.1).

You will need:
Steel bar 1.9cm ($\frac{3}{4}$") diameter, 30cm (12") long.
Hand or electric drill with 3mm ($\frac{1}{8}$") bit.
13mm ($\frac{1}{2}$") plywood 10cm x 30cm (5"x 12").
Aluminium channel (U-shape in section), 1.25cm ($\frac{1}{2}$") wide, 2.5cm (1") high, 30cm (12") long.
Ten 2.5cm (1") nails.
Set square.
Three No.4 screws 9mm ($\frac{3}{8}$") long.
Two pieces of wood 50mm x 25mm (2"x 1"), 30cm (12") long.
Pencil, hammer, screwdriver.
☐ First attach the aluminium channel to the plywood to make a support for the bar. Drill three holes evenly spaced along the aluminium channel, and drill three corresponding holes along the centre of the plywood base to accommodate the screws.
☐ Position the aluminium channel on the plywood and screw in place.
☐ To make the rests for the acrylic sheet while it is being heated, nail the two pieces of wood either side of the aluminium support, 1.25cm ($\frac{1}{2}$") away from it.
When a piece of acrylic is placed on the rests there should be a gap of 6mm ($\frac{1}{4}$") between the bar and the underside of the acrylic sheet to prevent the acrylic touching the bar during heating.
☐ Using a set square draw a line across the top of the two wooden rests at one end and at right angles to the steel bar.
☐ Half sink four nails along this line (fig.2).

The egg rack and recipe book stand are easily made from acrylic sheet and will be an asset in any kitchen. Designs by Norman Fisher.

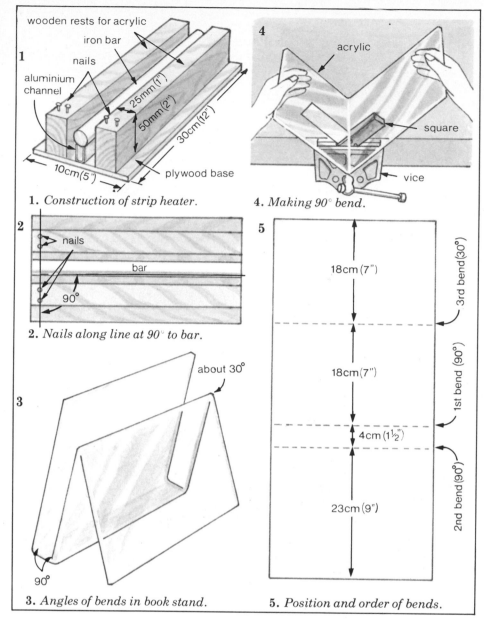

1. *Construction of strip heater.*

2. *Nails along line at 90° to bar.*

3. *Angles of bends in book stand.*

4. *Making 90° bend.*

5. *Position and order of bends.*

If the acrylic sheet is butted up against these nails during heating, this will ensure that the bend will be at right angles to the edge of the acrylic.

Recipe book stand

This book stand will protect your recipe books from grease and food marks, and will make a recipe easier to follow while you are cooking. It is made by cutting a rectangle of acrylic sheet and making three bends across the width of the rectangle—two of 90° and one of 30° (fig.3). The stand is 23.5cm (9$\frac{1}{4}$") high.

You will need:
Strip heater.
Burner on gas cooker or blowlamp for heating bar.
Carpenter's square.
Pair of pliers.
Transparent acrylic sheet 28cm x 63cm x 6mm (11"x 24$\frac{1}{2}$"x $\frac{1}{4}$").
Hack saw and vice.
Fine silicon carbide paper.

Metal polish such as Brasso.
Cloth for polishing.
G-clamp.
Chinagraph pencil.
Two pieces of wood to protect the acrylic from pressure while in the vice.
Asbestos gloves.
☐ Leaving the protective paper on the acrylic, cut out the acrylic rectangle and polish the edges following instructions given on page 240.
☐ Peel off the protective adhesive paper.
Bending. The acrylic is now ready to be heated and bent into the required shape. To obtain the two bends of 90° the heated acrylic will be held against a carpenter's square in a vice (fig.4). The bend of 30° is judged by eye, and the angle can vary as long as the book stand will actually stand up.
☐ Using a chinagraph pencil, lightly mark out the positions for the three bends (fig.5) on the surface of the acrylic.

Egg rack

This egg rack involves cutting out a rectangle of acrylic sheet, drilling eight holes to take eggs, and then bending along two lines to make 'legs' for the rack.

You will need:
Transparent acrylic sheet 35.2cm x 12cm x 9mm (14″ x 5″ x ⅜″).
Strip heater.
Burner on gas cooker or blowlamp.
Pair of pliers.
Steel rule.
Carpenter's square.
4cm (1½″) diameter hole cutter such as those made by Enox. These are sold in tool shops for cutting holes in metal tanks.
Electric drill such as by Black & Decker.
Wood file.
Fine silicon carbide paper.
Metal polish such as Brasso.
Dowel 2.5cm (1″) diameter, about 10cm (4″) long.
Two pieces of plywood 6mm (¼″) thick, one 20cm x 8cm (8″ x 3″) and one 25cm x 18cm (10″ x 7″).
G-clamp.
Vice.
Hack saw.
Pencil.
Chinagraph pencil.
☐ Leaving the protective adhesive paper on the surface of the acrylic, cut out required shape following instructions on page 243.
☐ Using pencil and ruler, mark out the positions of the centre of each hole on the protective paper (fig.6).
☐ Place the acrylic in the vice with a piece of wood on each side to protect the surface of the acrylic from pressure (fig.7). Make sure that there is wood behind the hole to be drilled—this will support the acrylic during drilling and prevent it splintering or cracking.
Cutting the holes. An electric drill is essential for this.
☐ Fix hole cutter (fig.8) on to electric drill.
In the centre of the hole cutter is a 6mm (¼″) drill which is the first thing to come into contact with the acrylic. Guide the point of the drill on to the position marked for the centre of the hole.
☐ Gently bring the rotating cutter into contact with the surface of the acrylic making sure that it is touching on all sides at once.
Friction of the cutting tool against the acrylic will generate heat, and may damage the acrylic by melting it if you are not careful. To avoid this happening, occasionally draw back the tool so that it can cool in the air.
☐ Drill each hole in this way.
Finishing. The inside edges of the drill holes must be smoothed and polished.
☐ Leaving the acrylic in the vice, and

☐ Secure carpenter's square in vice.
☐ Remove the steel bar from the strip heater.
☐ Put on asbestos gloves and hold steel bar with pliers over a burner on a gas cooker, or heat with a blowlamp, until it is nearly red hot (for about ten minutes). Try to heat the bar evenly by running it backwards and forwards in the flame. If the bar is not of an even heat, the bend in the acrylic will be irregular. It is a good idea to overheat the bar and let it cool down so that the heat will even out.
☐ Replace the heated bar in the strip heater on the aluminium support.
☐ Place the acrylic sheet on the strip heater so that the line for the first bend is exactly over the steel bar. Butt the edge of the acrylic against the nails to ensure that the bend will be straight.
If the surface of the acrylic starts to blister, this means that the bar is too hot.
☐ Once the acrylic is soft (after about one minute) remove from the strip heater and, holding the sheet on either side of the heated line, start to bend the acrylic.

The recipe book stand will hold a cook book open while in use and protect it from grease and food marks.

☐ Hold the acrylic against the carpenter's square to make a bend of 90° (see fig.4).
☐ After a few minutes, dip the acrylic in cold water or hold under a running tap to cool and harden the bend.
(If the bend has gone cloudy, or has cracked, this means that the acrylic was not hot enough.)
☐ Position the acrylic over the bar for the second bend.
☐ When the acrylic is hot enough, remove from the strip heater, and bend against the carpenter's square to obtain another angle of 90°.
You must now bend the piece of acrylic that will prop up the book stand. This must be a bend of about 30°.
☐ Heat the bar, and bend the acrylic along the line as before. Hold the acrylic against the carpenter's square to obtain an angle of 90° and then bend further until the angle is about 30°. Cool and harden as before and the recipe book stand is complete.

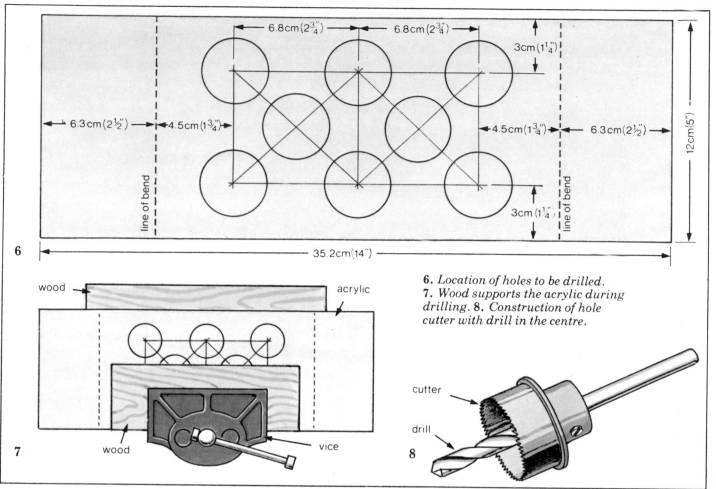

6. *Location of holes to be drilled.*
7. *Wood supports the acrylic during drilling.* 8. *Construction of hole cutter with drill in the centre.*

using the steel rule scrape off any scratches or surface blisters caused by the cutter. To do this insert the ruler through one of the holes, and holding the ruler in both hands on either side of the sheet, scrape away the inside surface.

It will be necessary to move the acrylic about in the vice to get at all the holes.

☐ When all the scratches and blisters have been removed, wrap a piece of fine silicon carbide paper round the piece of dowel, put a few drops of water on it and sand down the insides of each hole.

☐ Polish the insides of the holes with metal polish on a rag wrapped round the piece of dowel.

☐ Smooth and polish the edges of the acrylic as for the recipe book stand.

Bending the legs. The bend lines are 6.3cm (2½″) from each end, see fig.6. As the acrylic is thicker for the egg rack, it will take longer to heat the acrylic for bending (about 2 minutes).

☐ Mark out the lines for the two bends with a chinagraph pencil.

☐ Bend each end to an angle of 90°, using a strip heater and carpenter's square as before.

This egg rack holds eight eggs, but the dimensions could easily be reduced or enlarged to hold less or more.

Pictures supplied by
American Museum in Britain: 120, 121TR, 121BR, 121BL
Asprey & Co: 219
Mike Benson: 49, 53TL, 53TR, 53BL
Theo Bergstrom: 140/1, 180, 181TL, 181R
Steven Bicknell: 19, 20, 23TL, 23BR, 30TL, 30TR, 31, 32/3, 34, 36, 38/9, 40, 42, 44TR, 45, 47TR, 54, 60, 61, 64, 89, 90, 91, 136, 152, 160, 168/9, 220, 223, 228, 231
Camera Press: 28, 29, 95, 158, 159, 179, 208/9T
Martin Chaffer: 24
Alan Duns: 212, 213TL
Ray Duns: 55, 56TL, 56BR, 86
Geoffrey Frosh: 17, 101, 132, 133, 135, 196, 198C, 210, 240, 241B
Melvin Grey: 4, 68, 94, 151, 208B, 222, 225, 229, 230B, 236
Nelson Hargreaves: 149
Harrison Drape-Super Crest: 12, 13, 14TL, 14/15 spread
Peter Heinz: 2, 138, 241T, 242, 243
Chris Holland: 200/1
Institute of Geological Studies: 217T (copyright permission)
L. Johnson (illust): 114
Paul Kemp: 18, 25, 27, 137, 154, 155, 193, 194, 197, 199, 214/5, 216TR, 216BL, 217B
David Levin: 184, 185
Chris Lewis: 76, 78, 79
Neil Lorimer: 128, 129, 130, 131, 163, 165, 232/3, 235
Sandra Lousada: 198T
Maison de Marie Claire: 186TL, 186BL
Maison de Marie Claire/Chanabeix: 213BR
Maison de Marie Claire/Galland: 109, 110, 111
Nigel Messitt: 48BL, 48TR, 53BR
Dick Miller: 142, 143, 162, 164T, 164BL, 202/3, 230B
Keith Morris: 116
Tony Moussoulides: 127
Julian Nieman: 6, 74
Alasdair Ogilvie: 81TL, 81BR, 104/5, 139, 237, 239
100 Idees de Marie Claire/Dirand: 84
100 Idees de Marie Claire/Mirand: 107, 124/5, 125TR
PAF International: 87, 174/5, 177, 234TL, 234BL
Picturepoint: 150
Rex Features: 209
Rufelete: 7, 10
Johnnie Ryan: 126T, 139T
Kim Sayer: 66/7, 69TL, 69CL, 134, 187, 188, 207, 218, 244, 246, 247
Transworld: 43, 47CR, 70, 75, 85, 88, 108
Jerry Tubby: 8, 57BL, 57RC, 58, 59TL, 59CL, 92, 93, 97, 99, 102, 106, 113T, 113L, 113CB, 113BR, 123TL, 123B, 145, 166, 186/7TR, 192, 211
Liz Whiting: 1, 47BL, 47BR, 182, 183, 186/7BR
ZEFA: 195

Illustrations by
Janet Allen
Clare Beck
Victoria Drew
Barbara Firth
Lesley Fox
Trevor Lawrence
Maggie McNalley
Coral Mula
Ropecraft
Paul Williams